Behind

Autobiography of a Musical Shapeshifter

Jimmy Ryan

NEW HAVEN PUBLISHING LTD

Published 2021
First Edition
NEW HAVEN PUBLISHING LTD
www.newhavenpublishingltd.com
newhavenpublishing@gmail.com

Cover design © Jimmy Ryan
https://rampagemusic.com

Acknowledgments

To Carly Simon for being my friend, and inspiration for over fifty years.

To Gavin Ryan for his enthusiasm about these stories and encouraging me to write this book.

To my wife Gitam for keeping me spiritually awake when it was so much easier to go to sleep.

To Ian Ryan for proving that talent and hard work are key ingredients to becoming an amazing musician. And making me laugh. A lot.

To Rob Fossum for his flawless technical and editorial advice

To Phil Kurnit lawyer extraordinaire who has been guiding my career since I was twenty-one.

To Randy Pyburn for his unwavering support and keeping me busy for the last twenty-three years.

To Dr. Phil Hirschhorn for suggesting the name *Behind* for this book and keeping my teeth straight.

To Sarah Healey for her meticulous attention to detail in editing this memoir.

To Teddie Dahlin for giving me the chance to share my story with the world.

Content

Introduction

On a wintery February evening in a trendy Brooklyn neighborhood, I found myself sitting in a bar, enjoying conversation and a beer with my oldest son, Gavin. Gav is a music lover and works for Atlantic Records and our conversations are usually about two things - politics and music. Fortunately, we are on the same page with both, so unless one of us has had a huge fight with our significant others, the conversations are light and convivial. This night, the topics are music and business. When we finish discussing Billie Eilish, Taylor Swift, the hot new artists coming out of Atlantic, and Viacom takeovers, with a little prompting I begin to tell him a story about some rock star that I had worked with in the past. He loves these stories and often urges me to tell him anything I can remember. About three sentences in, he stops me: "Why don't you..." he pauses... "Actually, I dare you to write a book about all this stuff you tell me. Hell, you've been doing this for what, sixty-two years? There has to be a book in there somewhere, no? You worked with people like Elton John, Carly Simon, Paul McCartney, Jim Croce, and all these people you've told me about - why not share these stories with the world?"

This is definitely not something I had ever considered. I ask him if he thinks anyone will care; does he think there's a market for stories from someone who worked with stars, but was not a household name? Then it occurred to me that many of these biographies are written by unrelated authors, not the artists themselves. I was a whole lot closer to the action than a researcher who writes a book based on interviews and articles. While I liked Gavin's idea, I warned him I couldn't write a "tell-all" hit piece. I like most of the stars I've worked with, and we've enjoyed some amazing times together. He says, "Just write down the stories you've told me and the many more I'm sure you've got stashed away in your memory banks! They're good and people will love them."

Then it occurred to both of us that there are things that I saw... There are moments that I shared with these artists and stars that were personal to us, and we are the only ones who were there, the only ones who know about them. Hence, they have never found their way into books, *Rolling Stone* or *People* magazine. Would these encounters be interesting to anyone but me? Gavin seemed to think his generation would devour them.

I took him up on his dare and started to scratch my head and tap away at my keyboard. Memories started coming back to me - silly things, intimate things, embarrassing things, childhood memories of my first

7

guitar and my first public performance at eleven years old. Then bigger things: slamming a dressing room door in Warren Beatty's face when he was acting like a jerk trying to get to Carly Simon, which may have been the inspiration for "You're So Vain". Sitting in Sly Stone's fur-lined bedroom in Beverly Hills, while Andy Newmark auditioned to be the drummer in Sly & The Family Stone. Yeah... it was pretty funny when Andy played Sly's practice pads, and Sly stood up and started dancing on his waterbed. He came this close to puncturing it and flooding the room and everything below it downstairs. A photo of the look on our faces would have been hilarious. Then I remembered my first outdoor concert at the Schaefer Festival in Central Park with Carly Simon - not so much the concert itself but my conversations backstage with George Harrison, Mike Love and Art Garfunkel. Would anyone be interested in the story about going to a party with Carly Simon at the Playboy Mansion in London? On acid? That was as crazy as you might expect. Also hilarious at times. It could be an interesting read.

It took almost a year, a long look back through diaries, journals, and calendars, as well as Wikipedia to make sure I had dates and locations correct. At some point, it all came together, and the flow started. I was thoroughly enjoying myself, sometimes laughing so loud I scared the cats out of the room. Whatever the catharsis was, a whole lifetime of memories about my time with these amazing artists came out and started filling up page after page.

The final result is a book of short, often funny recollections, geared to entertain, while showing insight into the minds of the amazing musicians and singers who shared the stage and studio with me. I designed it so the reader can skip around all they like. Each of the stories for the most part stands on its own. Some will make more sense if you read them in order, but it's not mandatory. Each section is named after a song that either directly relates to the artist I'll be talking about or signals the gist of what I'm about to reveal, without necessarily being sung by the star in question.

With that, I offer you a seat next to me in the studio, on the tour bus, on the plane and in my mind as I wind through the never-before-heard stories of the lives and interactions I've had with heroes and heroines of rock & roll. I will illustrate the confusion and contradictions, the love and the hate, the amazing music, and the unusual and vastly insightful minds of those who created the songs that marked our youth and still make us happy when we hear them. Let's start with a tale about four testosterone-laced teenagers and a motel...

Chapter One
Beginnings

I Fought The Law, and the Law Won

It was the spring of 1967, and we were the champions! No longer a hometown, sock hop, cover band - things were looking up. "Younger Girl" was by every description a hit. We had made it into the national top ten, and to number two on NY radio. The band was now enjoying an extended run of packed venues and cheering fans. We always did well in the Northeast and often played in upstate NY. Glens Falls, a popular year-round resort area, a hot spot for music, and at the time, a small, local community with a conservative leaning, would host us for the gig I will now describe. Kenny Gorka, Chris Darway, Jack Decker, our manager Jerry Davis and me, Jimmy Ryan, were on the road. Collectively, we were the rock band known as The Critters.

On a cloudy Friday morning, we left Westfield, New Jersey in our vintage Pontiac airport stretch limo, motored up the scenic NY State Throughway and arrived in Glens Falls mid afternoon. We were early for the load-in and needed a few odds and ends, so we checked into our motel, then headed into town to get what we needed. The local mom & pop general store suited our needs, so we let ourselves in, looked around, and found everything on our lists - bottle opener, a jeweler's screwdriver to tighten my glasses, potato chips and soda. Band manager and resident adult, Jerry Davis, browsed the aisles, spotting a small but well-stocked guns and ammo section. He thought about his home in Hillside, NJ, where lurked an annoying blue jay in his backyard. This little feathered nuisance kept buzz-bombing his wife's equally annoying, nasty, yapping, shaved-like-a-pimp-dog poodle and scaring the piss out of her. At first, he considered blowing the

The Critters' Pontiac Airport Limo,
"The Beast"

9

bird away with lethal firepower. But in a rare, Sierra Club moment of compassion, he decided to go easy on the errant little jay and limited his assault purchase to a BB rifle. Soon the little bugger would feel the agonizing sting of a speeding copper bead in his butt and leave the damn poodle alone. We didn't notice Jerry throwing the BB gun in the back and wouldn't have cared if we did. We left the store and proceeded to the hall to set up for the show.

Our evening performance was a killer, and the crowd cheered us like heroes. We did two encores, took our bows, waved goodbye to our fans and headed back to the motel. I was exhausted, so I hopped into bed and switched on the TV to catch a bit of Johnny Carson, while Chris, my roommate for the night, unpacked. Then came the sound of a fist on the door. "BLAM, BLAM, BLAM." Chris and I looked at each other, WTF?? Chris got up, walked to the door, started to open it but got knocked out of the way by our Jerry, the commando bonehead, BB gun wielding manager who fired several shots in my direction. The first rounds splintered a glass ashtray, also breaking the glass on the two ugly pictures over our beds. The second and final insult round pierced the can of Orange Crush on my nightstand. The perforated can peed orange liquid all over the broken glass, the nightstand, my watch, my guitar picks and change and found its way to the motel carpeting. Cute. He and my other band mates then took turns levying the same assaults on each other's rooms. It wasn't quite up to The Who or Van Halen doing their well known, "level the motel" routine, but they were pleased with their rampage-lite stupidity, and I was so tired I didn't give a shit. Whatever. I switched off the TV and fell asleep.

The next morning, we decided to just throw twenty-dollar bills on the dressers and leave the mess for the maids. It was breakfast time; we were famished, and being seasoned road rats, we were ready to brave the local diner. Kenny, our resident groupie magnet, had picked up two cute-but-barely-fifteen-year-old girls the night before, and was smart enough to not bring them to the motel. He was, however, not smart enough to exclude them from brunch. We picked up the two, way too sexy for their age, illegals on a corner not far from the diner. Rolling into the diner parking lot, we stepped out of the limo in slo-mo, hair to the wind like Fabio with our little groupies and made our grand entrance like the superstars we always wanted to be. Upon my request, a waitress and bus girl slid two tables together, set out napkins, salt and pepper, ketchup, diner grade coffee mugs and aluminum ware for all, and we took our seats. We ordered a typical road rat breakfast - eggs, bacon, pancakes, coffee, more coffee, wolfed it all down, and after forty-five minutes of non-stop, high pitched, limited vocabulary, run-on sentences from our two perky little barely teens, we were done. I paid the tab, and we

10

swaggered out all cool, climbed into our limo, drove a half-mile or so, dropped the groupies off where we had picked them up about a block from their houses so they wouldn't catch hell from their parents and made our way back towards the Throughway. We were happy, full and heading home.

After a few blocks we heard Chris, who was driving, quietly say, "Shit." I knew that tone and it took little to realize that the swirling beacons and police wailer, loud enough to be heard through the airtight limo windows and coming from behind us, belonged to a state trouper to whom we were of interest. We pull over, he opens his door, gets out and slowly struts up like Clint Eastwood with a pole up his ass, looks the limo over, head to tail, peers inside - front seat, back seat, and in his toughest, subdued yet confident macho voice, treats Chris to an unemotional "License and Registration" with no "please." Chris complies. Magnum Force looks it over, stuffs it in his pocket and with a mildly disinterested tone tells Chris to follow him in his squad car. Then a second police car arrives... then a third. You could say we were now giving this scenario our undivided attention as we threw a few hypotheses around while soiling ourselves. Did they see the two statutories get out of the limo and decide we had sampled them in glorious rock 'n' roll fashion? Was this about to get deadly serious? Our garish white Pontiac airport limo was now surrounded by four patrol cruisers, rolling through the quiet town of Glens Falls and headed for God knows where. Too bad there was no TV video crew to document our ridiculous motorcade.

In about five minutes, we found ourselves in the parking lot of the State Police campus, complete with a courthouse and the Warren County State Prison. Blood pressure/heart rate elevated. The arresting trouper ordered us out of the limo and had us lean against it, hands and legs spread, reality TV fashion, while the other troupers looked on. That's when central casting kicked in. As if he were in a cheesy, direct-to-VHS B-Movie, up struts a fifty-something, crew cut, chiseled chin, steel browed, cheap suited, butt-ugly grimacing detective who, without introducing himself, spews out every curse word in the English language. "What the fuck do we have here?" "Is this the kind of sissies Jersey sends us these days?" "Whadaya faggots sit down to piss?" "Fucking disgraceful." "Get them out of my sight before I puke." Was it our long hair? It was still the mid-sixties after all, and let's face it - Glens Falls was not London. We had foolishly forgotten to wear our crew cut wigs.

The disgusted detective turned, mumbling more profanities, and headed back to wherever he came from, and four cops escorted us into the station to address our as yet unknown crimes. We were then taken to separate rooms, each with our own personal intimidator. Always the joker and always trying to lighten things up, I said to the officer, who looked like my dad:" Gee sir, can't we just replace the burned-out taillight, pay the ticket and be on our faggy way?"

I got a somewhat cynical smile out of him, but he countered with, "You think this is funny? You're a comedian? You kids are in a big heap of trouble."

I replied, "What did we do? What are the charges? We weren't speeding and our turn signals work fine as far as I know."

He sneered, "Malicious mischief, son. You really pissed off the motel owner with your little shooting spree, and he's pressing charges. You can get three to five for that up here."

I quietly freaked to myself, "Jesus F$%#ing Christ, he did not just say three to five years!!" Now I'm not smiling, I'm not joking, and I'm not happy. I pleaded, "Oh, come on, we'll replace the stupid ninety-nine cent crap paintings, clean the rug and buy twenty new ash trays for the idiot motel owner. Let's not get crazy here!"

Now he's laughing but doesn't explain why. After reading me my rights, he simply says, "Follow me, son." He leads me to a wall-mounted phone for my one call. I call our band lawyer, Phil Kurnit. He's upset, but says he'll get right on it. I would have preferred a plan, but that was it - CLICK. Interrogator dude now leads me to the fingerprinting station - cold, black grease on my slowly rolling fingertips, well secured in the vice grip of fingerprinting dude, immortalizing my unique identifiers in ten little blocks on the print page. I am then escorted into the next room where I get my close-up taken by the Warren County jail photographer, front, profile, next. Another room with a very tall counter about as high as my chin, attended by Jabba The Hut. I am instructed to empty my pockets, rings, belt and watch into a big brown envelope and sign across the seal. I comply. He takes it from me with a grunt, and my escort and I begin my utterly miserable "dead man walking" passage to the clink. We are about to do hard time for intent to kill a blue jay and the collateral damage of a few broken ashtrays and a soiled carpet.

We arrive in an unnumbered cellblock with bars, walls, floor and ceiling all painted the same - government grade, lizard shit green. My cell consists of a sink and an ice-cold, piss covered toilet without a seat, complete with an assortment of pubic hairs. The "bunk" comes with one war surplus, rat-ass, dried snot wool blanket over a bare, grey and white striped, body-fluid-stained mattress. In complete horror, I drag myself into my new, sweet Jesus please, very temporary accommodations, sit down on the steel wall hung bed and am struck by the smell of fetid body odor. It was wafting up from the disgusting blanket, a chilling reminder of previous unwashed tenants, no doubt murderers, rapists, child molesters and worse. This was no white collar, Paris Hilton halfway

12

house. This was the place that blues songs were written about, and we were trapped here with a cast of characters sporting the scariest resumes I would ever hear.

We spent the first night by ourselves in our individual cells; we had not seen nor spoken to each other in about eighteen hours. I slept well (in my clothes) despite my fears, worries and the ever-present BO wafting up from my blanket, but did not wake up to the sound of singing robins. Prisons have their own unique alarm clocks. The wake-up call is a sequential banging of metal and gears, "CLANG, vrreeee, CLANG, vrreeee, CLANG, vrreeee," the sound of the automatic, three-inch diameter steel lockdown bolts crashing open. I thought someone was slamming my cell bars with an aluminum baseball bat. Talk about a violent, wake up and feel like shit moment.

Once everybody was up, we were ordered to strip, handed towels, a tiny bar of soap and a welded shut scrape razor with no shaving cream, and marched with a group of other naked men into the community showers. Astonishingly, everyone was cheerful and joking, basically making light of an otherwise horrible and humiliating situation. The constant comment from anyone we spoke to was, "You'll get used to it." We showered, dried off, marched semi-naked back to our cells and got dressed. Unfortunately for us, the Warren County State Prison had our suitcases, so we had two options - spend the day naked, or get back into our dirty clothes - no clean underwear, nice crispy sox.

Breakfast time. We were marched down to the dining hall, seated in comfortable leather chairs to well-appointed tables with fine silverware, linen napkins and beautiful antique china, then served eggs Benedict, French toast, fresh squeezed orange juice, imported gourmet coffee, choice of umpteen cereals, fresh croissants... NOT!! Steel chairs, steel tables and steel guards everywhere. Plastic trays and utensils were handed to us to enjoy a buffet of corned pig intestine hash, lizard eggs seasoned with rat turds, meadow muffins and some lukewarm mystery liquid that might have been coffee in the Jurassic period, but now had aged into the kind of swill that resembled what oil rigs dump into the Gulf when they explode. Encouragement from our cellmates abounded: "You'll get used to it."

With our delicious and nutritious first meal in Chez Clink out of the way, we had lots of leisure time to reflect on personal matters like suicide, insanity, starvation, goiter, rickets and maybe getting a fucking lawyer, STAT. I put in the first request for Phil Kurnit and was immediately advised that if I brought in one of those "highfalutin 'NY lawyers" the judge would likely hit us with the maximum sentence. The solution was a local, alcoholic ambulance chaser who regularly played golf with the judge and who rumor had it was generous in sharing fees with the bench when charges and sentences went his way. We reluctantly agreed, and they escorted us into the windowless interrogation room. A few minutes later, our vodka marinated public defender staggered in and plopped down on one of the comfy steel chairs. Despite the alcohol on his breath, he seemed very confident and knew what he was doing. He coached us to say in court exactly what he instructed, word for word, to neither embellish nor omit any testimony, and promised things would "work out" if we did. I said, "But Jesus, all this for a couple of ashtrays and a few excremental works of 'art 'that couldn't even pass for trashcan liners?" After a moment or two of silence and with a quizzical expression he said, "What did you just say?" I repeated my question. He said, "Uh, what about the smashed TV, ripped out sink and cracked toilet?" We all looked at each other in horror, W... T... A... F???

We can only guess at this point what had followed our relatively minor acts of BB gun terrorism. Apparently, there had been a bit of vandalism at the motel from rock groups in the past. The owner hated bands, kids, music and fun, and since it was the beginning of the season, decided to make an example of us. After we checked out and the maids reported the broken glass, he allegedly entered one of the rooms, saw the minor damage and decided to embellish a little. Someone, not us, smashed a TV and ripped a sink right out of the wall. He then called the state police, claiming we had nearly blown up the motel. And of course, the rest is history. Through no doing on our part, we had officially joined the ranks of Keith Moon, Pete Townshend, Roger Daltrey, and all those bands that made a practice of redecorating hotel rooms in Unabomber chic.

The days did not pass quickly in our stinky little holiday home from hell. After a week of "You'll get used to it" from gentlemen who in their former lives had hobbies like yanking out their girlfriends 'eyeballs, our day in court had finally arrived. A guard delivered our suitcases to our cells and instructed us to change into not as dirty underwear and our crumpled corduroy band suits. Today, we would stand before the local magistrate and be told our fate. What a sight for sore eyes. We looked and smelled like we had been sleeping in a dumpster for two weeks.

The trial was brief. We spoke our well-rehearsed lines to the judge, and it went exactly as Vodka Vic said it would. He suspended our three-year sentence with a year's probation, no hard time, records expunged after a year of good behavior, a not too stiff fine, a restitution bill to be paid to the shithead motel jerk and a legal fee of, you guessed it - exactly the amount we earned on the previous week's gig. The last item on the penal to-do list was the press. The judge instructed us to make a public apology on national TV, and the guys elected me to deliver it by a unanimous vote of, "I'm not fucking doing that!" After giving it some thought, here's what I said:

"My name is Jimmy Ryan. My band, The Critters, had the pleasure of performing in this wonderful town of Glens Falls a week ago. During our stay, and in the spirit of good fun, we went a little overboard, and *some* damage was done to the property of one of the fine citizens of Glens Falls. The motel management was fair in not making it too tough on us once we admitted to creating *some* of the damage cited in their complaint. For our part in this unfortunate event, we are REALLY sorry. As guests of the State of NY this week, we were comfortable and treated well, despite some laundry issues. The motel management also wants potential visitors of Glens Falls to know that as peace-loving, small-town folk, they will not be disrespected by scoundrels like The Critters, and will seek swift justice if anything like the events of the past week takes place in the future. Keith Moon, you have been warned.

"Younger Girl" had started slipping off the charts a few weeks prior to our little adventure in hell, but when the news hit the airwaves, we rocketed right back into the top ten. Who says soft rock bands can't break ashtrays?

A couple of years ago, I took my kids skiing at Whiteface Mountain, Lake Placid. As we were driving up the NY State Throughway, I saw the sign for the exit to Glens Falls and said to myself, wouldn't it be fun to take a quick trip down memory lane, drive by the mom-and-pop general store, the diner, Bates motel...? Then I had another thought. What would I do if I got pulled over?

Piano Man

So how did I end up in a band like The Critters? Influences. Mom, Dad, and my two sisters were hobby musicians. All sang, all played piano, some played and sang better than others - some form of music was almost always playing around my house. The bulk of it was annoying, so as a child, I didn't show much interest. My parents loved to listen to hokey music from artists like Bent Fabric (Alley Cat) and Lawrence Welk. Since my room was upstairs, far away from the kitchen where they kept a radio, I just ignored it. The birth of my interest in music as something other than old people noise came in 1950 when I was four. One summer morning, I was hanging out in the living room, playing with an assortment of toys, and a catchy song came on my mom's kitchen radio. I think it might have been "Goodnight Irene" or "The Tennessee Waltz", both far better than Mr. Welk and his musical therapy for insomnia, so my ears perked up. I bumbled my way over the letter blocks, dog-eared Dick And Jane books and Howdy Doody puppet and made my

15

way to the family's upright piano. I liked this loud piece of musical furniture, but until this point, never had the urge to interact with it. As I recall, it was a 1932, moldy smelling upright Knabe, and the yellowed and cracked ivory keys were just about level with my nose. With tiny fingers, about half the width of the white keys, I reached up and started tapping out the melody I had been hearing from the kitchen. How did I know which keys to press? I don't recall ever touching the piano before that, but after a try or two, I got the melody right, and Mom noticed. She was upbeat and complimentary, which lit a lightbulb in my little attention-obsessed head. I didn't visualize a fabulous career as the next Rachmaninov, but something significant had just happened and it inspired me. Mom just went back to scrubbing out stubborn water spots on the previous night's cocktail tumblers. It was the Cold War years, so she was likely obsessing about the possibility of Russians dropping the Bomb on our Livonia, MI house. But in all her worried imaginings, she came up for air long enough to notice what just happened. She and I both discovered I had some musical ability. For the moment, it went no further.

Video Killed the Radio Star

It's now 1955, and I'm nine. My parents bought a TV, and if I was home, its tubes never got cold. It was a black and white Sylvania, and state-of-the-art. By 1953, the TV networks started broadcasting some shows in color, but like any new technology, it took a few years for the breakthrough to grab the consumer wallet and the price to come down. My parents weren't ready to take the expensive plunge to color, so it was black and white for now.

I was an early TV addict, firing it up when I got home from school and keeping it cranking out shows until bedtime, with a few breaks for dinner and homework. I had my list of favorite shows - *Disneyland, I Love Lucy, Gunsmoke*, and dramas like *Dragnet*. My sister Marilyn and I watched *The Mickey Mouse Club* every day after school, but the big ones for me were *American Bandstand* and *The Ed Sullivan Show*. If anyone got me hooked on music, it would be Dick Clark. He personified cool and had the best artists on his show. There was Jerry Lee Lewis - brilliant songwriter, talented piano player, and amazing performer. Fats Domino, fun, funny, fat and another classic songwriter, but unlike Jerry Lee, he didn't do much beyond sitting, playing, singing and smiling. Bill Haley and the Comets, with their "Rock Around the Clock"? Awesome! Bobby Darin, Connie Francis, and many more did their thing while the Bandstand kids danced the Stroll, the Madison, the Jive and the Jitterbug, and I was mesmerized. I heard songs like "Come and Go With Me" by the Dell Vikings, "Long Tall Sally" by Little Richard, "Why Do Fools Fall In Love" by Frankie Lymon, and there was Chuck Berry. He played a beautiful, blond Gibson ES-350 guitar and did his classic "Duck Walk" while singing his timeless rockers. The single artist that inspired me to start guitar, though, was Elvis. Seeing him for the first time on *Ed Sullivan* on September 9th, 1956 was a life changer. I could not believe how exciting and soul shaking his music, his voice, his persona, and his band were, and I couldn't get enough of his amazing guitarist, Scotty Moore. Scotty's solo on "Hound Dog" had my jaw on the floor. I just loved his speed and the intricacy of his solos. But The King? I wanted to be him, period, or at least do what he was doing. I had to get a guitar, and I had to learn to play. The old Knabe upright was not for me. Piano was for my sisters and parents. I wanted a guitar, and I wanted it now!

Mom and Dad were excited about my budding ambition and wanted to help. On a grey, wintery Saturday afternoon in February 1956, they took me down to the local music store. Through the window, I saw a beautiful, light green Gretsch hollow body electric guitar hanging high on the wall. I was drooling, but Dad made it clear that I had to earn a guitar like that. No problem. I was damn well determined and ready to go. We went in, looked around, negotiated with a salesman and closed the deal. They rented a cheap acoustic guitar for me, booked a few lessons, and I set to work... doing horrible, boring and useless three-notes-on-one-string exercises, graduating to silly "A B C D E F G" and "Twinkle Twinkle Little Star" songs. This was not Elvis! This was CRAP, and though I begrudgingly agreed to continue, I spent most of my practice time trying to figure out rock 'n' roll chords and ignoring my lessons. My parents were well aware of my frustration with the B-grade music store teacher, so they enrolled me in the prestigious Jack Moore Guitar School across town. It was a good fit, and I started making progress.

I enjoyed my lessons and being part of the Saturday morning band. The music was challenging and often interesting, but the rebel in me would not rest. I went through several of Jack's teachers and never settled on what I would call a winner. The problem was I didn't see the need nor value of reading music, so I devised a sneaky little cheat. I would ask my teachers to play me the song du jour, so I could get the "feel" of it. I was born with a musical gene, and my ability to hear, memorize and play back whatever I heard was genetic - I didn't learn it; it was imbedded in my DNA. So, as requested, my teacher would play the song on the sheet music, then I would stare at the music stand and dish back what I heard them play. I got away with it most of the time, but Jack's wife, Virginia, who also taught, was as sharp as an FBI operative. She had a hunch about what I was doing. Agent Virginia set a trap. She played the song we were about to tackle... wrong. With a sly smile, executing the song as I had asked, she inserted some random alternate notes mixed in with what was on the sheet music. On the return volley I repeated her mistakes verbatim instead of playing what was on the page. She then revealed her ruse. Busted and red faced, I stared at the floor, as she read me my guitar school Mirandas. "You will learn to read music, or don't let the door smack you in the ass on the way out." If I were to continue, I'd have to commit to practicing the page. I acquiesced like a good little curmudgeon, but much to my surprise, it didn't end up being a terrible burden. In learning to read, I could access many more titles that I wouldn't have discovered any other way. I was growing as a real musician, instead of posing like one with my former three chord vocabulary. No question, the reading skill was valuable, but I never enjoyed it. My reading didn't improve until my adult years, but I got through the lessons.

Though I wasn't his best student, Jack Moore believed in me. He knew I had no ambition to be a musical academic. I would never be part

The Jack Moore Guitar School 1958.
I'm top row, center next to Jack Moore (standing)

of an orchestra like Lawrence Welk's, so now and then, he'd give me an opportunity to play what I wanted. Once a year, he would put together a show where the entire guitar school, some eighteen guitarists, would set up like an orchestra. In this case, he rented The Gross School auditorium (seriously) on June 21, 1958 and put on a student concert. We had an odd and unusual sound - ragged clusters of strumming acoustic guitars from amateur to advanced students, with melody and harmony played by various electric guitars and ten-string electric lap steels. Listening to the steels take the lead, I often felt we had a kind of "drunk in Hawaii" sound. In its own weird way, it was unique and often enjoyable. We would perform songs like "Steel Guitar Rag", which showed off the more accomplished steel players, and ballads like Connie Francis's "My Happiness". As part of these concerts, Mr. Moore would let me showcase a song of my choice. For the summer 1958 concert, I got together with my friend, Billy Rankin, another kindred spirit and guitar school student, and worked out a two-man version of "Guitar Boogie Shuffle". I played lead, he played rhythm. We were just barely good enough to pull it off, but despite nerves and jitters, we got up in front of the audience, took a couple of deep breaths, counted it in, and three minutes and four shaking hands later, we nailed it. With all the middle-of-the-road music in the concert, no one expected a foot stomping rocker. I shredded the flashy ending riff, we both exhaled, and the audience erupted in cheers and sustained applause! The crowd was only parents, friends and relatives, but it was a thrill like no other. This was big, and I was getting more and more hooked. Sixty-three years later, I still remember it like a first kiss.

Getting back to my idols, another name arises - Buddy Holly. He was amazing and became even more important to me than Elvis. I had to take

Billy Rankin and Me - 1958

a few points away from The King, because he wore the guitar more than he played it. Using it as a prop, he just hung it around his neck while gyrating. Scotty Moore, his lead and rhythm guitarist, did the heavy lifting. But Buddy Holly actually played his Fender Stratocaster with a rock-solid sense of timing, rhythm and that wonderful twang. He wrote his own songs, and that inspired me. His chord progressions were fresh, his solos were perfect, not too flashy, just right for the songs. His singing style was imitated by many future artists who sold far more records than he did. His voice was like no other. John Lennon and Paul McCartney were of the same opinion - they listed him as one of their most prominent influences.

I first heard Buddy Holly's recording of "That'll Be The Day" coming out of a car radio as I came out of church, after my brother Dick's wedding. A friend of Dick's had it blasting from his red MG TD convertible, parked in front of St. Cletus. Dick and his bride, Ruth, had just married there, and I was one of the altar boys. To my ears, the song was a groundbreaker. I ran up to the car and asked Mr. MG who it was, but he didn't know. Standing by his car mesmerized, I listened till the last chord, when the DJ blurted out "That was Buddy Holly and the Crickets with their new hit, 'That'll Be The Day'." Throughout the weekend, I kept waiting for it to play on the radio again, but no luck. On Monday after school, with the song still in my head, I took my allowance down to the local record store and bought the 45 RPM single. Rushing home on my bike, I threw it on the old Silvertone phonograph and played it over and over. By the time I finished, I had almost worn it out. But... I now had the song memorized, so attempting to play it on my guitar was next. My first shot at the opening riff sounded like a chimpanzee playing with his elbows, but after a few days of practice, I nailed it. Then I noticed that Buddy's strings weren't ringing out when he played rhythm. The sound was tight, chunky, and throbbing. How was he doing that? At the guitar school, we just strummed open chords. We had little finesse, letting our strings just ring through the chord changes like amateur folkies at a coffee shop. This was a different, more sophisticated technique. His guitar sounded like it was pumping and muted, but when I played the same chords on my guitar, it just sounded slushy. What was I missing? On October 28, 1958, *American Bandstand* provided the answer. Dick Clark flashed his classic smile into the ABC cameras and announced, "From Lubbock, Texas, here are Buddy Holly and the Crickets, performing 'It's So Easy 'and 'Heartbeat'." As the band played through the songs, Buddy's strumming arm hardly moved. The heel of his hand was resting on the bridge, pivoting, not strumming... That was it! Use your palm to mute the strings. I grabbed my guitar, gave it a try, and it worked! Once I saw how he did it, the application was a cinch, and now I had a whole new style in my repertoire.

This was a fantastic discovery for me, but I was not alone - so many guitarists, from The Beatles to Eric Clapton to Steve Vai, made use of this style. It's a staple in most guitar-oriented pop and especially heavy metal music. Rick Ocasek's eighth-note muted rhythm was a Cars signature, and he can thank Buddy Holly for the inspiration. What would a Metallica or Ozzie Osbourne record be without it? Buddy may not have invented this technique, but he was the first to popularize it on multimillion selling records!

The Shadow of My Mom

Because my dad was a sales engineer, and because his employer, The Diehl Company, liked to move people around, we changed states almost every four years. Here's what my childhood residence record looked like: 1946-1950, Plainfield, NJ. 1950-1955 Livonia, MI. 1955-1960, LaGrange, IL. 1960-1963, Port Washington, NY. 1963-1968, Westfield, NJ. (with a second residence in the dorms at Villanova) 1968-1973, New York City. After that my moves were my doing, not my parents', but they were almost as frequent, starting with London, England in 1973. As you can imagine, with all that moving, I had some challenging social issues. No sooner would I make friends and establish relationships, than Dad would announce the next move, and it would be "Pack up, we're out of here." Fate wasn't always unkind, though. Each time we moved, things got a little better for me, but the initial phase of each new town left the entire family feeling lonely. My parents established no lasting friendships, so dinners with their friends or neighbors were rare. This involuntary pulling away from close friends and being thrown into new schools and cafeterias full of strangers was making me miserable. I never knew where it was ok to park my tray and eat lunch, and the result of making a mistake was rejection and humiliation. I was shy, and incapable of just walking up to people and introducing myself, so I always found a table of unpopular, nerdy kids, happy that I would join them. There were pretty girls everywhere, but I was invisible to them. I needed a solution, because this shit was getting old, fast, and despite my fears, I wasn't about to spend the rest of my life as human wallpaper.

By the time we moved to Port Washington, I could play like a pro, at least by the standards of pop music in 1961. Practicing day and night, I knew my way around the fretboard, not like Joe Satriani, but at least in a surfing Ventures kind of way. I had no friends yet, so sitting in my room and playing along with records occupied the bulk of my time. I was also bullied a little. Greasers were the scary, ever present alternate life forms in those days. Gangs were forming, and we lived next to Manorhaven, where the tough and surly Italian kids lived. I often feared seeing the glimmer of a switch blade while walking home from school, and "Little Professor" was a taunt I heard more than once from one or more of the school thugs. I was skinny and wore thick glasses that made my eyes bulge, I sucked at sports, and I did not exude confidence. But then… my guitar gently whispered, "I can help you with that."

A few weeks into ninth grade, Mom showed up after school and marched me down to the principal, Mr. Allen's office. In a humiliating gesture to flaunt my talent, we must have appeared to him like an organ grinder and monkey. After a discussion between them, with me squirming in my chair, they booked me on a "Beehive," which is a social mixer, not a concert venue. I felt that familiar sense of fear and intimidation rising. She said my band would be happy to perform for the kids. What??? I'm not kidding. I had no band, I didn't know any musicians, and she was booking this non-existent entity for a gig three weeks out. Let's see - create a band, come up with a half-hour set, rehearse it to perfection and do it all in three weeks while juggling schoolwork. I could have killed her.

Marvin Lubinsky was a kid who lived seven houses down on my block. He was my first Port Washington friend, was popular and knew a lot of kids. Introducing me to Bruce Leslie, who owned a set of drums, and Doug MacLeod, who owned a cheap Harmony guitar, Marv was rapidly becoming my best friend. Now... I did not say Doug played a guitar, and I did not say Bruce played drums, but they did the best they could. I spent a lot of time with the radio in my room/isolation ward, and with the gift of being able to play by ear, I knew most of the pop tunes of the day. I set out to teach the guys as much as I could in our limited amount of time, but I knew it would be up to me to carry the show. As much as I'd love to say I was the Buddy Holly in the band... I wasn't - I had not yet learned to sing. No one in the band sang, so it would be a risky instrumental set. Dance bands without singers can be fine if you're talking about Duke Ellington, but we were far from that. You can't play "Walk, Don't Run" and "Sleepwalk" all night without clearing the dance floor, and yet... that's what we were about to do.

Somehow, after many hours of after-school rehearsal, individual instruction, and teenage enthusiasm, we pulled it together and knocked out a ragged twenty, not thirty-minute set. When the fateful evening arrived, and it was time to plug and play, I was in the state of white-knuckled terror. The guys were cool and popular - that helped the optics, but no one would mistake them for The Ventures, and they were as nervous as I was. Mostly it was me, playing like I had four hands, Doug strumming away at something, I'm not sure what, and Bruce bashing away, not great, but not terrible either. Doug's dad bought him a Fender Bassman amp for the occasion, which helped. It was a loud, great sounding box with four ten-inch speakers and 45 watts of slam-the-back-row power. He shared it with me, and I glommed the loud channel. To my amazement, the kids loved us. We thought we sucked, but the crowning moment was on the following Monday. I was hanging out on the playground with Marvin and Bruce, and one of the scariest, mangiest, six-foot, chain-and-switch-blade gorillas in the school approached us. I was bracing myself for a bullying, but to everyone's surprise, he smiled and said, "Hey man, that thing you did Friday night? That was pretty cool. I thought you were just some little faggot, but you're ok. Keep it coming." Then he reached out to shake my hand. This playing guitar thing was changing my life.

Not to be unkind to my early musician friends, I would like to point out, as a footnote, that Doug MacLeod went on to be a world-renowned blues artist, and Bruce Leslie, a chancellor of several universities. They did just fine, despite some early growing pains in the music world.

Brooklyn Dodgers

We're up to the spring of 1960. I was a ninth grader at John Philip Sousa junior high, a fabulous Fliptone (the name we gave our little band), and first chair alto sax in the school orchestra. We were preparing for a concert featuring Ravel's *Bolero*. Yes, I said alto sax in an orchestra featuring Ravel. Saxophones in orchestras are like bullhorns in a confessional - loud, crass and unwelcome. But not in this orchestra. We were a marching band on chairs - all wind instruments and percussion. Saxes in this case were de rigueur. Also, the tubas and trumpets were the loudmouths, not the woodwinds. I was among kindred musical louts, making those awful, out of tune sounds junior high marching bands make when they try to play classical music. I'm kidding. Actually, we weren't all that bad. Many of us were practice junkies, so we carried our weight with honor and good intonation. I enjoyed sax, but I never got good enough to play in a rock band, certainly not like King Curtis or Bobby Keys of The Rolling Stones. Unfortunately, with school, I didn't have time to practice and perfect two instruments. After *Bolero*, I dropped the sax and devoted my full attention to the guitar.

Then the fun started. With the help of our rhythm guitarist Pete's dad, a music business attorney, we landed an audition to be part of the biggest show of the year. It was the Brooklyn Paramount Easter Parade of Stars. These shows would run from 10am to 11pm, for ten straight days, over Easter vacation. In previous years, the show had broken all ticket sales records, selling out most of their shows. This was the chance of our short lifetimes and we were stoked.

On that fateful Saturday in April, we packed our guitars, drums and amps into two cars, and our dads drove us into Brooklyn. The Paramount was in an iffy neighborhood at the intersection of Flatbush and DeKalb Avenues in downtown Brooklyn, but we couldn't care less. Murray the K and Clay Cole, the show's hosts and big-time celebrities in their own right, were about to discover us! To share the stage with so many superstars like Little Anthony and the Imperials, Ben E. King, Bobby Rydell, Johnny Mathis and Bobby Vee, was unimaginable a week ago. I'd also like to point out here that Bruce, Doug and Pete had been practicing, and they were getting really good at their instruments.

The producers scheduled our audition for 1:20pm, and they were running on time. We heard our name over the PA, "Next band, The Fliptones! Please set up and be ready to play in ten minutes!" We dragged our gear from the wings of the stage out to the center where the previous band was clearing off, set up, plugged in and let it rip. As I looked out into the empty seats in this vast theater, I felt this was a turning point in my life. Soon, screaming fans would fill these rows, and we would be among the stars for whom they were cheering. With this fantasy blazing in my mind, I played my little butt off. No fears, no mistakes, confident and cocky. My band mates were in a similar frame of mind, and we crushed it. Though there were only a handful of people holding the audition, they clapped and said, impressive set, guys, thank you! We packed up our gear, reloaded the cars, and our dads took us out for pizza to celebrate a job well done.

The next day the call came. My mom answered the phone, at first confused by who was calling, and then I saw her frown. I didn't realize it was one of the show staff calling, and I asked her, "Who was that?"

She hesitated, then said it was Murray the K's secretary.

My heart stopped. "AND....?"

"You passed the audition and you're invited to join the show."

I let out a whoop, leaping and dancing around the room. I didn't know how we'd fit into the show and didn't care. But Mom remained expressionless and did not join in the dance.

When Dad came home from work, she gave him the news in private, then called the other parents. I was up in my room, happy, clueless and practicing for my Brooklyn Paramount debut.

Dad shouted, "Jimmy, can you please come downstairs, we'd like to talk to you."

Those words never led to anything good. Mom and Dad were sitting together on the sofa, so I straddled a chair across from them.

"What's up?"

They glanced at each other with sad eyes, and Mom said to Dad, "Go on, tell him, dear." He looked at me, paused, then dropped the bomb.

"We're turning down the offer, Jimmy. We're so proud that you passed the audition, but all the parents agreed - you're too young. Maybe you can try again when you're a bit older."

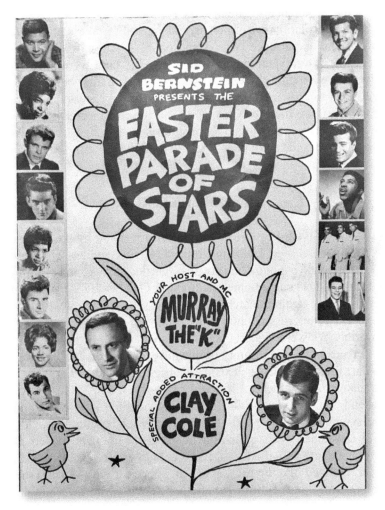

I was devastated by their ill-conceived, dictatorial decision and made my feelings clear. How could they tear up our heaven-sent invitation to the big time? Were they crazy? I argued and argued, but my protests fell on deaf ears. The Brooklyn Paramount would go on without The Fliptones.

To this day I'll never understand why, with parental supervision, we couldn't have just played the damn ten days and been done with it. We'd miss school, but so what? I'm sure our teachers and guidance counselors would have applauded our accomplishment and considered it a valuable life experience. We'd be like exchange students, studying the foreign culture of Brooklyn and the world of live entertainment. This onetime event for ten days out of our lives, a chance for an incredible, life enhancing experience - gone in sixty seconds.

As a consolation prize, our parents agreed to take us to one of the shows. The experience was stand-on-our-chairs awesome, though bittersweet. Twenty famous artists, many of whom were in my record collection, were right there, live on stage, singing their hearts out. I had never been to a rock concert before - star-struck, cheering and dancing in the aisles like there was no world outside this theater. During those two hours of musical joy, I almost forgot, if things had turned out differently, I would have been up there with them.

How I Won The West

We lived in Port Washington for about three years, and somehow I knew my time there was ending. That three-to-four-year mark had always signified change, and this time was no different. Dad came home one night in October 1962 and announced Diehl had once again transferred him. This time it was across the river to New Jersey, not cross-country, but far enough to require another family relocation. We were to start packing immediately.

Let's examine the insanity of this move for a moment. In Port, I was popular; I had a steady girlfriend, a successful band and good grades. I was also in a high school fraternity that threw kick-ass parties every weekend. My life was on fire in the best possible way. Mom and Dad were sympathetic, but it didn't matter. On Monday morning, Oct 15th, 1962, I watched with a sinking heart as the movers loaded all our possessions into an Allied Van. I said goodbye to my girlfriend, Barbara Kaiser, climbed into the passenger seat of the car with Mom in the back and began my journey into yet another new life... in the middle of my junior year!

Our new address was 62 Westbrook Rd., Westfield, NJ. For me, it was an immediate catastrophe, but for my three older sibs, Elva, Dick and Marilyn, it made little difference. Elva left for college when I was eight and never moved back. Bermuda was her new home in paradise. Dick got married in Livonia many years ago and was now enjoying his new life in California. Marilyn was at Merrimack College in Massachusetts with new friends and her future husband, so what did she care? I might as well have been in Siberia, staring at my bedroom walls, again with no friends and joining unfamiliar classes in the middle of a semester. It was deja vu, walking around the school cafeteria looking for a place to park my tray to the repeated refrain, "Someone is sitting there." My options were to feel sorry for myself, which I was more than happy to do, or come up with some way to improve the situation. Once again, my guitar quietly whispered, "I can help you with that."

As I ground through the school days, I found that if I surrendered to the situation, I could sometimes avoid crushing depression. But as long as I was mentally renegotiating the move, my life remained a misery. I wasn't good at sports, so I had limited after-school options. There was a marching band, and I joined it, but again, I didn't love playing sax. I loved playing guitar, and because I had time, I practiced long and hard. I would come home after school, put on the radio and just jam with whatever was on the air, usually top forty. The calluses on my fingertips were becoming like hardened old leather, and my coordination and agility were improving daily. For a time, I started listening to jazz, trying to keep up with legendary guitar players like Johnny Smith. I even bought one of his teaching methods, but that period of my life passed quickly. I was a rocker, and jazz was just too calm and intellectual for me. There were the French Romantic players like Django Reinhardt, who I could listen to all day, but traditional bebop jazz just didn't have the fire I was looking for. Pop and rock were in my wheelhouse, and I was doing what it took to become proficient. We call it wood shedding. You take your instrument out to the shed, close the door and don't come out till you're playing like a pro.

While practicing guitar like a fanatic was an excellent career move, my social life was a big zero. Eventually I would have to put the guitar down and face cold reality - I had no friends. I did, however, have one connection that I had not yet explored. On my last day in Port, Barbara gave me the phone number of her cousin, Maria, who went to Holy Trinity school in Westfield... it was time to make the call. I went downstairs, grabbed the kitchen wall phone with the eighty-foot curly cord, sat down with it in the dining room and dialed her number. I identified myself, and she said, "You're Barbara's boyfriend? I'd love to meet you. My school's doing a hayride on Friday night. If you're not busy, please come and join us!"

THAT was what I needed to hear. Join them, I did, and it was a blast. She introduced me to a couple of her friends, one of whom was a guitarist in a band, Paul Iovino. We became immediate buddies. We talked guitars and stars most of the ride, and I all but ignored Maria. Her popularity kept her surrounded by guys, so she didn't even notice. Towards the end of the evening Paul told me his band, The Vibra-Tones, were playing the following night at the Knights of Columbus Hall. "Would I like to hear them?" If so, he would put me on the guest list. Of course, I said yes, but I also asked if I could bring my guitar and maybe sit in for a song. He looked at me with squinted eyes, some hesitation... then smiled and said, "Sure, why not?

27

I practiced three hours the next day, so I'd be warmed up and ready. Big night, new crowd, new band - no way was I going to blow this one. And this time, I was in charge, not Mommy Dearest. Choosing your path is so much better than having it chosen for you!

The evening arrived, and I showed up fashionably late. The ticket lady at the front door checked me off on the guest list, and I strutted in, dressed in my cool best, guitar in its case and ready for the challenge. I saw Maria hanging out near the stage with a group of friends, so I wandered over and thanked her again for the previous night's invitation. She was warm and friendly and introduced me to several more of her friends, while the band played Chuck Berry's "Johnnie B Goode". They were doing a decent rendition of the song but were loud as hell. Conversation was impossible. The best we could manage was to smile, bob our heads to the music, or grab a partner and dance. I chose to just lean back on the edge of the stage, poised and ready.

Thirty minutes later, the band took a break. I went backstage, cornered Paul and asked if I could sit in for the next song. Again he hesitated slightly... thought about it... then said, "Are you sure you're up to this?" - his way of saying, "Do you think you're good enough to play with my band?"

I laughed and said, "Fuck you, I'll wipe the stage up with you."

That got his Italian hackles up." Ok, wise guy. You're on," he said with a "we'll see" grin.

The other guitarist, Wally, was happy to stay on break and hang with his homies. I walked out onto the small stage, guitar over my shoulder, maneuvered around the drums and plugged into Wally's amp. When the other players were in place I said, "Do you guys know 'Guitar Boogie Shuffle' [my old favorite from the Jack Moore Guitar School days]? It's just a simple blues shuffle in E."

All they heard was "simple blues shuffle in E" and nodded, "Uh, yeah, sure."

I gave them a preview of the tempo, snapped my fingers, tapped my foot, and counted it in:" A one, a two, a one, two, three, four," and slammed into the opening riff, probably louder and more aggressive than they were expecting. The song was pretty complicated, with jazzy phrases at a fast clip, but no worries. This had been my showcase piece for years, and I knew it backwards and forwards. The crowd jumped to their feet and started dancing, while the band did their best to keep up. They looked a little shocked at this skinny stranger with thick glasses blowing through the complex riffs. When it was done and the applause ended, I got the "Cool, man!" "Good job!" "Wow. Yeah man!" from the guys.

Paul just stood by his amp, nodding his head, and finally said, "Not

28

bad for a dumb Irishman," then with a smile and a handshake, "Really good, man."

I left the stage with a big, shit-eating grin on my face. The rest of the evening seemed like a dream, almost as if I had always lived there. I had friends again and felt like I was right where I belonged. Paul continued the high praises for what he called my "slam dunk," and started introducing me as his new favorite guitarist.

The outcome was not what I expected, nor even hoped for. Paul called me the following evening and broke the news that Wally had quit the band. With guilty butterflies churning in my stomach, I said to Paul, "I hope it wasn't because of me. I wasn't trying to replace him. I just wanted to meet some new people, jam with a good band, and have some fun."

He replied, "No. He just wasn't into it anymore. But now we're short one band member. Would you like to join The Vibra-Tones as our new lead guitarist?"

"Really? Sure. That would be great!" I couldn't resist - "Are you sure I'm up to it?"

He laughed and returned my "fuck you" from the previous night, and said, "Band practice is next Saturday morning at my house. We start at 10am. Bring your guitar and amp, and if you have a mike, bring that too. We could use some vocals."

After months of feeling unpopular, unwanted and lonely, that Knights of Columbus dance turned my life around. I was beaming when I gave Mom and Dad the news. They were thrilled and congratulated me. They were also quite relieved. Mom knew how badly the move had affected me and didn't know what to do about it. Dad was always emotionally clueless, so he wasn't much help. But in my heart, I was learning that I had been given something that was unique, something magical that would carry me through much of what life dumped at my doorstep. With that dawning realization, I felt extremely grateful. And my guitar gently whispered, "You're welcome."

Ch Ch Changes

The Vibra-Tones did not hold together well after I joined. I was a serious musician, and if I was going to do this, my condition would be that everyone with me would be equally committed. Several weren't and over time they either dropped out or were fired. We started with the bass player and drummer, but it didn't stop there. We had heard about a pianist named Chris Darway who lived in the next town, Scotch Plains. Paul and I thought adding a keyboardist could help us expand into new musical territory, so we contacted Chris and held an informal audition. It went very well. We knew from the first song that Chris was our man. He was quirky, a great pianist, sang (a little), wrote some original songs and was enthusiastic about joining the band. He was also an excellent artist.

Next came the drummer. Chris had a drummer friend named Jack Decker who he had been jamming with over the last year and requested we give him a tryout. We set up an informal audition at Chris 'house, picked a song, counted it in, and within seconds, Jack blew us away. He created complex and original rhythms I'd never seen a kid do and fit them right in with otherwise simple pop songs. He was a winner. As with Chris, Jack was more than happy to join the band. He was a free agent and ready to rock.

The next replacement was bass. Our current bassist, Paul Battalora, was a friend of Wally's and when Wally quit, after a short time, he quit in solidarity. Paul knew a "greaser" named Kenny Gorka who played bass. If you're not familiar with the term, "greaser" would be the kid that looked like the Fonz in *Happy Days*. Then of course there was the movie, *Grease*. Now mind you, I was on the other side of the high school political spectrum, a "rah-rah," with my white Levi's, madras shirts and short, well combed hair. This was a stretch for me. With my experience in Port of often being bullied and threatened by the greasers there, I was in "whoa" mode on this one. Paul, who was somewhere in the middle between the rahs and the greasers, urged me to try Kenny. He pointed out that Kenny might bring in a new audience for us, since to date we were only attracting the clean-cut kids. I decided it couldn't hurt to keep an open mind.

Kenny had a superb 1960 Fender Jazz Bass and a loud, thumping Ampeg Bass amp, and knew his way around a fingerboard. He was also a super nice guy who only looked and dressed like John Travolta for effect. Being a ladies' man, not a fighter, he diffused all my BS prejudices against anyone who didn't dress like me. I had not yet reached the age of introspection, but having my judgment pleasantly overturned was an awakening of sorts. Kenny and I became immediate friends and remained so until his death in 2015.

The Vibra-Tones sounded like the top bands on the radio, and our work schedule reflected it. That summer, we landed a job playing on the food court deck of the Union Drive-In Theater every Wednesday evening from June to the end of August. Not only did they pay us, but we got free snacks and could stay to watch the movie. Money was not an issue, because we were all in high school, living with our parents. We were in it for the joy of performing, and our enthusiasm and energy were the proof. People loved us. They came to the drive-in as much for The Vibra-

Tones as for the movie. Well, to be honest, most of the kids our age came to the drive-in for the opportunity to get a little... or a lot. We were no different and brought dates to every show.

One evening, Chris and I lamented that there were several songs that we liked that had sax solos, and we were lacking in that area. A couple of them were in our set, one being "Harlem Nocturne". Though I played sax passably in the high school band, my sax chops were not up to this tune. We brought up the idea of getting a sax player with Paul. To our surprise, he had an old friend from nearby Plainfield, whose band had just split up. This was exciting news. Paul called him and invited him to come to a practice and jam. His name was Bob Podstawski. Bob was another winner. Not only could he play well, he was also a keyboardist, percussionist and a talented singer.

Then it got weird. Bob had only played with serious musicians and had no desire to downgrade with us. Once he joined, it became apparent that someone in the band was holding us back. We all knew who it was, and with reluctance, we had to own up. It was the founder, manager, and only original Vibra-Tone left - the guy who got me this job in the first place and changed my life - Paul. This was difficult for me. Paul was my friend, he took me under his wing, introduced me to innumerable people, many of whom became close friends, and was the one getting us bookings. But Paul was the weak link. He did everything well except play and sing. Bob called me one afternoon, and with as much tact as he could muster said:

"Jimmy - this is kind of awkward, but I'm having a problem with Paul's playing. I know he's your friend and introduced us, but he keeps messing up the chords to our songs. We know he doesn't practice. He's in it for the partying, not the music. Would you be open to hearing the guitarist that was in my previous band that just broke up? He's a lot better than Paul."

Ahh, that sinking feeling. I was sixteen and had never been confronted with this kind of dilemma - imperil a friendship for the sake of personal gain or settle for the status quo. I gave Bob a vague, "Let me think about this for a day or two" answer. He was right, but we were approaching crossroads. If we kept Paul, the band would continue to be good, but never great. With that decision, Bob would likely quit. Or, I could hold The Vibra-Tones as my business, my career, and the livelihood of four other band mates. That would serve the greater good. To help move things along, Bob brought me a record that his band had cut that featured his friend. It was a no-brainer. His friend was an amazing singer, a great guitarist and wrote songs. An audition would just be a formality for someone of this caliber. Nonetheless, we had him over to Chris 'house, plugged in, played a couple of songs we all knew, and it

31

was an immediate yes. His name was Don Ciccone. We all acknowledged that his joining The Vibra-Tones would be a substantial upgrade.

We left that audition feeling both elated and sad, as we knew there was a difficult task facing us. The four of us, Chris, Jack, Kenny and I met the following Saturday morning at my house and took a vote. It was unanimous: Paul was out; Don was in. We invited Paul over and broke the news to him. He didn't take it any better than we expected. We told him about Don, aired our feelings about his lack of commitment to his voice and instrument, and made it clear we were serious about making this an actual career, not a side job. He understood, we shook hands, and that was that.

Don was a fascinating character. He was good looking, a great singer, charming and a rich kid. His dad had a close association with the shadowy side of car dealerships, and his family owned a fancy restaurant. They lived on Belvedere Ave in Plainfield, NJ in an enormous mansion on a hill, with a bowling alley in the basement. There was a ballroom-like space in the East Wing for us to rehearse, and even an underground tunnel to their garage at the bottom of the hill. This garage sported a turntable. You could drive in, hit a button, and within a few seconds, an electric motor would wheel your car around, facing outward. This place was designed for quick escapes. Shadowy side of car dealerships.

Don's dad passed away before we met, so I never had the pleasure of shaking his limp, ice cold hand. Don rarely spoke of him, but when he did, the words "love" and "great loss" were not part of the conversation. We were grateful for Don and this amazing rehearsal space and didn't much care about how it was acquired, nor its creepy history. But if I paid attention to the hairs on the back of my neck and occasional goose bumps, I'd say the mansion had some unresolved issues. Don once casually mentioned that there were encounters in its history with some Discarnate Americans. Little things like hearing bowling balls crashing into pins in the basement when only he and his sister were home and both upstairs. Then he'd go down to inspect and find all pins standing and balls on the rack. Goose bumps and hairs tingling on the back of my neck.

Since there was no one left from the original Vibra-Tones, we changed our name to something more consistent with the times - The Critters. It was kind of a dumb name, but right in line with The Beatles, The Animals, The Crickets, etc.

The Critters, 1964 - L to R: Me, Chris Darway, Kenny Gorka, Don Ciccone, Jack Decker, Bob Podstawski

Behind the Music

Our popularity continued to grow, and a big part of it was performing original songs. Don wrote a song called "Georgiana" which was a regular in the set, as well as "I'm Gonna Give", a collaboration between Don and me. Things were going well, but we felt that to take it to the next level a manager would be helpful and should be on the top of the to-do list. Paul used to handle that role, but now he was gone, and none of us had any music business connections. We thought if we could find a bigger venue to play than our usual school dances, we might increase our odds of being seen by managers and/or agents scouting for new talent.

There was a very popular dance hall in Union, NJ called The Flagship. They built it to look like a small ocean liner and parked it in the middle of Route 22. Among all the stores, gas stations and strip malls on Route 22, people held it as either a state monument or a hideous eyesore, depending on your sense of humor. In the image below, it looks like it's sitting on water. It's not. That's pavement. Over the years several businesses called it home, but currently it was the hottest teen club in the area. This was what we were looking for, so I cold called the ticket office. With a short phone call and a slick sales pitch, I landed us a booking, and in two weeks we were on the Flagship stage rocking our little teenage

The Flagship Dance Hall

butts off.

But that wasn't the point. The point was finding a manager, and as luck would have it, a local manager and promoter had heard of us and was in attendance. He loved our show and offered to manage us. Mission accomplished! The Jerry Davis I mentioned in the first chapter was now on our payroll... or should I say, we were on his.

On the promotion side of Jerry Davis 'resume was a venue he booked called The Elizabeth Elks Bandstand. It was on Westfield Avenue in Elizabeth, NJ, an old building kept in good condition, with good acoustics, and an ideal venue for dances/concerts. He offered us the job as the house band, and we eagerly accepted.

One of our first concerts, Feb 1965, was with Clay Cole, the well-known DJ and TV personality that I almost met at the Brooklyn Paramount fiasco when I was a Fliptone. Tickets were $2 in advance and $2.50 at the door. He would host the show with Tony Orlando ("Halfway To Paradise") and Bobby Lewis ("Tossin 'and Turnin'") as the main attractions, and as offered, we would be the backup band, an oddly satisfying role. The kids would focus on the singers, so we could relax and just play. It went very well, and the audience loved it. We enjoyed meeting these stars and providing their musical backup, and I wish it had been memorable. It wasn't.

The next show was The Ronettes and this one had my undivided attention. "Be My Baby" and "Walking In The Rain" rocketed them into world fame, and I was among their biggest fans. The opportunity to hang with them would have been inconceivable a month before, but here we were, eighteen years old, getting ready to be their backup band. *Ed Sullivan* had featured them as well as *Shindig* and *Hullabaloo*, and now they were our responsibility.

The Ronettes. L to R Nedra Talley, Ronnie Spector, Estelle Bennett

We arrived early that day so we'd be set up and ready to go when they walked in. It would just be the three women, no managers, assistants, agents or music directors, and because they sent us a set list in advance, we were well prepared. I remember sitting with them in their dressing room with my guitar, running through their songs, and trying to capture all the nuances of their records. Their lead singer, Ronnie Bennett (later Spector), was having problems with her throat that day and was sipping hot lemon tea. She seemed a little on edge, and during rehearsal, she only sang a few words of each verse and chorus to save her voice. This was not unusual for lead singers, so the other two Ronettes, Estelle, Ronnie's sister, and Nedra, their cousin, filled in the blanks. I was star struck and in love; comforting and reassuring her came easily.

We were the opener as always and cruised through our set without a hitch. The kids danced and cheered and made us feel welcome and wonderful. Then out came The Ronettes. I was a little nervous, but not enough to blow it. It was their show, and we were just the house band. If it didn't go well, we would be blameless. It went very well. They blew the kids away. Just being who they were, dressed to kill and looking sexy and gorgeous might have been enough, but these were super pro singers with a string of top forty hits. To look and sound that good made them unique among pop stars, and the day belonged to them.

After their encore, we all gathered backstage for the usual high-five, "good show, good show" thing. Ronnie then turned to thank me for the support and encouragement I had given her pre-show. She shared that this was a heavy responsibility she never dreamed of as a little girl and sometimes didn't handle the nerves so well. She had to be on top of her game, or the show would collapse. Estelle and Nedra could hold their own on backups but didn't have Ronnie's sound and wouldn't be able to cover for her if her voice failed.

I loved this day, this show, this meeting one of my favorite groups, and I'm disappointed our paths haven't crossed since. But Ronnie is still performing and can now claim an additional credit. She survived an abusive marriage with one of the most famous record producers of all time, the late Phil Spector. His world-famous "wall of sound" graced Ronettes records, The Righteous Brothers records and even The Beatles. Phil was also responsible for shooting and killing actor Lana Clarkson in 2003. He died in prison on January 16, 2021, while serving nineteen years to life. We are all grateful that Ronnie survived and is still charming audiences with her amazing voice and hit legacy. The Ronettes were inducted into the Rock and Roll Hall of Fame in 2007.

We continued doing the Elks club shows for about a year. I was at Villanova University pursuing an engineering degree, and Elizabeth was about ninety miles away. Getting home to do these gigs was a challenge but rewarding. Don and I were roommates, and Bob lived across the hall, so we all traveled together. Chris attended Philadelphia College of Art, so he had a slightly shorter commute. Jack and Kenny lived in Cranford and Clark, NJ, so their drive only took twenty minutes.

The Elks show that turned the tide for The Critters was one that I had brushed aside initially. After backing up artists like Little Anthony and The Ronettes, it would have been hard to impress me. So when we found out that next show we'd be backing up Jay and the Americans, I responded, "meh." Not that I didn't want to do it. I did, and I liked their music. They just weren't in my record collection - a fine singing group but not my taste.

On show day, we set up early as usual, and were ready long before Jay and the Americans arrived. When they did, they were far more prepared, calm and professional than many of their predecessors. Kenny Vance, their guitarist and musical director, made our jobs easy. We rehearsed onstage, not in the dressing room like with The Ronettes, with live mikes and excellent direction from Kenny. By the time they let the kids in, it seemed like we were about to start our second show, not our first.

We opened as always, but much to our surprise, Jay and his girlfriend, Iris, didn't stay in the dressing room with the others. They stood in the wings and took in our entire performance. That was a first. Most acts stay sequestered until the last minute and rarely watch the

Jay and the Americans

opener. During the break between our show and The Americans, Iris was particularly complimentary. She asked if we could hang around for a chat when The Americans finished their show. It seemed like a simple, friendly gesture, perhaps some tips on how to improve our show, so I said, "Sure."

After the show, as we were heading for the door, Iris and Jay pulled Jerry Davis and me aside, again complimenting and thanking us.

Iris asked, "Has a record company ever approached you guys?"

I said, "We had a deal last summer with Musicor, but when our song 'Georgiana 'bombed, the label dropped us."

Her eyebrows went up, "That's very surprising. I don't know how that happened, but I might be able to help you guys."

"How?" I asked.

She said, "I work for a production company called Kama Sutra. Let's exchange phone numbers, and I'll be in touch."

Jerry handed her his business card. Two days later she contacted us and said we had an audition at a midtown rehearsal studio with her boss, Frank Mell (actual name Frankie Meluso), at 1pm the following Tuesday. We were sort of excited, but who was Kama Sutra? It seemed like a long shot, but we had nothing to lose; we agreed. Little did we realize that Kama Sutra signed the hit band The Lovin 'Spoonful who were riding an enormous wave of success.

Iris pulled an extraordinarily creative, if not devious, maneuver. The day after our show, she booked a rehearsal studio, snuck into Frank's office while he was out and wrote the booking into his datebook. As he headed out for lunch the day of the audition, she said, "Don't forget your 1 o'clock with The Critters."

He replied "The who? What are you talking about?"

In her best motherly voice, she said, "Oh Frank. You told me to make this appointment last week. You don't remember? They're that amazing band that everybody's talking about. Jay and I saw them last month. They're wonderful. Anyway, 1pm at the usual studio. Don't be late."

Frank, feeling embarrassed about his alleged memory lapse and trusting his faithful assistant, said, "Ok, if that's what I told you," and out he left scratching his head.

Frank Mell had a weird vibe, professional but cold. He showed little emotion and acted like a big shot. Being kids and naive, we assumed that's how a big record company exec acts. He didn't impress us, but we perked up after the audition when he said, "You're great. I want to sign you. You certainly impressed my secretary and her boyfriend, Jay Black, and I've heard enough. How can we get in touch?" Jerry Davis had his card already drawn and on its way into Frank Mell's chilly little hand.

That night we had a muted celebration. Though Kama Sutra boasted a few hits, it wasn't Columbia, Capitol or Atlantic Records. Still, if they did so well with The Lovin' Spoonful, this might work. A week later, they sent us a one-page contract. The words, exploitive and predatory, don't give a full picture of this comical piece of toilet paper. I'm surprised it didn't begin with the words "You have the right to remain silent." The title line read:" Standard Recording Agreement", and they assured us that every artist in the business signed this exact document. It afforded us a *generous* royalty rate of 3.5% of sales, and all recording and "other" expenses would be deducted from our 3.5% share before we would be paid any royalties. That meant they would pocket 96.5% of the expense-free profits if we had a hit. The only recompense was that if we bombed, they would eat all expenses and we could leave, owing nothing. Our parents looked it over with no idea how to interpret such a document. It seemed very one-sided but appeared to be a real offer. With some apprehension, they let us sign. Once again, we were recording artists, and the future was looking better. Why it never occurred to any of us to consult a lawyer remains a mystery, and subsequently, we never made a penny despite three top forty hits. More on that later.

Poetry In Motion

During the previous year, Don had encouraged me to write. I had no experience, but being a huge music fan, I had a lot of role models, especially the Brits. I started writing with a passion, mostly about my ex-girlfriend Laura. She and I had broken up recently and I was devastated. The songs were mostly about her as well as other depressing subjects. They weren't cheery, but they helped me soothe my depression, and the band seemed to like them. With titles like "I'll Wear A Silly Grin", a salute to Smokey Robinson's "Tracks Of My Tears", I hoped they'd attract lovelorn teenagers like myself. I penned another naïve little ditty called "Forever, or No More", a song with a lyric that spoke of romantic loyalty. "True Love Is So Hard To Find" "He'll Make You Cry" and "It Just Won't Be That Way" rounded out my cathartic contribution. Don and I wrote one of our best songs in our Villanova dorm during a lunch break called "Gone For A While". Excellent music IMHO, but again, doomy lyrics.

Our day finally arrived. We piled into our cars and headed into New York City, the Big Apple, to make our first record with Kama Sutra. The recording session would take place in a famous midtown music building,

Artie Ripp

1650 Broadway. It housed many record companies, publishers and composers, and boasted a world class recording studio in the basement. We pulled into the ground-level garage, unloaded our amps, guitars and drums, hauled everything into the elevator and punched the "B" button for Allegro Recording. As we dragged our gear out of the elevator and down the narrow hallway, the studio owner and engineer, Bruce Staples, and our record company rep, Artie Ripp, met us at the studio door. Artie was the Kama Sutra exec who convinced us that the "Standard Agreement" we had signed with them was in fact standard. Later, we discovered it was anything but. Also, Artie changed his original surname from Marcus to Ripp. Why? We found out two years later. His deep, scary voice and often cold and calculating demeanor should have been a red flag. We ignored the signs, trying to keep an open mind.

The session did not turn out to be what we expected. It was a "demo" session, one in which we would quickly record our original songs in rough format and pick the best one for a subsequent session. Despite our slight disappointment, recording went well, and we had a productive day. Having picked the best song of the lot, Kama Sutra booked our first real session for two weeks later at Bell Sound in NYC. They hired a producer named Jerry Ragovoy to work with us - a superb writer, and an insightful producer, and we had a wonderful experience. Jerry wrote hits like "Time Is On My Side" by The Stones and "Another Little Piece of My

Heart" made famous by Janis Joplin. We loved Jerry, and he made mostly great suggestions. Some were a little bizarre, some logical, but all improved our chosen song, one of mine, called "It Just Won't Be That Way". Was it a mind-blowing, destined for the Top of the Pops song? Nah. It was just ok. The production was first rate, but a better song would have been helpful. We didn't have one yet. To succeed beyond the teen dance circuit, we had to write catchier, more commercial songs. Chalk it up to a learning experience and an encouraging first step.

Later that month, Artie sent us a song written by Jackie DeShannon called "Children And Flowers", which would be our recording project for the next session. He didn't ask for our opinion. He told us, "Keep writing, but until you come up with some hits, I'm going to keep looking for commercial songs to help you break through." Once we established ourselves, we could start weaning our audience away from the hot AM radio ear candy and introduce the

The Critters at Bell Sound Studios, 1965

more introspective stuff. I didn't love this song and asked if I could rearrange it. Though Jackie was an excellent writer, and the song had good lyrics, the chord changes were just too basic for my taste - C-Em-F-G through all the verses, C-Am-F-G for the choruses. I found it boring. In an effort to spiff it up, I changed the chords. My labor paid off. When I played it on my twelve string with a different beat, Artie treated me to a rare display of excitement. With his stamp of approval, I taught it to the guys, and we headed back to the studio for the second round.

How you set up a studio in those days was critical to the final record. Bruce isolated the amps and drums with sound dampening baffles for maximum control of each instrument. That way, if he wanted more low end on the bass guitar, that adjustment wouldn't affect the rest of us and add dull mush to the guitar, piano or drums. This was so important, because state-of-the-art recording machines in those days only had four tracks. With none of the conveniences of the computer-based, multi-track disc recording wonders of today, Bruce had to dial up a killer mix on the console before we recorded our final take. He'd also have to dial it up quickly. If we nailed it on the second run-through/take, but the sound wasn't there yet, we would have two options: do it again and hope we could keep up the energy, or release the record as is and hope no one noticed the questionable sound. Many records fit that latter description - stellar performances but mediocre sound. There could only be minimal adjustment post recording, because several instruments shared the same track, i.e., bass and drums on one track, guitars and keyboards on a second, leaving two tracks open for lead and background vocals. One thing to note about the above - even with superb recording technique, a bad performance/song will still be bad. By contrast, a great performance will still be great even on a tinny, mono AM radio speaker. That's the reason MP3 audio is just fine for most people in this modern age. Though the sound is inferior to a CD, convenience and portability win the day, and most people wouldn't be able to tell the difference.

In almost all recording sessions, the band will play a song over and over, each time making minor or major adjustments. When a band performs a song that many times, again, one of two things happens - the musicians either become frustrated and bored, and the session deteriorates, or everybody maintains their focus and it gets better and better. Our excitement at just being in this amazing studio kept us razor focused, so every run-through got better. After rehearsing for a little while, working out parts while Bruce adjusted the sound, the recording began:" Children And Flowers, take one." We'd count it in and give it our best shot. On completion, Artie would say, "Good take. Let's hit those opening chords a little stronger and run it again. Take two..." This one crashed when one of us played a wrong chord in the chorus. "Take three..." - a good one overall, so we took a break to listen and maybe exchange some suggestions. We parked our instruments, and shuffled into the control room, a high-tech conglomeration of tape machines, small humming fans, a space age recording console covered in knobs, switches, meters and tiny lights... and the main attraction, four massive speakers mounted on the wall near the ceiling. Reaching over to the four-track machine, Bruce pressed the play button. The tape made a hissing sound as it glided over the record/playback/erase heads, then the slate, "take three," and the song began. As the first chords struck our ears, we looked wide-eyed at each other. It was like listening to a hit radio station on huge speakers. Bruce knew all the classic recording tricks, overdrive the tape machine just a little to add edge, use audio compression to make the track punchier, add concert hall reverb and crank the bass and kick drum. We could not believe how good Bruce and Artie made us sound. That was all the inspiration we needed - get back out there, strap on our instruments and kill it.

We now had a kick-ass backing track - time to sing. How I ended up the lead singer on this track baffled me, since in my opinion, Don was the better singer. But there I was, standing at the mike. Artie seemed to think my sound best fit the song, so we just went with it. I had a high pitched, nasal kid's voice in those days, and in listening to a recording, some found it hard to tell if I was male or female. Not a bad thing, because like it or hate it, I had a unique voice. Because I spent hours rehearsing the song over the previous days, I didn't need many tries to get to what I thought was an excellent performance. Pitch and timing were not issues. My approach to singing was. For me, being naïve and a newbie, this should be a mechanical/intellectual task. If my vocal was accurate, and well-executed, it served its purpose. Or so spoke "The Little Professor." It never occurred to me that this almost mathematical approach might leave the vocal accurate but unemotional, flat and sterile. I didn't understand what Don meant when he said, "You need to just 'feel 'what you're singing."

"Don, what does that even mean? It's in tune and I got all the words right, didn't I?"

"Stop being so clinical and let yourself go."

Then he dropped the bomb - "Think about Laura" (my ex).

I wasn't even a little bit over her, and his suggestion was like a stab in the heart.

The breakup with Laura was the devastating image that left me with shoulders slumped, looking down at the floor and swallowing hard. Bruce knew he only had seconds to capture the moment, so he hit record, and the reels started rolling. I heard the intro in my headphones and sang, "You came in riding on a white dove's wing." I was on the verge of crying through the entire performance. Never in my life had I felt so exposed and yet somehow safe in those surroundings. The guys were close friends and were behind me, 100%. I got out of my own way and sang from my heart. As unnerving as it was, the Laura prod got the job done. When I listened to this new take, I had only one thought - drop the calculator and go hug someone.

Music is not an accounting lecture. It can be the invisible magic that awakens the heart, a catalyst for joy, fear, anger, violence, sex and an entire universe of emotions. It can also suck. If a song doesn't move you, what is the point of listening? But if a singer can allow themselves to be vulnerable, unguarded, and sing the lyrics like they were in the arms of a dear lover, or on their knees at a loved one's grave, they will blaze a trail straight to your heart. That's what made Don such a great singer. Despite growing up surrounded by wealth, he also grew up surrounded by trouble. He shared much of his life's challenges with me, and was never far from his pain, least of all when he was performing. And he taught me how to sing.

When "Children and Flowers" was complete and Kama Sutra set a release date, we did what we usually did - we went back to college. For me, this was a heavy-hearted departure. I loved NYC, the restaurants, the clubs, the concert halls, all of it. At the time, Villanova was a small, boring Catholic college. I was barely interested and barely studying. Instead, I'd sit in my dorm and play guitar, listen to the radio and tape songs I liked on my Wollensak reel-to-reel tape recorder. My marks weren't stellar, and my enthusiasm for calculus and chemistry took a distant second place to my enthusiasm for unsedated eye surgery.

About two weeks after its release, Kenny, our bassist, called and said he had been in touch with the record company, and we should tune in to WKBW-Buffalo tonight for a surprise. That was a challenge. Buffalo was 365 miles away, and AM radio waves rarely traveled that far. How were we supposed to listen to a station two states away? I asked one of my engineer buddies if there was any workaround to hearing the station, and he had a brilliant solution. It was a cloudy day. WKBW had a fifty-thousand-watt transmitter. If luck was with us, we could tune in at night and make the connection. With the ionosphere reflecting certain frequencies of radio waves, the earth acts like a trampoline, helping to bounce the waves between the ground and the ionosphere, all around the planet. The reflection characteristics of the ionosphere change at night, enhancing the ability to pick up distant, high-wattage radio stations. With WKBW's massive transmitter and a little luck, the broadcast would bounce down to Villanova like a basketball. We put it to the test at around 9pm, and sure enough, aside from some static, the station's call letters and jingle came in loud and clear. Ok, great. Now what? Kenny didn't give us any further information.

Then we heard it. "This is Joey Reynolds [in his goofy comedic voice] and you're listening to WKBW Buffalo, New York. Here's our pick of the week, a new band called The Critters with their debut song, 'Children and Flowers'!" WTF?? We were the pick song of the week on a fifty-thousand-watt station? Don, Bob and I gathered in our dorm room listening with our eyes bulging like Sponge Bob Squarepants. This was almost too good to be true.

Everything changed in that 2.5 minutes of ionosphere-assisted bliss. We were no longer the Knights of Columbus Vibra-Tones from Westfield, Plainfield and Scotch Plains. We were in rotation on a major radio station, no less than The Beatles and The Stones. YES!! Ok, now what?

I'd like to say this was where we experienced that meteoric rise to fame, taking the express elevator to the top of the charts on our way to hall of fame status, but nope, not this time. The song only made it to #85 on the Billboard charts. Still, not bad for our first shot with the Kama Sutra team. We performed the song live a few times, but it just wasn't a big hit with our audiences.

Dick Clark gave us a super boost on *American Bandstand* by entering it in his famous "Rate A Record" contest. I watched him place the placard with our name and song title up on the board, and the song began

Dick Clark's American Bandstand,
rating our record.

to play. Kids moved out on the floor, started dancing, and it looked like a winning situation. But when the song finished, the moment of truth arrived, and it wasn't good. Dick walked over to the two teenage judges to get their vote. The first, a young lady curiously named Melody, said:

"I gave it a 60, and I didn't like it cuz it sounded like floating."

Dick Clark: "Is that bad? You don't like people to sound like they're floating?"

Melody: "No, I just didn't like it."

Dick Clark to second judge, Sam: "Do you agree with her?"

Sam: "I gave it a 65. I didn't think it was that good."

Boom! "Children And Flowers" got the virtual Frisbee toss straight into the bargain bin. Did that stop us? Did we give up and go home? Nope. We were undeterred. The Critters started out as a high school sock hop band, and we now had a song that made it into the Billboard top 100. So we hadn't achieved that coveted stardom... yet. To quote Tracy McMillan, "Everything works out in the end. If it hasn't worked out yet, then it's not the end." Remember that quality people often talk about?

Thick skin? We took the rejection in our stride and were ready for the next round.

Chapter Two
Hits & Misses

Mr. Dieingly Sad

Once again we returned to 1650 Broadway, Allegro Sound. This time was different. We weren't newbies anymore, and the respect we were given was quite inspiring. Bruce Staples congratulated us and wanted to hear all about our adventures since we last met, and Artie Ripp, to our surprise, was charming. Everyone involved was excited about taking the next step. Don came forward and said he had written a new song that he thought we might like. In our concerts we had been doing a David Raksin song called "Laura"; no relation to my ex-girlfriend, but an old standard. We performed it to a bossa nova beat and it went over very well with our fans. Don took the framework of that song and worked it up into an original. He gave it an unusual, word-warped title, "Mr. Dieingly Sad". He played it for us, and

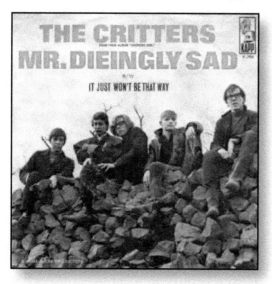

we all agreed it should be our next recording. Kenny rarely felt confident about his bass playing in a studio environment, so he sat this one out. Chris didn't think a piano fit the song, so he also sat it out. Bruce miked up Don's acoustic guitar, I picked up Kenny's bass, Jack picked up a pair of shakers and sat down at his drum kit with one stick to hit the rim of his snare while he played the shakers and bass drum. We ran through it a couple of times, making changes here and there, and got to a place where we liked it. Bruce hit record:" Mr. Dieingly Sad, take one."

It was a beautiful but uncomplicated song. We only did a couple of takes until we had a good foundation for vocals. Hearing the playback of our simple track on the huge speakers was a wonderful and inspiring experience. You realize that we're talking about 1966. Most records were mono (one track, not two like modern stereo), because AM radio was mono. Neither hi-fi FM radio nor stereo had caught on yet, so we were used to hearing songs on table radios with one four-inch speaker. So to listen to the instruments spread out over these four huge Altec Lansing speakers was, for young suburban musicians, almost a life altering experience!

Bruce set up a single microphone, Don put on his headphones, said a few words, and Bruce fed him the music track to see if it was at a good level in his headphones. With thumbs up from Don, we began tracking the vocal. For those who have never done this, tracking vocals is almost always a patchwork process. First, we had Don sing the entire song a few times to warm up. Then we focused on the details. Bruce always recorded a rehearsal take for reference. That way if the singer didn't like the mike or the sound, he could adjust it before we started recording for real. Don was an excellent singer, so we didn't have to do many takes on his vocal. As I recall, we punched in a word or phrase here and there, had him re-sing a verse and chorus, and that was it.

On to the background vocals! Since we had worked out the parts ahead of time, recording them was straightforward. We just sang the parts with feeling, and that was that... until we went into the control room to listen. We opened the heavy soundproof door to, "Holy shit, what the hell was that?"

I said, "Oh man, they sounded good out there, did we screw something up? Was I flat?"

Bruce and Artie practically spat their coffee across the room. "No, Jimmy, you were not flat. Please sit down and listen."

Artie's wife, Iris, was there for the session and she just looked at us with her hand over her heart, shaking her head. She said, "This is one of the most beautiful songs I've ever heard. Artie, honey, play it for them!" Bruce hit play, and again I was transported by the sound of the huge studio speakers, each one playing back a different group of instruments and voices. We did well. It was one of those moments in the studio when you're certain you have a hit. It sounded so good, it gave me chills. Hats off to Don, his voice and writing talent were going to finally put us on that proverbial express elevator. Or so we thought.

In the days that followed, much to our annoyance, Artie started meddling with the backing track. He said Jack was not a good drummer, and the timing in the track was inconsistent. I wanted to call bullshit, but I chose to be respectful and see what he had in mind. He brought in studio musicians to replace our parts while playing along with what we did. Think about that for a moment. If these musicians followed our track, they would have to create the same timing inconsistencies, or they would

47

be out of sync with our vocals. We didn't take bets, but I was right. The new parts didn't improve the song. They sounded stiff and mechanical, because instead of playing with their hearts, the studio guys were doing their best to memorize and duplicate what we did while trying to follow our "shaky" timing. That's never a good way to record, and that was what all concluded at the end of the session. Artie included a vibraphone player among the new band who had some good ideas for improving the track. He was the only studio musician who made the cut. In the end, we kept our original track plus the vibes and that became the record.

Though Artie never conceded that the track worked fine in its original form, he dropped the argument. But then came the next hurdle. He didn't think "Mr. Dieingly Sad" was a commercial enough record for a second release. He felt we needed something more catchy, upbeat, and instantly likable. In his opinion, "Children And Flowers" had not done as well as we hoped, and in order to get interest from national radio stations, we'd have to have something that immediately caught their attention. We thought we had it with "Mr. Dieingly Sad"; but we weren't in charge. Don had written several other songs, and we collaborated on a couple, so we started playing Artie what we had. Nothing seemed to stimulate his interest. He said we should regroup in a week after he'd had some time to think about it and consult with other writers. This plan annoyed me. I liked our songs, as did Don and the rest of the band, but we were still novices. As such, we gave Artie the benefit of the doubt.

I'll interject here that Don found college more than he could handle. He was a physics major, and that line of study was not for part-timers. His heart was in making music, not quantum particle theory, so early in our third semester, he dropped out of Villanova. I was the last man standing, since Bob had left after the first semester. I attended summer school to repair a failing calculus grade, so in some ways I was determined to stick it out. To no one's surprise, when my two musical buddies were no longer in school with me, my grade average jumped from 1.8 to 3.5. My new friends were not band mates. They were serious students with a strong desire to succeed, and their work ethic soon rubbed off on me. I was still writing and practicing but paying much more attention to my studies.

Younger Girl

In the middle of that week Don called me and said Artie had come up with a good song for us to do. I asked what it was. He said the Lovin' Spoonful recorded a song on their first album called "Younger Girl" and Artie thought we could do a great cover of it. I knew the song, as I was a big fan of the Spoonful. What did we have to lose? I agreed to take the usual train home after class on Friday night and be ready to go into the studio Saturday morning.

"Younger Girl" was an easy song to sing and play. It only had four chords, so we just had to come up with an arrangement that was acceptable, and we'd be good to go. They elected me to sing the lead this time, since Don had done "Mr. Dieingly Sad". The song work-up came effortlessly, and we started recording our version. It sounded good to us, but got the "meh" line of muted disapproval from producer Artie.

We ran the clock out on studio time, so the session came to an end. I went back to school the next day and just figured we'd go with "Mr. Dieingly Sad" as per the original plan.

Didn't happen.

Again, the call from Don." Artie wants to hit 'Younger Girl' again on Saturday. You good to come home?" I said, "Fine." So again, the Friday night train to my parents' house in Westfield, and into the city on Saturday morning. We set up and

started experimenting with other ways to play the backing track. When we came up with a good alternate arrangement, Bruce hit record. After a few takes, we got the thumbs up and I recorded another lead vocal. I can't say I was super excited. I didn't want to record a cover song in the first place, even if it was a great Lovin'Spoonful song. My feelings must have shown in my vocal performance - I'd have done better with pneumonia. I asked Artie, "What do you think?" Out came another "meh." At this point, fed up and tired, I announced I'd be going back to school and would not be interested in recording "Younger Girl" again. I said either version would work fine; they should just pick one and go with it. That point of view, delivered with a tad of attitude, didn't meet with a standing ovation, but I didn't care. I packed my guitar and headed home. Again, on Sunday afternoon, I got on the train back to Villanova and put the whole annoying kerfuffle behind me.

49

I thought that was the end, but Don called me the following Thursday:

"'Younger Girl' turned out great. Recording it was a smart decision."

This surprised me, and I asked him which one of the two versions they chose... Silence.

Then, "Jim, didn't Artie tell you?"

"What? Tell me what?" Another pause.

"We did a new version with studio musicians. Nobody told you? We called in a big-time arranger and he put together a ten-piece band for the session. It's fantastic! I think you're going to like it."

I said, "Wow, I didn't see that coming. So when do I do my lead vocal?"

Again, the damn pause on the line. "Uh, I did the lead vocal. Artie wanted to try my voice to see if it would work better for the song. Everybody likes it."

Jesus. What the actual fuck? I said, "Well, are we going to do any background vocals at least?"

No pause this time; the bomb had already exploded. "They're done. Kenny and I did them."

Try to imagine the venom coursing through my body upon hearing this news. I was not in love with the song, and I felt betrayed and furious. As I was the de facto leader of this band, the final say on what we did or didn't do, until this moment, rested with me. I had brought Don and Kenny into the band, and I was standing in the dorm phone booth trying to hold this news as anything other than a mutiny. The second record release by MY band, The Critters, would not contain any contribution from me - I had been completely sidelined. Don was apologetic and had no idea why Artie hadn't discussed it with me, but the lesson was now obvious. The previous week, I copped an attitude with Artie, an established record producer and record company owner. I disrespected his opinion, and with only a shrug of his shoulders, he dismissed mine. His money was paying for our recordings, and we weren't at the stage where we could call the shots on big decisions like this. Artie never apologized, nor did he bring it up. He did what he thought was best for the band and didn't care how I took it. We have long since made up, and I doubt he even realized how angry and humiliated I felt. I learned the hard way that copping an attitude in a professional situation rarely ends well. What escaped my notice was the fact that Chris and Kenny, playing no part in "Mr. Dieingly Sad", couldn't care less about that recording or this one. Why was I so upset? Just a bruised ego, I guess. No one would suspect my absence on the record unless I told them. If it was as good as Don said, I would reap tremendous benefit without the slightest effort. The present day me sees this at a glance, but the me in those days took

50

quite a while to get over himself.

Once I got around to listening to "Younger Girl", I must admit I was impressed. The arrangement was completely different from the Lovin ' Spoonful's and was quite original. Vinnie Bell, one of my favorite session guitarists, played a strange and wonderful sounding solo, and the song was arranged by the legendary Jimmy Wisner. It really sounded like a hit. So now what? We had just released a record that, from my perspective, was by somebody else. We were about to embark on a career as imposters. To add to the dilemma, Don, no longer in college, got reclassified to 1A. In military terms, that meant you were fresh meat for the draft. Fearing that he would be called up and sent to Vietnam, he enlisted in the Air Force. Our lead singer for "Mr. Dieingly Sad" and "Younger Girl" was gone before either record was released. Chris and I were still in college, so we were not of interest to the military. Uncle Sam gave us the IIS student deferment. Kenny's dad was killed in action in the Korean War, so as a sole survivor of a dead veteran, he had a permanent deferment. Jack was a question mark that we hadn't thought about, but the bottom line was The Critters were down to four members. That meant that Kenny and I were the new lead singers, and background vocals would not be terrific. This was all new to us, and we did not have an immediate plan. So Chris and I went back to school.

Where The Action Is

We're now up to March, 1966. Cell phones did not yet exist, and the school didn't allow land lines in our dorm rooms. The entire floor shared one phone booth at the end of the hall. This was never a big problem, because we rarely called home or anywhere else unless we needed money. Most of our friends were here, so we would just wander into their rooms if we wanted to talk. One afternoon, I was in the dorm, studying for a chemistry test, and I heard the familiar jangling payphone bell echoing down the hallway. After a few rounds, it stopped, and I went back to my formulas. Then I heard a shout, "Ryan! It's for you!" No one ever called me on that phone, so I felt some anticipation. Who could it be now? I paused my studies and jogged down to the phone booth in my flip-flops. There was nobody around, and whoever answered the call had left the receiver dangling from its vandal-proof spiral chrome cord. Hoisting it up, I pressed the cold plastic receiver to my ear and said:

"Hello?"

"Hi Jimmy, it's Marilyn." (My sister.) "Are you sitting down?"

"No, I'm standing up in a dingy, stale beer smelling, Villanova dorm phone booth. Why?"

"'Younger Girl' is the pick hit of the week on WBZ here in Boston!"

"Wait... what? No way!"

Oh boy, deja vu. I was cautious, holding back my excitement for now. We chatted for a few minutes, I thanked her for the call, and we said our goodbyes. Putting the receiver on the hook, I stood there in the phone booth for a minute staring at the wall. Butterflies. Heart rate elevated. There was a stifled scream aching to come out, but I stuffed it. This time I would not get my hopes up. Bullshit. My hopes were boiling over. And I was ready to do an Irish jig down the hallway back to my room. But first, three calls - Chris, Jack and Kenny. Collect. I had no change for the payphone.

WBZ wasn't a fifty-kilowatt station like WBLS. We couldn't tune in at night and hear them say, "Here's that fab band, The Critters, with our WBZ pick of the week, 'Younger Girl'," but we were seriously stoked with this news. Over the next month, "Younger Girl" started climbing up the charts, and bookings were coming in. Did we just step into that proverbial express elevator? Sort of.

As I mentioned earlier, I was a huge fan of Dick Clark, and *American Bandstand*. They were the primary source of the musical discoveries that shaped my career. Ironically, until I wrote this book, I did not know "Children And Flowers" received a thumbs down on that very show. I discovered it while doing research for this book. I only knew it bombed, and now I can see that show had to be at least part of the reason. Nonetheless, our paths with Mr. Clark would cross again under much better circumstances. A tour celebrating his new show, *Where The Action Is*, would hit the road in July 1966. Kama Sutra's publicity department had been in touch with the booking agent for the tour and got us a place on the bus. Because of the success of "Younger Girl" we would hit the road with The Young Rascals, Paul Revere and the Raiders, BJ Thomas, The Knickerbockers, Shades of Blue, and on one occasion, The Kinks and The Dave Clark Five, plus a handful of popular acts from the time. Until then, we had never done a tour; just one nighters, out and back.

We didn't gloat because we weren't all that confident. Having lost the lead singer of our big hit, we were only a four-piece band with limited vocals. The bizarre events that took place during this tour would haunt us for the month we were out, and many months in the aftermath. Jerry Davis handled the booking. He told us we would not need any equipment other than our instruments, and The Young Rascals would be happy to let us use their drums and amps. Jerry overlooked one detail. He neither asked Sid Bernstein, their manager, nor any of The Rascals if this was ok. He just assumed it would be. When we were setting up for the first gig of the tour, an outdoor fair on Long Island, the tour manager approached us and asked where he could find our amps. We told him about the alleged permission, and he gave us that look - the little squint and very slight tilt of the head when someone doesn't want to be disrespectful, but it's obvious they think you're full of shit. I moved quickly from the mental "uh oh" to a full-blown anxiety attack. In a microsecond, a frightening possibility appeared on my radar. Had somebody dropped a very large ball? In that instant, I imagined thirty painful days of The Critters playing unplugged, no amps, no drums, no acoustic instruments... but hey, at least we had mediocre vocals. Gene Cornish, The Rascals 'guitarist, overheard some of the conversation, and wandered over. I jumped on it. "Hi Gene. Great to meet you. We're big fans of you guys. Please tell [tour manager] what our manager agreed with you guys about using your amps and drums."

"What are you talking about?"

"Your amps. You agreed to let us use your amps."

"Uh, still have no idea what you're talking about. I never spoke to your manager, and no one has said Jack to us about this."

He was not happy with our assumption nor the miscommunication among staff. Me, in my mind: "FUCK!! Jerry Bullshit Davis. Again." Gene, seeing me squirming and getting a little pale, offered: "Look, I don't know who your manger talked to, but it wasn't any of us. I don't want to be a hard-ass, and I can see you're in a bind, so you can use our stuff on one condition. You set it up and pack it back into the truck after each gig." He was telling me that in order for us to be in the show, we would have to be their roadies. Final offer.

Gene Cornish brought a Fender Twin amp for their show. It weighed about three and a half tons and when you tried to pick it up, you felt like it was bolted to the stage. It did not ship with wheels, and none were retrofitted. That was the light item. Felix Cavaliere, their lead singer, had a Hammond organ. It weighed as much as an eighteen-wheeler, and we were skinny, out of shape musicians who would get winded climbing one flight of stairs. Nevertheless, this was our thirty-day fate. I recalled the cheerful Warren County State Prison mantra:" You'll get used to it."

We did get used to it. Eventually. After some days of heavy lifting, dislocated vertebrae, torn ligaments, crushed spinal disks, multiple hernias and a little help from the tour truck driver, it became our humbling little routine, something I so looked forward to at 11pm, after a three-and-a-half-hour show.

The bands and the Action Kids (cast from the TV show) all rode in a regular Greyhound style bus. Not a fancy tour bus. Just an ordinary bus with regular bench style seats, no tables, no bunks, and a stank-ass porta potty in the back. We were booked throughout the South and East, often driving all night after a show. I'm not good at sleeping sitting upright on benches, so I was becoming exhausted. In the moment's stress, an idea came to me. It involved a borrowed pillow from one of our motels and my newly developed biceps. On one of the long night drives, I tested the bus overhead rack for strength with a couple of chin-ups. When it didn't budge, I advanced the experiment to phase two. Pushing everything in the overhead rack back about six feet from my seat, I tossed the pillow up there with my best hook shot. The next challenge? Follow the pillow. Remember, this rack was at eye level to a six-footer, so getting up there would be a challenge. But in my red-eyed, sleepless desperation, I was highly motivated. With a quick hop up on the seat while holding the vertical rack support, I lifted my left leg onto the seat back, then the right, then swung my left leg up onto the rack, hoisted myself up and squeezed into the cramped space. I had barely enough room to turn or move, but at least it was a horizontal surface. Kind of like a bunk in a torture chamber. Comfortable? Nope, but better than the church pew bus bench.

July in the South, and barely functional air conditioning obviated the need for a blanket. Did I sleep? Yes, but not as well as I would have in a feather bed at the Ritz Carlton. An overhead rack is a hard, flat surface with no padding. Still, better than the bench. Did anyone care? Actually, most were impressed, but no one else followed. It would be an obvious risk putting more than one person up there. The chances of the rack coming crashing down on top of people below were pretty good, so no one followed suit. I had this cozy, squeezed-in space to myself for the rest of the tour. Well, not the entire tour.

After a few nights sleeping on what felt like a door, I developed a stiff back. I knew going back to sleeping on the bench would be even worse, so I came up with another, even more dangerous solution. In packing the tour truck, I noticed that the Hammond organ had a thick, padded cover, as did its Leslie speaker cabinet, which was the same height. I pushed them together and made myself a bed in the back of the truck, a reckless and stupid move. If the truck had to stop fast, I would become a human torpedo, slamming my head into the front wall of the truck. If we got into an accident and the truck tipped or flipped, the heavy equipment would no longer be below me. After some brief weightlessness, it would come to rest on the newly two-dimensional me. I only slept in the truck a couple of times, because despite the padding, the equipment vehicle had truck suspension, not cushy bus suspension. Any bumps in the road were amplified in the back, so unless we were on smooth blacktop, it could feel like trying to sleep on a Texas bar room mechanical bull turned up to eleven. One time the organ and I got bounced into the air by the truck, cruising way too fast over a speed bump. Fortunately, my leg didn't land between any of the equipment, or it would have been crushed. Think panini. No one seemed concerned. People in the 60s were pretty chill when it came to motor vehicle safety - no seatbelts, no airbags and lots of nice, jagged switches on the hard steel dashboards with few rules about where you rode in a vehicle. If I wanted to sleep in the luggage compartment under the bus with the suitcases and personal paraphernalia, the driver would have happily opened the bay doors and said, "Climb in. I'll wake you up when we get to Little Rock." Luckily, we stayed in motels about half of the time or we would have had to rename the tour "Where The Zombies Are."

Despite the less than royal accommodations, the tour was going well. The shows almost always sold out, and some venues were huge. For me, the thrill was seeing and learning what works and what doesn't from the other bands. We all watched and complimented each other's performances, and a particularly enjoyable part of the tour was hanging out after shows and giving each other tips. These were big name acts, skilled at performing, so feedback was rarely negative. Everyone's shows improved with the implementation of this sage advice from admiring new friends.

The long drives on the tour bus were rarely sight-seeing extravaganzas. Whether dozing off, reading books or staring at the inside of their eyelids, no one payed much attention to travel beyond their current item of focus. That changed one hot and sweaty afternoon, several hours into our Florida travel day. As we pulled up and came to a stop, the bus driver hit a button, opening the pneumatic door with a whoosh, clicked on the PA and announced, "Attention Action cast and crew - Welcome to paradise!" All stopped what they were doing and turned to face the glorious porte-cochère just beyond the right side of the bus. The words "Eden Roc" were blazoned on the edifice. We were in Miami Beach. In seconds everyone poured out on the pavement, gazing at the extraordinary opulence of one of Florida's finest high-end hotels. The tour manager announced with a grin, "This will be our home for the next two nights."

What a well-earned treat! The art déco lobby reeked of wealth, and check-in took no time. Everything was pre-arranged, so upon giving the concierge our names, he handed us our keys. Unlike the funky motels in the Deep South that had been the norm until today, our rooms, all super luxurious, had views of the turquoise ocean from the fourteenth floor, and no mold or cockroaches in the showers - a road rat's dream! ABC chose the Eden Roc for the view and the extensive pool area, ideal for filming. Dick Clark himself would soon be there with cameras, recording equipment, and a full production crew. The show would be taped and broadcast on national television! I had forgotten about this event, so you can imagine my excitement. What an opportunity, a first for us. Sure,

"Children And Flowers" got a few spins on *American Bandstand*, but only made it into the top 100. This time, in Dick Clark's universe, we would be featured artists with a hit record, guests of honor with no condescension from clueless teenage music critics!

After checking into our rooms, I wandered down to the pool deck to watch the load-in. Though we were taping the following day, the crew needed a day's lead time to get everything set up. I was amazed how organized, methodical, smooth and casual the process was. No one rushed. Dick Clark was famous for his easygoing, unflappable manner, even in awkward moments on TV. He hired a crew with the same mellow mentality. That, or his manner rubbed off on everyone who worked with him. I can assure you, production crews are not always this relaxed! It just made us feel safe, special and in the right place at the right time!

The evening of our arrival was uneventful, save a walk on the beach under the beautiful, clear, star-filled Miami sky. July, usually a hot month for FL, brought balmy weather, perfect for this outdoor event. Fresh air made a pleasant change from bus fumes, and my bed was, well, an actual bed. Needless to say, we were not inspired to break any ashtrays. Our 2pm camera call for the following day gave us extra time to sleep in and enjoy a leisurely breakfast. Unlike the Warren County Clink, the Eden Roc served fresh OJ, croissants, gourmet coffee, eggs Florentine, and yes, linen napkins and tablecloths. Unless you booked in the $100k per gig category, hotel stays like this were rare. For average artists, a Holiday Inn or Motel 6 would be the norm.

us in our brown suits

After killing what was left of the morning in slugs on the beach mode, it was time to get ready for our ABC TV closeup. What to wear? For us, casual-neat made the most sense. The Rolling Stones, with their immense popularity, had long since done away with suits and formal show dress, so following their lead, most bands performed in lightly accessorized street clothes.

56

We started the tour performing in old-school brown matching suits, but for this show, outdoors in the Florida heat, suits made no sense. We decided on cool shirts, white jeans and Beatle boots.

Our camera call was upon us, so we popped out of our adjoining rooms on time, dressed and ready for our timeslot. Into the ornate brass and mahogany-adorned elevator we marched, heading down to the lobby, then out onto the bustling pool deck where the production was taking place. My engineering alter-ego took in all the intertwined cables with fascination as we walked around TV monitors, huge cameras, crew, makeup people, script people, and onlookers. We were so proud and excited to be part of this mass gathering of TV professionals, creating our little episode of one of the most popular shows on daytime TV. As soon as we stepped through the big glass pool entrance doors and onto the deck, a production assistant approached us with her clipboard in hand and directed us to a small makeup cabana for a quick, light dusting. Everybody would benefit from a cover up for their oily, pasty, tan-free, tour-worn faces. The process would be quick and painless, a natural look being the day's choice. Outdoor shoots are like that. Heavy makeup in a sunny setting looks artificial and pretentious, so a little concealer for the pimples, a little powder, and we were done.

1966 -The Critters on the set at the Eden Roc Hotel, taping Younger Girl

Our job was about as easy as it gets. Another assistant led us to an open area in front of the upper deck, overlooking the pool. From there, we would simply look into the cameras with the Action Kids and audience dancing and smiling behind us and... LIP SYNC!!?? I couldn't believe it. Talk about a punctured bliss bubble! I expected a full setup like our shows - equipment, lights, mikes, the works, but nope, not for location TV in 1966. Today would be phony to the max. No drums, no keyboard, no bass, just me with my Mexican twelve-string and the guys standing by my side pretending to play with no instruments. One of the camera operators explained to me that the technology needed to make a live musical performance sound even minimally acceptable was way beyond the scope of this shoot. The crowd noise, wind noise, and dead outdoor sound with no natural reverberation would not do us any sonic favors. I argued that Ed Sullivan always had artists perform live on his Sunday Night in-theater shows. He pointed out that Ed Sullivan had a full, state-of-the-art audio setup and studio, giving bands at least a fighting chance of sounding good. Apparently low-tech was good enough for a minimally discriminating teen audience and was also the way to keep these shoots profitable. They would just play our records through the speakers near the cameras, and we would pretend to sing along. When the show aired, the kids would hear our records in full sonic glory while seeing us pretend to perform them "live." As far as they were concerned, we would sound great, just like our records!

Resigned to embracing the absurd, I tried to make the best of the situation. I played the real chords on my guitar and sang the songs as I would have on stage. Jack tapped his drumsticks on the railing. Chris mimed playing keyboard on Jack's and Kenny's back while side-talking and laughing. Dumb as a brick, but it's how all these shows were done in those days. We slugged through it like musical clowns, and once I gave up trying to be cool, we did have fun. You can still summon our performances from that day on YouTube. Search "The Critters, Dick Clark," and enjoy them in all their grainy, lip-syncing black and white glory.

All the acts shared our plight. The Action Kids, our dancing faux audience, didn't quite qualify as go-go dancers, because there were no cages and it wasn't an all-female cast. Go-guys shared the deck - handsome, ripped young Paul Newman types that flexed in the background while the girls danced. Despite the absurd assumption that kids wouldn't know the difference, the rest of the shoot went like clockwork. Each band performed two songs to keep the show down to an hour. The highlight for me was Paul Revere and the Raiders. They weren't part of the regular tour, so this was the first time they joined us. When I say they killed it, that would be an understatement. They climbed

58

up on the tall risers in full revolutionary war dress and George Washington hats and did their songs, leaping around the stage, swinging guitars at each other's heads, dancing in circles and looking like they actually were performing live. That is genuine commitment to your vocation if I ever saw it. Those outfits in the hot summer sun, combined with the Flying Wallenda dance routines? Everyone was in awe. Even the amazing Rascals couldn't top that. They closed the show with cheers and whistles from everyone on the pool deck, cast and crew! That evening, the entire tour and crew celebrated in the large hotel restaurant, with toasts, jokes and lighthearted rehashing of the previous week's road trials and annoyances. We enjoyed a nice bonding experience in a casual setting, a welcome contrast to alternating work nights with endless hours riding in an uncomfortable bus full of cranky passengers. A good time was had by all!

Another event stands out, with not such a fond memory. As you recall, Bob Podstawski, our saxophonist, left Villanova after the first semester, acquiring a 1A draft qualification and having to leave the band to join the Air Force. Don Ciccone made it through the first year at Villanova but dropped out hoping to have a full-time career as a rock star. He ended up in the same boat as Bob, an Air Force recruit. The six Critters had been reduced to four, like sitting ducks, picked off, one by one, by a military sharpshooter. We reluctantly accepted our temporary fate but didn't plan to keep it that way forever. As soon as we had some downtime, we'd rethink and regroup.

On an infamous morning, the third week in July 1966, Jack came down to breakfast looking a little more pale than usual. Considering our diet, sleep schedule and lack of sun, that was quite an accomplishment. He sat down at the table with a particularly glum expression on his face. Again, always wanting to lighten things up, I joked, "What's up with you? Did you just find out your girlfriend's been cheating on you?"

He said, "Worse." Still thinking he might have contracted crabs from a groupie or drunk too much the night before, I prodded, "Really? What could be worse than that?"

"I've been drafted."

I almost choked on the words and dropped the F-bomb right there in the hotel restaurant. "Oh FUCK, NOOO!"

In those days, being drafted had real death sentence potential. With the Vietnam war raging, just toss a coin. With luck, you'd be fueling helicopters in Japan, or without luck, you'd be wading in the malaria infested swamps in a country we were attacking for no obvious reason, killing people who had no idea why we were there. The assumed reason, based on all the double talk from our government, was they were "commies," or we were trying to prevent them from getting swallowed up by commies. Why we gave a shit is beyond me. Maybe something to do with their proximity to Red China and Mao. It is befuddling that we lost that war, and now "communist" Vietnam has become a desirable tourist destination.

I asked Jack how soon after the tour he would have to report for duty. He let out one of those depressing, defeated laughs and said, "After the tour? How about I have to report to Fort Dix tomorrow morning? I booked my flight and I'm out of here in an hour." Now the original six-man Critters would be down to three. We were completely blown away, reaching for the panic button on full red alert. How would we finish the tour? Did our career just end before we even released "Mr. Dieingly Sad"?

A couple of BJ Thomas's band members were sitting at the next table and overheard our conversation. One of them, BJ's drummer Willie Ornelas, slid his chair around and said, "Jack - I can't believe this just happened. I'm so sorry, but I think I can help you guys out. I've seen your show fifteen times. I'm pretty sure I could play it even without a rehearsal. How about I just take over drums for the rest of the tour? I love your music and it would be fun for me."

I said, "Do you think BJ would mind?"

He replied, "No one would mind under these circumstances. You could get any drummer in the show to help you out."

We agreed it could be a good solution, and Jack seemed relieved. He felt that he'd let us down, but in reality, he just got clobbered with a massive dose of bad luck. We were sad, but not angry. The show would go on without him. And Uncle Sam had once again failed to destroy the invincible Critters!

I'll share one last incident to wrap up the Dick Clark tour. The show was booked at a big convention hall somewhere in Arkansas. We had finished our performance, and the Knickerbockers were now onstage. BJ's band was getting ready to follow them, and I walked into the men's room where they were spiffing up for their grand entrance. Minding my business, I proceeded over to the nearest urinal. As I peed, our substitute drummer, Willie, thought it would be cute to light an M80 firecracker. The "M" stands for military. M80s, also known as ashcans, are used by the United States Army to simulate explosions, gunfire and hand grenades during training exercises. They are loud. Very loud. We were in a men's room with hard tile walls. Very reverberant. Things sound much louder in men's rooms. He took out his lighter and lit the fuse. I was facing the urinal with my back to him, so I had no idea what was going on. I just heard the clink of his Zippo lighter opening, the zzit of the thumb wheel, fizzz for a couple of seconds, and BOOM!! The little fucking mini bomb exploded a foot from my right ear. I screamed in pain.

Every curse word in the dictionary came roaring out of my mouth, as I clumsily zipped my fly. In a blind rage, I lunged towards him, fists clenched, ready to deck him, when the other band members stepped in between us and tried to calm me down. It was so mind-numbingly ignorant and inconsiderate to blow off any fireworks in an acoustic environment that amplified and reverberated even quiet sounds, leave alone a military grade explosive. The bad news - it killed my ability to hear high frequencies in that ear for many years. Ears are not supposed to regain hearing after an injury like that, but for some magical reason, after several years, mine did. In the interim, I had to turn my head sideways when mixing audio and listen with my left ear to each speaker individually to be sure the equalization and levels were consistent. Eventually I stopped doing that, because stereo mixes sounded like stereo again. An ENT tested my ears, and to my amazement, I had regained most of my hearing. Though Willie continued to perform with us on the remaining dates, he and I did not exchange phone numbers after the tour.

The Critters, 1966

Audiences are an odd lot. If a band sounds good, they tend to not ask questions about what they are seeing, within reason. If you recall The Spencer Davis Group, who had several hits, including "Gimme Some Lovin'" and "I'm a Man", the lead singer, keyboardist and composer was Steve Winwood. Steve left the band in 1967 to form Traffic, yet Spencer Davis continued performing for decades with various unrelated musicians. I doubt many asked where Winwood was, because Spencer Davis stood center stage. His band, his name, his call, good enough. The average person would probably be unaware Winwood ever performed with that band. Our situation was similar. Don Ciccone sang lead on our two biggest hits. We played them every night of this tour. The tour brochure contained two full-page pictures of us, both with Don in the foreground, both featuring five band members. But there were only four of us on stage, and in the final week, only three. Not one autograph-seeking fan brought up the discrepancy. They asked for four, and later three autographs, thanked us and went on their way. The lonely picture of Don remained conspicuously autograph-free in all those brochures, and neither a question nor a complaint was heard.

Don't Let The Rain Fall Down On Me

We finished the tour on a pleasant note despite my hearing injury and Jack's departure. Our next task would be finding a new, permanent drummer. It turned out to be a surprisingly straightforward task. Through the grapevine and our rising fame, we had many submissions for the job. After a couple of auditions, we decided on a young drummer from Irvington, NJ named Jeff Pelosi. Not only was he an excellent musician, he had a super high falsetto. His normal singing voice was average for lead vocals, but for backgrounds, especially the high notes, his voice could soar. We gave him copies of our records as well as some tapes from live performances, and he learned the show in no time. Although we loved Jack, our brother from high school days, Jeff had the advantage of being able to sing. We now had another voice to fill out our background vocals. We didn't stop there. Chris loved talking to audiences from the front of the stage. He also enjoyed playing autoharp on "Younger Girl" and conga and percussion for other songs more than keyboards. So he wouldn't have to keep coming out from behind his piano to MC the show, he suggested we audition some singing keyboard players, bringing the band back up to five members. Again, it ended up being no big deal. After a few auditions, we settled on Bobby Spinella from Brooklyn. Bobby came with classical training, unlike the rest of us, so he brought a lot of well received musical expertise to the game. He also brought an amusing dose of Brooklyn/Italian gangsta mentality, which often had us in stitches laughing.

I'm going to digress again, but don't worry. It will all come together shortly. After the *Where The Action Is* tour, Artie Ripp wanted us to go back in the studio and do some more recording. We created several singles, including "Marrying Kind of Love" and "Bad Misunderstanding". We also recorded a song of mine, which I wrote at Villanova just before I took my sabbatical. Here's what happened: One fine fall afternoon, after a full day of classes finishing with English Lit, I stepped out of Tolentine Hall into what I thought would be beautiful fall weather. It wasn't. In fact, it was quite dark. I looked up to see clouds forming in an ominous sky. A deluge was imminent. I was wearing a jacket and tie, as per Villanova regulations, and no raincoat nor umbrella. The walk to my dorm, Sullivan Hall, would be about ten minutes. With my strong, eighteen-year-old legs, I started a very swift walk/trot. No good. Not fast enough. The thunder clapped and within seconds my formerly polished Bass Weejuns splashed through mud puddles three inches deep in a downpour. My sports coat looked like I'd worn it scuba diving, my books were getting soaked, and I was pissed. In the first place, I hated English Lit, and it was my English class's fault I couldn't be back at the dorm, watching the storm from my cosy, dry room. When I finally arrived, soaked and miserable, I had to strip off all my wet and clingy clothes including underwear and dripping sox. Once in dry clothes, I just sat on my bunk hating everything in the universe and feeling sorry for myself. My Mexican 12-string was leaning against the wall, so I grabbed it, tuned the low E down to a D and started angrily throwing chords and melodies around. In a short while a song began to emerge. Rain... something about the damn rain... I hated rain..." Don't Let The Rain Fall Down on Me". That was it - melody, chords, and within a short time, lyrics. In my pissy, disgruntled, rain-soaked mood, I had written a complete song in about forty-five minutes, an all-time record for me.

Sometimes when I'm angry, I just don't want to get over it. I want to fume and feed my righteous indignation with all the reasons I was wronged. That's how I felt about not bringing an umbrella and getting soaked. But upon completing the song, instead of wallowing in self-pity, I was beaming. A damn good song came out of that waterlogged fiasco, and it had hit potential.

Back to Artie Ripp. During the above mentioned singles sessions, I pulled Artie aside and told him about the storm experience and the resulting song. He laughed and said, "Let's hear it!" I had not yet played it for the band, so it was just me, Artie and my trusty 12-string cranking out my new song, unplugged. His smile spoke volumes. He loved it and wanted to record it as a possible single for the band. After the "Younger Girl" fiasco, my enthusiasm for The Critters was returning.

"Don't Let The Rain Fall Down on Me" was a complex song. It had unusual chords and plenty of them. I wasn't confident the guys could do it justice, nor was Artie, so we called in an arranger, Artie Butler, and about seven studio musicians. Fortunately, my fellow Critters didn't complain. I would be the band leader and play guitar.

The recording date came around and I found myself surrounded by the best studio musicians in NY - Joe Mack on bass, Sal DeTroia on rhythm, Gary Chester on drums, and many others - some of the most famous musicians you never heard of. Unnamed and unrecognized outside of the business, their second homes were the NY recording studios, and they created hit after hit, day after day. Despite being the foundation for so many international hit records, they never wanted nor

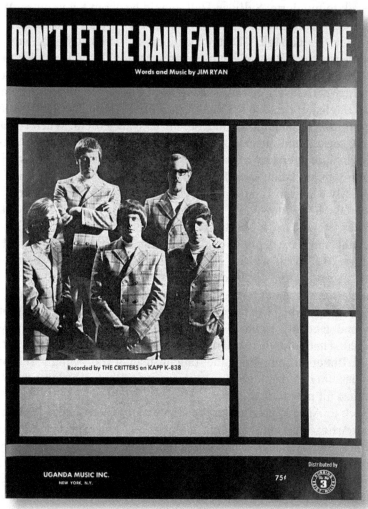

needed credit. They came in, did their job and left, moving on to the next session. By the seventies, record labels started recognizing them as musical heroes and insisted on listing them on album credits. I liked this idea of working in the background with many artists. Trying to stay enthusiastic about being the main attraction was becoming tiring and tedious, and I was getting burned out. Life as a studio musician seemed like it would be much more fun and a lot easier than trying to be a superstar! Wheels were starting to turn in my head.

The "Don't Let The Rain Fall Down On Me" session was a marvel. I couldn't have asked for a better band, and the arrangement - better than anything I would have come up with. The recorded sound was another story. Once again, I found myself hating the bass sound. It was that NY, AM radio, thin, cut-through-everything tinny nonsense; I called it banjo bass. I loved Joe Mack's playing, but the engineer did him no favors with the sound. I wanted a rich, full McCartney bass sound, but they overruled my request. I dropped the argument, hoping to resurrect it when it came time to mix. In the meantime, I taught the singers (also the producers) Pete Anders, Vini Poncia, and our Kenny Gorka the vocal background parts and we sang a couple of layers. Time ran out on the session, so I quickly did a one-take reference lead vocal to be replaced on our next session.

The song ended up in the can, meaning it wouldn't be released for a while, but also not rejected - just shelved for later. Instead, we released the two Anders and Poncia songs, "Marrying Kind of Love" which made it into the early 100s, and "Bad Misunderstanding" which made it to #55. Neither moved us closer to hall of fame status.

Artie kept trying to supplement our repertoire with outside material, continually pressing the need for hit singles. During the recording of our first album, he sent two writers to the studio, Gary Bonner and Alan Gordon, to play me a song. We sat down in the studio lounge and Gary pulled out a guitar. They said they loved The Critters and thought a particular song they had just finished would be perfect for us. Gary started playing, they both started singing and I sat back and listened. When it was done, I told them I loved the chorus, but the chords in the verse were a bit too commonplace for my taste. Would they consider changing them? They declined, saying they thought the chords really worked well with the lyrics. We tossed ideas back and forth, but in the end we reached an impasse. I said, "I think it's a good song, and I'm sure you'll find someone who'll be happy to record it." We shook hands, and said goodbye. After they left, the chorus kept going round and round in my mind, "I can't see me lovin 'nobody but you for all my life!" I wondered if maybe I had been a little rash.

In another studio where The Turtles were recording, they closed the deal. I've made some poor judgment calls in my day, but this one tops the lot. The Turtles recorded the song and had a massive hit, rocketing them to stardom. Bloody hell. As a joke in my later years, I made up a self-owning parody (sung to the tune of "Happy Together"):

If I could turn back time,
I would,
I'd tell those guys I love their song,
It's really good,
Then we'd have that humongous hit,
Just like we should,
Oh, what was I thinking?

I'd take my time machine,
Back to that night,
And tell them give that song to us,
We'd sing it right,
Don't give it to The Turtles please!
They're way too light,
Oh, what was I thinking??

(Chorus) I can see my brain wasn't working at all,
When I said NO!
Black and blue from banging my head on the wall,
Cuz I said no...

Amid our slow slip into obscurity, we received our first royalty statement. Our income for record sales came to zero. With two hit singles and a successful album, we allegedly still owed Kama Sutra money. The numbers quoted on our statement made no sense, so we called in a lawyer and an accountant to go in swinging for us. An audit began, and our team discovered quite a few large, questionable entries in the books. There were expenses incurred by other bands, and travel and tour charges in cities we had never played. That, plus the inexplicably lowball sales numbers, convinced us that Kama Sutra was mathematically challenged or cheating us with both the original bullshit recording contract and now the creative accounting. When our lawyer Phil Kurnit (mentioned in the Glens Falls fiasco) saw that contract, his eyes rolled almost into the back of his head. He said he would never have let us sign this indefensible piece of crap if he represented us. He also told us that recording contracts are usually many pages long, and no legitimate contract would start with the words "Standard Recording Agreement". Topping off the bad news, he dropped the fact that most record deals are closer to 12% - 15% for a new artist, not 3.5%. Kama Sutra had been shady to the max, and with this deal and their well-cooked books, we'd make no money no matter how many records we sold.

In a formal letter, Phil Kurnit informed them that The Critters would be severing their relationship with Kama Sutra. With no desire for litigation, considering the egg all over their faces, they bid us farewell. They also dropped a "we wouldn't want anyone to get hurt" threat, but their conditions for staying safe were unclear. That was the end of an otherwise very successful record deal. Well... successful for the fame. The money? Not so much.

A short time later I was in my '66 Austin Healey, bombing around Westfield and listening to WABC NY. I almost drove into a tree when I heard the famous ABC disk jockey, Dan Ingram, announce, "You remember these guys, The Critters? We haven't had a hit from them for a while, but it looks like they've been busy. This one's a winner. Here's The Critters with their new single, 'Don't Let The Rain Fall Down On Me'!" And the song began. There was my electric twelve-string playing the intro, then me singing "A raindrop falls from the sky..." And after a couple of minutes, it ended with me pulled over to the side of the road and my jaw in my lap. W.T.A.F? They released it in our absence? How could they do that? I never even did a final vocal... But damn, it sounded awfully good on my tinny Austin Healey radio. A small, almost imperceptible grin was forming on my face, truncating my little tantrum. I wrote a song in the dorm amidst a pile of wet clothes on the floor. It took me forty-five minutes, and it was now playing on the biggest station in NY. Yeah, try to stay mad.

Counting the Cars on the New Jersey Turnpike

Just to backtrack a little, music had always been my first choice for a career, but I had no interest in music college. This was before the world considered rock a legitimate art form, so music colleges taught mainly classical and jazz. No thanks. So I considered being an engineer as a responsible Plan B. I was fascinated by electricity, especially electric guitars, and why not? All the men in my family had engineering degrees of one kind or another. I felt some some pressure to comply, but nothing overt. No one in my extended family pursued music as a profession, so I had no mentors of that kind - only super smart, highly educated and successful college graduates. The silent assumption was always that I would attend college like the rest of my family. Though I showed talent, music was considered a hobby - not in my mind! College was a safety net, not a trapeze. I paid my tuition by gigging with my guitar. In that first small way, I proved to myself that I could make a living with music, even under the pressure of trying to do it simultaneously with my studies... for a while. After about two years, it became clear that I couldn't handle both an engineering curriculum and a music career. The juggling scheme collapsed. My grades suffered because I put performing first, school second. Having a hit with "Younger Girl" lent some credibility to my pathetic 1.8 cumulative average, but it also meant I'd have to endure summer school. Mom and Dad were uncharacteristically patient with my perfect impression of a moron, so to keep the peace at home, I went back to school in the fall. But in my heart, I knew I would never be an electrical engineer. The ejection seat got triggered by a concealed message from the gods.

In October that year, just before homecoming celebrations, the Dean of Engineering brought the entire college of engineers into the field house to welcome us back. We sat and listened to his pep talk for about forty-five minutes, as he raved about our futures. There was aerospace, automotive, the dawn of computing, electronic wonders to be conceived and created by us! Engineers were in tremendous demand, and he wanted to let us know the world was waiting with open arms. Then the gods spoke to me through his lips. He said, "I can't think of any more rewarding career than engineering - ok, maybe being a rock star would be better, but, ..." and that was the last thing I heard. My mind was racing. The Dean had spoken. I'm done, out of here, hitting the road to become a rock star, damn the consequences.

In November 1966, the month of my 20th birthday, I sat down in my dorm with close friends and roommates and told them I was going to take a sabbatical. It didn't go so well. They tried to convince me that the perils and risks of dumping a sure shot like college for a long shot like music were not worth it. After a half hour discussion, they admitted they just cared about me and did not want me to leave. I appreciated their concern, and their arguments made sense, but not enough to change my mind. I had dropped the bomb on my parents the night before, and they were about as enthusiastic as my friends. They did not, however, stand in my way, and the following day, Dad agreed to come and get me. I packed my clothes, books and guitars, hauled them out to the car, loaded them into the trunk, and we headed north. It was a quiet drive home, with Dad planning for my inevitable failure, and me planning for my first concert at Madison Square Garden. As the sun set on the New Jersey Turnpike, the moment was mine. I was now a full-time musician, I had a hit record, and I was feeling empowered for the first time in my life.

Though things were going well for The Critters, the Vietnam War still raged on. Chris had left college to tour and record with us, but with that, his IIS student deferment got revoked, and he was now reclassified 1A. That meant he was likely to be drafted. Soon. Unlike Don and Bob, he had no interest in enlisting in one of the other armed forces, so with regrets, he quit the band and hightailed it back to Philadelphia College of Art. They zipped his paperwork through and got him reclassified back to IIS. Ironically, while attending PCA, getting his degree, the draft system changed to a lottery, and he received his number - 300. By the time they got anywhere near that number, the Vietnam War ended, and with it, the draft.

We were beginning to feel like the North American version of Menudo, a Latin American band famous for their age-out formula. As soon as a member turned sixteen, they were replaced by someone between twelve and fifteen. Though our guys didn't succumb to age limits, they left regularly and always for frustrating reasons. It kept happening over and over. We were back down to four members with only two originals, Kenny and me. The disappointing final phase was upon us, and it didn't last long.

After leaving Kama Sutra, we began scouting for a new record deal. Our accounting and legal team went to work for us, so much of the shopping took place in the background while we continued to gig. Phil Kurnit represented a label called Project 3, and with some arm twisting, talked us into signing with them. They had money but no major pop artists. We were pop artists and could use the money, so we signed with them in hopes of a win/win.

Sadly, it wasn't. We produced two more albums and no more hits. Project 3 spent some money to buy us but were clueless about how to spend some money to promote us and get our records on the air. It was a bad choice to not pursue a bigger, more established label, and after about a year and a half, we cut our losses - another record deal in the rear-view mirror.

One incredibly fortuitous situation evolved out of The Critters fiasco. I met a man named Dan Armstrong. He played bass, repaired guitars and owned an NYC guitar store. In the previous year, when a thief stole our instruments and amps after a gig at Rutgers University, we came to Dan for replacements. Through some unexpected twists and turns, he ended up being the producer of our third album. It was odd recording with a storekeeper, but as it turned out, Dan was a

Dan Armstrong with
me in the background

super-talented musician, arranger, and producer. He and I had very similar musical tastes, so recording with him was a pleasure. Though he wasn't able to squeeze any more hits out of us, Dan and I went on to become lifelong friends. But The Critters had exceeded their "best if used by" date.

That spring, after several shows for Long Island high school senior proms, I pulled the plug. I did not know what I would do with myself, but I couldn't stand another gig with what remained of the band. We rose from Knights of Columbus sock hops to national fame, then sank back down to doing high school proms, and I couldn't continue. For me, unemployment and financial insecurity would be better than a slow, painful descent into irrelevance.

Before you get the impression that it was all bad, I'll toss in one of our last gigs to honor a fellow performer from whom I learned more about singing and performing in one hour than than I did in much of my previous career.

We were hired to do a concert at Hunter College in NYC. Playing any gig in NYC would be fun, but this one was special. The roster was Booker T. & the M.G.'s, Otis Redding and us. Any artist would feel intimidated in the company of these greats, but it didn't end up being a problem. We just did our show the way we did, and the crowd responded very well. A hit is a hit, no matter the genre, so our chart action with "Younger Girl" and "Mr. Dieingly Sad" carried the day. But Booker T wasn't as exciting as I thought he would be. He was certainly a talented musician, and Steve Cropper, his guitarist, and Duck Dunn, his bass player, were legendary. The problem was listening to an hour of groove instrumental music. It wasn't jazz, and it wasn't rock. It was just groove. The crowd liked it, but there were no standing ovations.

Otis was the main attraction, and he was up next. One little problem. His band had not shown up yet. There were no cell phones in those days, so he couldn't contact them to see what the problem was. Traffic? An accident? No one knew. After fifteen minutes, Otis said to hell with it. He would go on without them. We all looked at each other with a big, "Huh? No band? What are you going to do? Tell jokes?" He said, "I'm going to do what I always do. Sing." I thought, ok then. This should be interesting.

He walked out on stage to loud cheers and just stood there looking around the audience, smiling and nodding his head in acknowledgment. Then he raised his hands to quiet everyone. Speaking in a muted but confident voice, he told the crowd his band hadn't shown up; they were nowhere to be found, and he had no way of contacting them. Not wanting to disappoint anyone, he said he would do his show without them. This man was going to do an entire R&B set without a band - not just unplugged - 100% a cappella. The crowd started murmuring, everyone looking at each other in disbelief, but he just stood there... eyes closed... head back... slowly reaching for the mike stand... waiting as the hall fell into complete silence. Then, softly..." I've been loving you... too long... and I don't wanna stop now..." You could hear a universal gasp and see the look of awe everywhere. His voice was almost preternatural. This was about as close to a spiritual experience as I have ever had watching an artist perform. Otis Redding was singing fro m his

Otis Redding

heart to every single person in that audience, and you could feel the wave of emotion enveloping everyone. Time stood still as he churned out hit after hit:" Sittin 'On The Dock of the Bay" "Try A Little Tenderness" "I Can't Turn You Loose" "Satisfaction" "So Hard To Handle" - just slapping his hands on his hips, stomping his feet and absolutely killing it. This Hunter College concert was not just a show. It was a once in a lifetime experience that no one there will ever forget. I am thankful that we opened this show, not closed it. There would be no point in following Otis. When he was done, the show was done. Nothing to do but go home completely fulfilled.

Juke Box Hero

The previous story was a peek into the kind of devotion and drive some have for being not only a rock star, but delivering their message straight from the heart. The audience leaves a performance like this uplifted, joyful and bonded to memories that could last a lifetime. But let's talk about what it's like for the artist. When one has the opportunity of performing a song, flawlessly executed in front of an adoring audience, the psychological reward is indescribable. It's like floating in an alternate dimension, feeling pure bliss. The pull of its gravity is unrelenting, irresistible. This is the payoff for the hard work and struggle. By contrast, in business, certainly in engineering, the climb up the corporate ladder can take years of slow, stressful work. The reward may be financial success, but for many, it's just a job, often a drag and not a cherished passion. That's how it was for my dad, and that's how it was not going to be for me.

The dream of creating one or more songs that could take me to the top of the world on the express elevator is what kept me going during the tough times. Even if we factor in the years of study, long hours of practice, unpleasant gigs, and disappointments, the idea that I might turn a dead end into a freaking parabola, rocketing me and my bandmates to number one on the charts with just one song going viral, well, ask any superstar if the risk and toil were worth it.

If, dear reader, you've never earned a standing ovation, let's just say nothing compares to ten thousand crazed fans cheering and shouting your name to help fill any empty spaces inside, even if it's only for a few moments. The rush of energy, looking out at those happy fans, or winning a Grammy, or signing a six or seven-figure contract, or selling out a stadium, is always temporary, short-lived, gone in a flash... but we entertainers must think it's worth it because we keep pursuing the dream. Shallow? In some ways yes, but if you think of music and entertainment as your job, would you rather be doing that or sitting in an office shuffling paper in a thankless job for a thankless company?

But... I learned the hard way that fame is not the antidote for one's foibles. If you are looking for that temporary high to cure all your ills, welcome. Those of us who have had a taste of fame will be happy to burst that bubble for you. Sure, it can be fun, and can bring some short-term happiness, but in the long run fame does not bring fulfillment. I am not suggesting you avoid it. I just want you to understand fame for what it is, and enjoy it if you've been blessed, but hold it lightly.

Let's put the parabolic rise to stardom aside for a moment and explore what makes some people want to be famous. For me, I was experiencing a void, something missing inside of me, and I hoped fame would fill that void. At every step up the ladder, it did... for a short while. Then it was back to staring into that empty space, longing for something bigger and better. My balance came with therapy and meditation, psychology and spiritual practice. I urge you from experience, ignore self-awareness at your peril. If fame was a panacea or cure for neurosis, movie stars, pop stars and politicians would be strong, clear-headed and sane. Most are not even close. This claim will surprise no one, least of all them. The phrase "sane artist" is almost an oxymoron. The number of overdoses, violent episodes, divorces, restraining orders, untimely deaths and general pandemonium that surrounds most "stars" is a given. Neurosis in the arts is endemic, whether the malfeasance makes it to the media or is a guarded secret among managers, agents and family. So, if you'd like to join the inmates at the institution called "The Arts" - by all means, come on in and join the fun... just come in with an understanding that it's a career, not a cure.

That crazy institution I reveal here has been good to me, despite its shortcomings. The Critters were an encouraging start, but though we could not sustain our success, it was a useful gateway. While searching for the elusive wormhole to stardom, an opportunity arose that allowed me to try something different - establish myself as a backup artist. This was the big shape-shift. I became a chameleon of sorts, getting very good at accompanying rock stars of multiple genres, writing background music for film and TV, and being an essential behind-the-scenes operator. Being stationed a few steps beyond the reach of the spotlight, not in it, has its benefits for longevity. So many stars fall from grace, but their failures have little effect on those who provide their musical support. We rarely go down with the ship. We dance in the shadows behind the artists, and when their careers crash, we move on, taking the call for the next recording session, the next concert with the next artist. Though this may sound uncompassionate, maybe a little jaded, I assert that if we don't participate in the profits, there is no reason to go down with the losses. My former clients 'misdeeds have never damaged my career. This is the beauty of being part of the team behind the stars.

The Critters chapter of my life is a collection of experiences I will treasure until the day I die. Sure, there were bad times and many disappointments, but only if the framing was exclusively around commercial success, not psychological growth. The education I received as a result of our adventures could never be taught in any school. It was a masters 'course in entrepreneurship, psychology, patience, relationships, music education, recording and electronics, but mostly a crash course in growing up. There was plenty of success, just not quite superstardom. I'm fine with that. I've written more about the downs than the ups, because frankly they're a lot funnier and more interesting, at least to me. The joy of receiving a check lasts about as long as it takes you to put it in the bank. You make the deposit, feel a little more secure, and then it's on to the next adventure. Not much growth there. But when something doesn't go to plan, if you're smart and paying attention, you eventually shift from damage control to introspection. We cross-examine ourselves, hoping to uncover our mistakes and not repeat them. Faced with the choice to beat ourselves up or learn and grow, hopefully we choose the latter. I did that examination and went deep. I took on Primal Therapy and studied Eastern Philosophy, learning to meditate in hopes of finding something better, more substantial than what commerce, finance and show business had to offer. It's a work in progress, but it's going very well. Though The Critters story would seem to have an unfortunate ending following several years of deterioration, in retrospect, it was more of a gain than a loss. I believe when a door closes behind you, another will open in front of you. The following stories will make my point.

Chapter Three
Role Reversal

Elephant Talk

On a Saturday night in June 1968, bored in Westfield, New Jersey, I decided to hop in my Austin Healey and take a ride into New York City. I headed East on route 22, then on to the Turnpike, through the Lincoln Tunnel, eventually pulling up and parking on West 46th Street. My friends were waiting when I arrived, looking forward to a relaxing evening at Steve Paul's Scene. Teddy Slatus, the evening's host, met us at the club entrance and led us down the stairs into the noisy, smokey, underground cavern, a haunt for many a rock star. I never paid to get in because, hey, I was one of The Critters! Famous people were always guests of honor. I worked it while it lasted. The room was filled with music fans and showbiz people, and the Chambers Brothers' "Time" echoed through the club over the sound system.

At around 10:30pm, while my friends and I sat at our table talking about the usual - girlfriends, politics, whatever, the canned music faded, and Steve Paul stepped up onto the small stage, tapping the center mike several times. Steve always sported a wide-eyed, spaced-out expression on his face as he looked at the ceiling awkwardly announcing each show. He, Skipper the black belt karate chopping bouncer and Tiny Tim comprised some of the quirky attractions that helped make the Scene popular and the go-to NY dive for John Lennon, Jimi Hendrix, Keith Emerson, Johnny Winter, Joe Cocker, The Rascals, Traffic, Pink Floyd, The Doors and many other rock stars of the day. Steve leaned into the mike." Good evening everybody. Thanks for coming out and joining us at the Scene. Please give a warm welcome to Elephant's Memory."

I thought, "Hmmm - not familiar with that name. Hope they're not too loud." After a few snare drum hits, the usual buzzes from plugging in live guitar jacks and the obligatory "testing, one-two, one-two," they kicked off their set with... a song no one knew. They were ok. I paid little attention to them, but when I looked up from my third lime and lager, I saw a tall, beautiful woman singing lead. It was an odd match - her voice was far more interesting than their music. No one in the band mentioned her name, but in a vote of who gets to stay on the island, I'd say with that voice, she was the keeper. I didn't give it much further thought and continued my conversation with my friends about Lyndon Johnson's resignation and how long it would be before the war in Vietnam would end.

Back to The Critters for a moment. On one of the final mixing sessions for that third and last Critters album, Dan Armstrong showed up with his girlfriend, who was a musician/singer. He wanted her to meet us, but mostly wanted to impress her with his production skills. I immediately recognized her as the Elephant's Memory lead singer I had seen earlier that year. Dan introduced her by her first name, Carly, as they took off their winter coats and scarves and settled into the control room sofa. When I told her how much I enjoyed hearing her that night at the Scene, she seemed to appreciate the compliment but confessed she hadn't done much in music since then. I was utterly baffled but had a strong feeling her current musical silence wouldn't last. During our

Paul Glanz & me

conversation, I fantasized, "wouldn't it be cool to be in a band with a singer who was that good?" I thoroughly enjoyed chatting with her while Dan made comments and suggestions to our engineer about the mixes. The evening ended on a happy, "hope to see you again soon" note. It would be a year before our paths would cross again.

I'm sure you've figured out by now, the Carly I'm talking about is Carly Simon. It's hard to imagine her fronting a hard rock band like Elephant's Memory, but that's what she was doing, albeit for only a short time. I'll now reveal the steps that led up to being her friend, guitarist, musical director, arranger and sometimes composer. It all started with Paul Glanz, our last Critters keyboardist.

Within a month or two of The Critters 'demise, Paul Glanz called me and asked, "Are you still playing bass? Have you kept it up?"

"Yep, I'm still thumping the sucker. Why?"

"I've got a gig for us if you're interested. It's a one-month tour of the Midwest with a British artist. The band would be me on Hammond Organ, you on bass, and some drummer named Carl Palmer."

He'd got my attention. I asked, "So who's this mystery artist?"

"Do you remember that song 'Fire? 'Big hit last year?"

"Of course. Arthur Brown. Number one record and one of my favorites. Hard to ignore that screaming intro, 'I AM THE GOD OF

HELL-FIRE, AND I BRING YOU - FIRE!!'"

"So? Are you interested? The money's good, and the songs are pretty easy."

"Absolutely. Tell me where to go, and I'll be there with bass and suitcase!"

Not only was I thrilled to have work, I'd be playing in a kick-ass band with a hit artist, and the show would be HIS, not mine. Working behind someone famous and getting out of that annoying spotlight would make me very happy.

After a week of weird but fun rehearsals peppered with pseudo demonic bullshit, we kicked off the tour on June 28, 1969, at New York Central Park's legendary Wollman Skating Rink - the Schaefer Music Festival. I was super excited to be playing bass, for me, an easier instrument than guitar, and to be free of having to carry the show. Arthur

Arthur Brown

Brown required us to dress in polyester blue warlock gowns to give the impression of mystical accomplices (more demonic bullshit). The summer heat could be an issue, so their thin fabric was a good choice. But to make sure I didn't roast, I just wore my undershorts and a T-shirt under the cloak, as did the others. I could have gone commando but chickened out at the last minute.

Arthur put on a wild show and wore a costume that looked like priest's vestments. But instead of a cross, he had a pentagram emblazoned on the front. He also wore a headdress that looked like a helmet with a large, U-shaped lyre on the top. I paid little attention to him as we cranked out song after song. I needed to focus on playing bass, which I had never done in a live setting, only in the studio. Offstage and out of sight of the audience, his roadie basted a second infernal headdress with jelly gas, and with the click of a lighter, whoosh, up the bugger went in flames. Arthur dashed over, took off his initial helmet, grabbed the burning one and carefully placed it on his head. Then he burst back onstage. So picture this skinny, wild-eyed dude, decked out in his pentagram priest's frock, leaping around the stage singing the "Fire" song with his head literally on fire. His antics were so padded-cell crazy, all I could do was laugh. In the previous week, we only rehearsed songs, not staging, so I was unaware I'd be a participant in a pyro-circus. He probably wanted us to act serious and threatening, to honor the spirit of the god of hellfire, but I just couldn't. This was more like the god of hell-farce. Then came the instrumental break. I had my eyes on Paul wailing on the organ and didn't notice Arthur dramatically hurl his flaming helmet in the air. Which way did he hurl it, you ask? Backwards. The bouncing bonfire landed behind me, but because we were quite loud and my attention was on Paul, I neither saw nor heard it land. When Paul finished his solo, I turned to face the audience and took a few unconscious steps backwards. The flaming headdress was now under my cloak, between my legs. Paul and Arthur looked at me in horror, as I felt the searing flames singeing my unclothed leg hairs and roasting my private parts right through my jockeys. I screamed and jumped in the air, leaping the hell away from the groin grill, still trying to play bass while praying my balls weren't on fire. The cool breeze under my frock and the immediate relief of only being over the mini inferno for a second or two quelled my fears, but that wasn't the end. The audience thought it was part of the act and couldn't decide whether to cheer or roll on the floor laughing. They did both. Picture people laughing and cheering, while I was screaming and leaping like a man possessed, and a stagehand running out with a fire extinguisher hosing the helmet and eyeing me to see if I too needed a blast of high pressure carbon dioxide in the crotch - all at once. Arthur decided it was fabulous and would become a regular part of the act. I decided he could go to hell like the song. I won. We never played burn-the-bass-player's-balls again.

For the remainder of the tour, we did a fun series of outdoor events, and I'll attempt to describe two additional weird incidents. We were in Michigan at the 1969 Saugatuck Pop Festival. Our showtime was coming up as we were hanging around behind the stage. The MC5 were blasting through their set to the delight of the sold-out festival audience, and Arthur had to take a leak.

I was several feet away, so he shouted, "Ryan, where are the fucking outhouses?"

I said, "I don't know. Do you want me to ask around?"

He replied, "Fuck it. I gotta go."

He then pulled out his penis in front of his wife, the entire backstage crew and performers and pissed on the side of one of the tents. I guess if he was the god of hellfire, this wasn't out of line with his job description. Amazing what you can get away with as a headliner. Like a dog to a fire hydrant, people barely noticed.

The other moment that stood out was an odd tribute by Iggy Pop, a fellow artist at this Michigan festival. He called his band Iggy and the Stooges, and at the time called himself "Iggy Stooge." Brian Jones, the rhythm guitarist for The Rolling Stones, had just drowned in a swimming pool, leaving Stones fans mourning all over the world. Iggy honored our sadness with a heartfelt, tender and sensitive dedication: "HERE'S TO BRIAN JONES, THE DEAD STONE!!" Such finesse. Such class. The silence and uniform mass of frowns from the audience was priceless. His almost comical insensitivity had the potential to alienate thousands of fans, but to my amazement, it didn't. He started another song, and it was as if it never happened.

Iggy's currency was shock and awe, so if he didn't say something idiotic or insane, people would have felt cheated. Despite hating his Brian Jones tribute, I enjoyed seeing him scream and writhe through his half hour set of pre-punk musical debauchery. This is the artist who sometimes slathered his body in peanut butter, barfed on his audiences and rolled around in broken glass on the stage, performing while bleeding all over himself and his band mates. Imagine Iggy in a car, pulled over for DWI: "You want a blood test? Here's your fucking blood test! [Scraaaaape]" Despite being a heroin addict and a self-destructive fool, he is still alive and well as I write this book, at 73 years old. Brian Jones will have to wait to thank him.

As planned, the tour ended after a few weeks and unfortunately, we heard no talk of future plans for Mr. Brown. And that drummer I mentioned earlier, Carl Palmer? Yep, he went on to form Atomic Rooster, and then Emerson, Lake and Palmer. Nice to have played with him in his early career.

I'd Like To Get To Know You

Once I returned to NY, my savings soon evaporated, and the pressure was back on to look for a day job, anything to sustain me until I could find another interesting and hopefully lucrative musical gig. I recalled Dan Armstrong had a popular music store in Greenwich Village and decided to inquire about a job. I gave him a call, and luck was on my side. He needed a store manager, and I got the gig. Now let's talk about Dan's girlfriend.

Carly would often show up at the store to meet him for dates, and occasionally I'd grab a guitar, and we'd sing a song or two together while waiting for Dan. She was only a year and a half older than me, but had so much more worldly experience, I often looked up to her like a big sister. In a very short time, we became close enough that we would share very personal experiences and feelings, her about her relationship with Dan and the loves of her past, and me about my relationships with the various women I was dating. We also had almost identical musical tastes, so I never found myself in a living room with her, having to listen to music that I hated. That may seem like an insignificant issue, but to a musician, it can be a very important litmus test for a relationship, both platonic and romantic. I had a similar relationship with Dan Armstrong, so the three of us got along like a functional family, something to which I was unaccustomed.

An amusing event happened between Carly and me during my days at the store. Towards the end of my time there, she came in saying she would like to buy a good acoustic guitar, and what would I recommend? I always loved Martins. Steven Stills played one with Crosby, Stills & Nash, and it sounded wonderful. She agreed, and I ordered her a Martin D-28 dreadnaught. The guitar arrived about a week later. I opened the case and took it out to tune it and get it ready for her. That's when the problem occurred. This Martin was too good. It sounded magical, and the selfish idea that I could never let this guitar go made me almost feel guilty. Almost. At the moment it belonged to the store, but not for long. I didn't want to have a tug-of-war with Carly, so I searched my devious mind for excuses to not part with it. The ultimate deterrent was sitting there right in my hands. Martins can be a little difficult to play out of the box, because the factory sets their strings a bit higher off the frets than most production guitars to ensure that they don't buzz. This can be adjusted by filing down the bridge, but that is not common knowledge and a delicate job, easy to botch. As such, Martins are not the first choice for people who don't play all the time with shoe leather finger calluses.

When Carly arrived to buy the guitar, I told her, "The guitar is here, but I'm not sure you're going to like it. The action is unusually high, making it difficult to play."

She picked it up, played a few chords and immediately agreed. She said, "I'm really sorry I made you order this. I don't like it. It hurts my fingers. Is there any chance you can send it back?"

I said, "Ya know... I don't mind it. Maybe I'll buy it. How about I order you a Guild which is also a great brand and easier to play?"

She was thrilled that she hadn't caused a problem, so I got on the phone and ordered an equivalent Guild for her. It arrived another week later, and when she picked it up to play, she loved it. Why not? It was a great guitar, and considerably easier on the fingers... until I filed down the Martin bridge and made it equally easy to play! Eventually I told her the story, and she took no offense. This was a win/win situation. We both got the guitars we wanted. Just a fun note: I paid $395 for that Martin D-28 in 1968. They currently sell for almost ten times that, so I'd say it was a good investment for price and usability. That guitar is on every single recording I have made to this day that required acoustic guitar. And a salute to how crazy collectors can be - David Gilmore of Pink Floyd sold his for $1.095 million.

I worked at the store for about a year, while developing a studio musician career during the evenings and days off. It was like being in music college. Our store clients were the big star guitarists and bassists of the day, and I used this to my advantage. As artists like Johnny Winter, Jack Bruce, Billy Squier and Joe Walsh would come in looking for a cool vintage Les Paul or Strat, I would hand them a primo instrument off the wall and then just watch them play, studying their technique. I learned a tremendous amount just being an observer, asking questions about how they practiced or played certain phrases.

Not only was this the equivalent of a music school, it was also a luthier school. Dan taught me how to re-fret guitars, grind, level and polish frets, straighten guitar necks, shave sound board braces in cheap Yamaha guitars to make them sound more like Martins, rewire pickups, pots and switches, and the best one - be part of the focus group for the design of his groundbreaking, clear plastic guitar. This was a revolutionary concept which used 1.5-inch clear lucite for the body of the guitar, a traditional maple neck, but the real kicker, removable, exchangeable pickups, each one sounding slightly different. There were two initial models - a guitar and a bass. Eventually they created black plastic versions, but those didn't sell well, and only a few were made. I snagged one of the first basses off the production line and still have it to this day. The originals are quite valuable among collectors. Unfortunately, there were two major problems with the instruments which doomed them to becoming beautiful wall decorations or lawn ornaments. The guitar, for some reason never solved, would not stay in tune. No matter how well you secured the strings, and no matter if you replaced the tuning heads with the most expensive ones on the market, the tuning would drift. That eliminated it from stage use, despite Keith Richards being one of the original endorsers. The other problem was with the bass. Very simply, it just didn't sound that good. It was ok, but no match for the good Fenders of the day. Mine remains in a case in the closet, quietly gaining value, while my current go-to bass is a Ken Smith.

Working at Dan Armstrong Guitars was the only day job I've ever held, and it was never meant to be the start of a career in retail. On my days off, I would hustle jingle companies and record producers for work. Eventually those contacts would pay off.

When The Moon Is In The Seventh House

Dan was an excellent bass player, and he had a hobby band with a studio musician named Charlie Brown. Charlie often came to the store to hang out, chat and explore newly acquired instruments. In the evenings and two afternoons per week, he was the guitarist in the original Broadway production of *Hair*. The show was a Tony nominee, the number one attraction, the most expensive ticket on Broadway, and Charlie was the guitarist in the show band. He heard me play around the store a few times, had jammed with Dan and me occasionally, and I did my best to impress. He was also aware of The Critters, so he knew I had a track record. One day he came in and asked me if I read music. I said yes, why? He said he was getting fed up with playing eight shows per week and wondered if I'd like to sub for him in *Hair* from time to time. Oh, hell yeah!

He explained the routine for bringing in a new sub, and the following night I began my training. The first step - watch the play from the audience, two or three times. What an emotional experience, seeing how the actors depicted young people coming to grips with the Vietnam War, losing friends, singing wonderful songs from their hearts and inviting the audience up on the stage to dance in the finale. Next step - sit on the bandstand and shadow him for about a week, reading the music over his shoulder, watching the play from the on-stage faux-trashed flatbed bandstand truck and memorizing his every move. A curious steel-beamed tower loomed over the stage from the back. During one of the songs, I would dress up in a Jimi Hendrix-style Hawaiian shirt, chains and necklaces and a headband, after which I'd climb the vertigo-vomit structure and play a histrionic-fueled solo. Content didn't matter much, as long as it was loud, and I swung my arms like Pete Townshend or an orangutan and acted like I was headlining an Altamont psilocybin festival.

After my basic training, the time had come to turn me loose. Charlie cleared it with the conductor and let me do the show on my own. Once I got past my nerves, I thought it went well. After three shows, however, the music director did not think it was going so well and told Charlie to find another sub. I was devastated and had to know why, so I pressed him, and he pressed her. The problem turned out to not be such a disaster. She said I was simply playing too loud and too much. Turning down and simplifying my parts, getting out of the way of the piano and wind instruments, would solve the problem. In her critique, she said my playing was a better fit for a four-piece rock band, filling up all the empty spaces with power chords. This job was nothing like that. It was a carefully arranged, intricate combination of instruments that worked in lock step with the singers on the stage. I just had to get out of the way. When Charlie explained the situation and what they required, I learned a fundamental rule in being a backup musician. Listen. Keep your ears open and find a place to create a part, not fill every place that's vacant. Music has three essential ingredients - notes, spaces and emotion. I was filling all the notes and all the spaces, and clueless about the resulting irritation emanating from the other musicians. Playing like that becomes boring after a very short time, especially in a production with a full orchestra and singers. In hopes of being reinstated, I promised to listen and adjust my approach, and they brought me back on probation. Acquiescing to the pressure, I cheerfully played only the written page at a reasonable volume and did so well that Charlie eventually turned the show over to me. He was bored with *Hair* and had enough session work that the play became more trouble than it was worth. I performed every show from then on, right up to closing night on July 1, 1972.

Just one quick and funny story before we put *Hair* to bed. In those days I was painfully shy. I had to muster up a lot of courage before I could ask a girl out, so being a chicken at dating, I spent a lot of time alone and lonely. There was an actress in the play that I loved to watch every night. She was a brilliant singer, quite attractive and single. I'll point out here that an odd and amusing part about the play was the famous nude scene. For me, it was no big deal because the band was seated on that flat bed truck facing stage right, perpendicular to the audience. When the cast undressed in the dark, I saw nothing, and when the lights came up for the shocking reveal, they were facing the audience. The name of the play was *Hair,* so everyone had long hair. From my perspective, all I saw were their backs. Male and female looked pretty much the same, but for thinner waists on some females. This world-renowned show of naked flesh, a Broadway first, ended act one, after which the cast would walk nonchalantly to the dressing room, carrying their clothes… not wearing them. Because we all shared one big dressing room, nudity had become as commonplace as being dressed.

One evening I got up my courage and decided to ask this actress out. After the nude scene and curtain down, I put my guitar on its stand and followed the parade of bare butts into the dressing room. I spotted her in a corner getting her clothes back on. As ridiculous as it was, having seen her every night in her birthday suit, I played the gentleman and waited until she was dressed. Wandering over with as much confidence as I could muster, I said "Hi!"

Then I dropped some irrelevant small talk, and with two left feet, said, "I love your singing. Would you like to have a drink or do lunch some time?"

She looked at me as if I had just called her a ho.

"Oh, rock on Jimi Hendrix. Aren't you so cool? Just play your fucking guitar and get out of my face."

I'm serious. That was her response to my show of interest. There is no dark corner in my morbid imagination that could have conjured up a worse outcome than this moment of stark, humiliating rejection in front of the entire half naked cast of *Hair* and several of the musicians. Jesus H. Christ. I didn't get mad. I was momentarily suspended in that weird delay between being smacked in the head by a two-by-four and the resulting pain.

Wide-eyed and in shock, I said, "Wow, didn't expect that. Sorry..." and slunk out of the dressing room with my head down as fast as my feet would carry me, holding my stomach and trying not to throw up.

I went out the stage door into the alleyway, leaned against the cold brick wall of the theater and lit up a cigarette. Jimmy Lewis, the bass player, was chatting with Idris Muhammad, the drummer, and they kind of chuckled when they saw me.

I took a deep puff, exhaled and said, "Well that was embarrassing."

Now they were cracking up.

"Oh come on guys, she was a little harsh, don't you think? Was I that bad?"

They looked wide-eyed at each other, surprised at my comment, and Idris turned to me and said, "Man, what did you expect?"

Now I was confused. "What did I expect? I expected she would give me her number, or at least politely decline. Why else would I have asked?"

It finally dawned on them I was missing an important piece of information. Jimmy broke the news: "Man - she's gay. A lesbian. Looks like she thought you were insulting her. Everyone in the cast knows she's gay. What were you thinking?"

Have you ever felt both stupid and relieved at the same time? I went from being hurt, angry and humiliated to a somewhat relieved face palm. "D'oh!" Considering what she thought I was doing, I no longer felt any sense of rejection or anger. If I thought some jerk was making fun of my sexual orientation in front of my friends, I'd probably let out a few choice words too. As our old Critters song opined, "What A Bad Misunderstanding."

I wanted to apologize immediately. She worked the far side of the stage in the second act, so I had no opportunity, and she left right after the show. In the interim, I think someone must have informed her of my cluelessness. The following night before the show, I was getting my guitar out, and she wandered over. Smiling, she said, "Sorry about last night. I was in a horrible mood, and I thought you were making fun of me. You're new here, so how would you know? I don't exactly wear a sign, 'Lesbian! Approach with caution!' Didn't mean to blow you away like that."

I smiled and said, "Thanks for saying that. I really appreciate it. No worries, I'm good." With a chuckle, I added, "But hey, if you ever change your sexual preference..." Haha, nooo, I did not say that.

The Times They Are a Changin'

Ok, back to Carly Simon. Having gathered enough recording session and Broadway orchestra work, I had enough income to quit the store. I left my job at Dan Armstrong Guitars with good wishes and congratulations from Dan. I felt a bit sorry about my timing though, because I soon learned that Carly had also handed in her resignation to Dan around the same time, ending their romantic relationship. Dan assured me it was ok. They were not getting along, and he was actually relieved to be free and available once again.

She and I stayed in touch over the next year, both enrolling in the same music copying course at the Juilliard School. We used to joke about why we were even taking the course, as neither of us had any ambition to be copyists (the people who create sheet music when needed for recording sessions or live performances). These days, it's all done much better with software programs, so if you were a professional copyist, you have about the same job security as a coal shoveler on a diesel train. Also, the jingle business thrived in those days. Carly and I often found ourselves standing side by side in studios, singing about dish soap and diapers, and occasionally, when we got a lucky break, making national cigarette commercials. They were legal then, and I smoked Winstons, so no foul. Eventually I quit, and both lungs are still functioning well.

One day in the spring of 1970, Carly called me to say Elektra Records had signed her to a singer/songwriter recording deal. I grinned ear to ear and cheered in my mind, "YES, FINALLY!!" She asked if I'd like to play guitar on her upcoming album. This time I said "YES" out loud.

Before my first recording with her, she played me a song she had just finished at Jimi Hendrix's studio, Electric Ladyland. The band consisted of Carly on piano, accompanied by an A-list group of studio musicians. From beginning to end, my jaw was nailed to the floor - it was spectacular. She'd never shared her original songs with me, so who knew she could write a song like this? I liked her Simon Sisters recordings, but this song was in a category all of its own. She titled it "That's The Way I Always Heard It Should Be" and it had all the ingredients of an enormous hit.

Though I didn't play on the entire album, I heard enough to know her music would be very important in her life and the lives of people all over the world. Her intimate perspective, her unusual and mesmerizing songwriting style and her beautiful voice would soon be charming the masses.

Fast forward, "That's The Way I Always Heard It Should Be" started climbing up the charts, and she was getting pressure from Elektra to perform live. In early March 1971, she called me and asked if I'd like to be her guitarist for a series of concerts at the famous Troubadour in LA. The gig was scheduled for the week of April 6th, and we'd be opening for Cat Stevens.

A dream had just come true. Not only would I meet and open for one of my favorite artists, but I'd be doing it with one of my favorite people, my old Juilliard and jingles, guitar store boss's girlfriend, Carly. She was about to begin a journey that would make history, rocketing her into international stardom - and I'd be tagging along with minimal responsibility. In The Critters, everything depended on me, and I grew to hate it. Some people are cut out for showboating, but when it becomes hard work with only moderate success, the spotlight is not such a great friend. I now had a gig where I could contribute, and be an integral part, but if it failed, I wouldn't share in that failure. I could choose to move on to the next artist.

She asked if I would help her put a band together. Two musician buddies came to mind. I suggested my former Critter pal and Arthur Brown keyboardist, Paul Glanz. Paul and I had also been jamming over the past few months with an excellent drummer named Andy Newmark. We called ourselves Ivory and had ambitions to become the next Emerson, Lake & Palmer, but Carly's offer seemed like a better opportunity. She invited us all to her apartment to try out the combination. After playing through a couple of her songs, Andy and Paul passed the audition with flying colors. Carly loved them both. But unfortunately, with as much talent and input as Andy brought to the table, budget concerns would prevent him from joining us on this first gig. Instead, we would be using Russ Kunkel, a legendary LA drummer who had just become available. His current tour with James Taylor got postponed due to James being involved in a motorcycle accident.

With this wonderful dream unfolding, Carly and I put together a set list, and she, Paul and I rehearsed it song by song, coming up with intricate instrumental parts, working out harmonies, having meals together, laughing and jamming and creating what would become her live band and the core for the recording of "Anticipation".

The days passed quickly. We became tighter and tighter, super excited about opening for Cat Stevens and playing at this famous LA venue that had showcased so many iconic stars over the years. On the morning of April 4th, we gathered at Carly's apartment on East 35th St. A limo picked us up, whisked its way through the twisted, intertwined and congested Long Island highways, and with all the comfort and luxury of rock stars we hoped we'd become, gently deposited us in front of American Airlines at LaGuardia Airport. The big time beckoned, and after the Critters debacle, I was ready.

We had an enjoyable but tiring six-hour flight to LA. That gave me time to read the book I brought, take in a movie and try to keep Carly from jumping out of her skin with flight fright. As we window gazed at the Colorado mountains below, we toasted to our exciting future with those little airline booze bottles you could suck on like Nik-L-Nips from the fifties. Thankfully, I had more than one, because during our final approach, Carly's death grip on my hand almost stopped the circulation. You've heard of Clapton's "Slowhand"? Call me "Bluehand". We both felt some relief when the wheels touched the runway at LAX.

Once we'd deplaned and retrieved our bags, Elektra took care of everything. A limo waited outside, ready to whisk us into Hollywood, and the city-of-dreams-and-fake-everything would be our host for the week. So far, the fake was minimal. Our Electra rep and watchdog, Steve Harris, and Carly's manager, Arlyne Rothberg, also came along to make sure things went smoothly for their budding artist. After a long ride in traffic from LAX, we pulled up in front of the famous Continental Hyatt House on Sunset Blvd. This would be our home for the week, and to me it seemed like Buckingham Palace. What did I know? As a kid, we always stayed at Howard Johnsons or Holiday Inns, and at least the Hyatt House room doors didn't open onto the parking lot. We also enjoyed the Hyatt's rooftop pool, providing an awesome retreat during our down time and a convenient place to gawk from behind our Wal-Mart sunglasses. From this vantage point you could see well up into the majestic Hollywood Hills, and down to the sprawling city of Los Angeles. Though not quite up to Movie Star standards, we loved it and it suited our needs perfectly. The room they picked for Carly, however, was a little creepy. It had a curious bed raised up on a platform, almost like a riser or stage, with a dark red velour bedspread and surrounded by four stanchions, connected by thick red velvet ropes. Every detail raised the question, "Is this a set for porn movies?" I'll stop there. This hotel was rock 'n' roll ground zero for traveling miscreants and had stories that might fill several chapters of this book all by itself, not to mention videos on the shelves of windowless stores.

The Hyatt cafeteria met our minimum standards, so we took our breakfast there. We spent the rest of the morning and early afternoon at the pool. 2:00pm - time to go to work, so we gathered our guitars and bass, hopped into the car and drove five minutes to the famous Troubadour. The club owner, Doug Weston, greeted us with an enormous bouquet of flowers and an expensive bottle of champagne. We truly felt welcome. Russ Kunkel had already set up, every bit the consummate professional we hoped he would be. He had already learned our songs the week before, and the sound check and run-through went without a hitch. Well, one hitch. They were one mike short. On songs that I sang backup (most), I had to sit on the stage floor and sing into my guitar mike. Yes, stiff neck and a silly look, but hey, it was Carly's show, not mine. It also put me eyeball level with the front tables, so I could stare at people and make them uncomfortable if they didn't clap loud enough!

We had a magical opening night with a full house, and our half-hour show brought deafening cheers and a standing ovation. For a new artist and support act, this was an incredible accomplishment. If Carly suffered any of her well-known stage fright, she showed no sign of it that night. She carried the show with grace and poise and received uniform rave reviews from the music press and the many Hollywood stars who came out to support her. Warren Beatty was one of them. Whatever you're thinking... Yep.

We played the Troubadour twice. For expediency, I'll conflate the two gigs and pretend the stories all came from one. So... Carly, Paul, Andy and I were gathered in our dressing room. There was an electric air of anticipation (pun intended) in the club, and we were doing last minute tune-ups and reshuffling a couple of songs in the set. A knock came on the door. Carly was preoccupied, so I said I'd get it. I opened the door and before me stood a gentleman in one of those flammable orange rayon shirts with a way too big collar and very large thick glasses.

I said, "Hi, can I help you?"

Rayon responds, "I'd like to see Carly."

I counter, "She's busy and we're just about to go on. She doesn't meet with fans or family before shows. Maybe check back afterwards."

Disgruntled and with a dismissive tone, he persists, "I said I'd like to see Carly."

I don't do well with condescension. He had activated my douche bag alert, which in turn activated my arm, shifting into slam the door in the asshole's face mode. I turned around, mumbling "Jerk," then looked across the room at Carly, whose facial expression was a mix of amazement, incredulity and a touch of wonder. Something important was about to be said. I waited. She began:

"Do you know who that was?"

"A badly dressed fan/jerk?" I replied.

"Mmm, well yes, maybe, but he does have a name, and he is a tiny bit famous."

"I doubt that," I said, still activated.

She dropped the bomb." Jesus, Jimmy, that was Warren Beatty."

It's just amazing how the introduction of one minor fact into a conversation can warp your mood, attitude, comfort, fear and damn near anything you had going on in your head prior to that moment of enlightenment. I went from smug and righteous to self-loathing and panic in the span of two words. W a r r e n B e a t t y. In a rush to save the day, I said:

"Ohhh shit! Give me a minute, I'll go grab him, apologize and bring him back."

To my surprise, she said, "No. Leave it. It serves him right for being rude. I'll bet no one ever responds to his crap like you just did. I loved it. He needed that."

Though Carly has made a career of obscuring the protagonist in "You're So Vain," I maintain that at very least, this encounter gave her the idea for the song. I ran this by her when she was writing her memoir, *Boys In The Trees*, and had asked me to help her remember some events. She neither confirmed nor denied.

Then there were the naughty boys. James Taylor came to one of our shows that week and was accompanied by his girlfriend, Joni Mitchell. Carly and James rekindled their old Martha's Vineyard childhood friendship that night, and he sat in during our set, singing "Don't Let Me Be Lonely Tonight". He also fell asleep on our dressing room floor. In deference to his well-known drug habits, we were willing to give him a pass and step over him. He was one of my faves, and I considered it an honor that he felt relaxed enough to crash on our floor, whatever the circumstances surrounding his narcolepsy. In watching Joni's reactions to the evening's events, she was less willing to give him a pass. The legendary Joni Mitchell was not amused and for good reason. The rest is history. I love James, but from what Carly has made public knowledge, he was about as faithful to her as he was to Joni. Fame seems to make committed, monogamous relationships quite a challenge.

As long as we're in gossip mode, Warren Beatty of rayon fame had Julie Christie on his arm that night. Who knows where she thought he was going when he came knocking at our door and got his circuits shorted? I have to believe Julie knew who she was dating. Based on what Carly told me and what she revealed in her book, anyone dating Warren had to be ok with polyamory because in those days he... oh hell, let's not go there. Assuming he's happily married to Annette Bening now, I'd have to believe all has long since been forgiven on everyone's part.

Quite a week for stargazing, though. In short, I met and had conversations with Cat Stevens, Warren Beatty, James Taylor, Joni Mitchell, Julie Christie, and let's throw in Candice Bergen for good measure. She was with Julie and Warren. I've never been a groupie, but at twenty-four, meeting and chatting with these incredibly talented people from my record collection and some of my favorite movies (Julie in *Dr. Zhivago*, Warren in *Bonnie & Clyde*, Candace in *Carnal Knowledge*), I admit it. I was impressed.

On to Cat Stevens. What a master singer songwriter. Quiet, somewhat introverted and with a unique perspective on the world. Like many artists, he started out as the product of the record industry pimp shop. Dressed like a nineteenth century English dandy, he cranked out insipid pop songs. Something happened around the time of *Mona Bone Jakon*, where he found his muse. Not just his songs and his singing voice, but also his dress and appearance. With *Tea For The Tillerman*, and the song "Wild World", a new artist bearing no resemblance to his former self was born. That's when I discovered him. I heard "Wild World" once on the radio and was hooked. I have a vivid memory of coming home to my 38th Street apartment with his album, throwing it on the turntable and fixing a salad with some generic supermarket dressing. The taste of the salad dressing remains as I hear the first cut on the album in my mind, "Where Do The Children Play". If I was ever going to be a drooling fan, this would have been the recipient artist. Then I met him.

I found him not very friendly and not particularly approachable. Shy or aloof? Probably both. His band was just the opposite and became close friends of mine when I moved to England. But we are here at the Troubadour now, it's 1971 and we're opening for him. We finished our set, got rid of the guitars and headed down to the audience to watch his show. I wanted him to be stone cold amazing. He wasn't, but I'll be kind in my review. Cat sang every bit as well as I expected, his voice rich and soulful. The band comprised some of the same players who performed on his album, and they reproduced their parts well. But Gerry Conway, his drummer, and Jean Roussel, his keyboardist, were missing - only Larry Steele on bass and Alun Davies on guitar. The sound was empty, not driving, missing percussion and not much like the records. He played "Wild World" on the piano, and without the punchy guitars and drums it was meh. I was very disappointed, not in the artist but in the performance and lineup. He said little beyond announcing the songs and kept his eyes closed most of the time, barely connecting with the audience. Regardless, I remained a huge fan of his records. Of this show, not so much. Note, Cat Stevens has changed his name a few times. We always called him Steve because his birth name was Steven Demetre Georgiou.

Carly's opinion was the opposite. She had an extracurricular interest in Cat Stevens and was not the least bit put off by his show. Did they hook up? Yes indeed. Did it amount to much other than a short tryst? Nah. Usually when this happens, people part and have little to do with each other in the future. Not so with Carly and Cat. They remained good friends and worked, hung out and enjoyed each other's company well into the future. As Carly illustrates in her book, she invited him to dinner at her apartment one evening. When he arrived, they would enjoy a very special dinner of chicken with cherries and a cream sauce Carly made from scratch, and she even threw in an expensive bottle of wine... and waited... and waited... Why was he so damn late? Annoyance and panic took over. She rushed into the bedroom, grabbed her guitar hoping to distract herself or channel her anger, and with a few chords and hummed melodies, out popped "Anticipation". As she tells it, she was afraid he would show up any minute, so she had to finish the song quickly. As with "Don't Let The Rain Fall Down On Me", the song just materialized and was finished in no time. Cat eventually showed up, but she didn't reveal the song at that time. He inspired her in ways he could not have imagined.

Our week in LA ended on a happy and successful note. Carly Simon was becoming a household name, and I shared some of that glory, co-creating her records, touring with her and cementing a lifelong friendship, all the while building my career as a studio and backup musician. The Critters were history, and I couldn't have been happier with my new life.

It's A Family Affair

What do you do when you're on a break from a gig at the Troubadour with one of the biggest rising stars in the USA? Why, you audition for Sly & the Family Stone, of course! I'm not kidding. Gerry Gibson, Sly's drummer, had left the band, and our Andy Newmark got a call from his friend, Pat Rizzo, Sly's sax player, that they were looking for a replacement. There were all kinds of internal conflicts going on within the band that could mean trouble on the horizon, but Andy knew nothing about them and was eager to jump in and audition. Here's the true story:

91

We would finish our first set with Carly, and after a quick equipment shuffle, Cat Stevens would come on and do an hour and fifteen minutes. Then, the first audience would exit, and the second would be seated, which takes about forty-five minutes. That leaves a two-hour window to get into our little Budget Rental car and head to 783 Bel Air Road, Sly Stone's Beverly Hills mansion. I volunteered to be Andy's wingman. The Troubadour isn't far from Beverly Hills, so the journey took about fourteen minutes. We pull up in front, park in the driveway with a few other cars, and look at each other.

Me: "You ready for this?"

Andy: "Yeah… I mean no… I mean I don't know. It's kind of weird just showing up."

Me: "Did Pat call Sly and tell him you were coming?"

Andy: "Not sure. Maybe."

Me: "Oh what the hell, let's ring the doorbell. What's the worst that can happen?"

Andy: "Ok. Yeah. Let's go."

We do that. We're met at the door by a very large gentleman who looks like he spends ten hours per day at the gym and hasn't had a pleasant thought in twenty years. He opens the door with a grimace and says, "What do you want?" Andy explains the call from Pat Rizzo and the possibility of auditioning for the drummer position and Mr. Big says, "Wait here," and closes the door. He comes back a few minutes later, still looking like he caught his wife cheating with the pool boy and makes the "my boss said to let you in" head gesture. He then walks away and leaves us standing in the vestibule. So far, so good. Everyone's being nice. A woman approaches from another room. It's Rose Stone, Sly's sister. She says in a fuck-you accent, "Go sit over there." Not wishing to be nosey and ask her if someone just punched her in the face, we oblige and take our seats on a narrow bench in the hallway. After about ten minutes, an older gentleman comes into the hallway, and without introductions or "welcome to the happy home of the Family Stone," simply says, "Sly will see you now. Go upstairs, first room on the right." That was Sly's dad, we found out later.

Stuck in what feels like a carnival funhouse, up the stairs we go, cautiously approaching the first room on the right. As we enter, we notice three men in suits sitting in chairs facing a large waterbed on which Sly is lying face-up, eyes closed. Are these people Sly's lawyers? Managers? Accountants? Have we walked in on a business meeting from the Twilight Zone? It's not clear whether Sly is asleep, unconscious or dead. The room's floor, ceiling and walls are covered in black fur. I'm sure it was insulation to keep Sly warm in the harsh and unforgiving Beverly Hills winters. Everyone looks up at the two, twenty-something, skinny white boys walking into this room from outer space, wondering what the hell we are doing there. By Sly's side is a bulging manila file folder with nothing written on the tab. Soon enough we learn about the contents of the folder. Sly partially awakens, and with one eye half-open, rolls over, and opens the folder to reveal a large mound of white powder. He scoops up a handful, puts it to his face and sniffs a deep inhale of whatever it is into his lungs... and flops back down onto his pillow. It's now smeared all over his mouth and nose like he had gone face down in a bowl of flour.

There are no free chairs in the room, so we sit on the rug with our backs to the wall. Quite comfortable with all that fur. I'm unable to take my eyes off of Sly's almost child-like, comical face with what I assume to be cocaine smeared all over it. I'm also wearing large, coke-bottle-bottom glasses that make my eyes seem a tad larger than they actually are. My pupils are probably dilated too. I guess I was gawking. My bad. Sly, now awake, lifts his head from the pillow, looks at me with an evil frown and blurts out, "What the fuck are you looking at?"

He lets out a coughing laugh and continues, "Yo, bug eyes - you look like you seen a ghost."

Nervous laughs erupt from the audience of three. He lifts his head up a bit more, looking down his white powdered nose, examining Andy, then me. His brow furrows a little, a pause, then in that deep, grainy Sly Stone voice he says, "Who the fuck are you? What the fuck are you doing here?"

Andy seizes the moment." I'm Andy, this is Jimmy. My friend, Pat Rizzo, told me you're looking for a drummer. I think I'm your man."

Sly mocks, "You... are my man? YOU? Are My Man?"

More snickers from the court of three.

Andy: "Yes."

Sly: "M'man says yes. Are you funky?"

Andy: "Yes."

Sly: "Show me, white boy."

Ouch! Ok, Sly has a set of practice pads in his bedroom. They're just grey rubber pads set up like drums with Toys 'R' Us cymbals, and they make a clicking noise, exactly what you would expect from hitting hard rubber with drumsticks. Andy looks at them with dread, but like I said in the car, "What's the worst that could happen?" Well, they could all laugh and tell us to get the fuck out of there. So what? Who cares? They're strangers, and Sly is so out of it, why take any of it seriously? Andy stands up, walks over to the pads, sits down and kicks into an amazingly intricate funk beat that even on the pads sounds like the hippest drum beat you ever heard. He had been listening to Tony Williams, a famous jazz drummer who perfected playing drum fills past the downbeat where most drummers usually hit a cymbal and go back to the normal beat. It's a clever way to make the fill sound cooler. He's nailing it like a pile driver. Sly gets up on the unstable surface of the waterbed and starts dancing. The waterbed is rolling like a vat of Jello in an earthquake. The three others track his movements with bulging eyes, ready to catch him before he loses his balance and impales himself on a bedpost.

Sly lets out a hoot and shouts, "You ARE funky. You a funky motherfucker. That's what I'm talking about. That's the shit. Play that shit. I love you, man. You in my band, motherfucker. You in the Family Stone."

After fifteen seconds, Andy plays another how-the-hell-did-he-do-that fill and ends with a hilarious splat on the crappy tin cymbal.

Andy says, "Thanks. Wow, that's great. Listen, I'm really sorry, but we're playing at the Troubadour tonight, and we have to get back for our second show. Can I leave my number?"

The others now demonstrate that they can in fact speak, and one of them approaches. He extends his hand and says, "Cool man. You made m'man happy. We'll be in touch."

Sly says nothing more. No hand shake. No congratulations. No discussion of upcoming gigs or rehearsals. He just collapses on the bed, takes in another handful from the manila folder, closes his eyes and resumes his waterbed stupor with the audience of three, in the black fur-lined room, at the top of the stairs, in the mansion on Belle Aire Road, in Beverly Hills, California… and we take our leave. I want to be overly friendly to Rose on the way out as a send up to her prison warden greeting when we arrived. But neither she nor anyone else is around. We let ourselves out. Before we get into our humble little rental car, we run into Sly's driver who is hanging out by his car in the driveway. Unlike his employers, he is friendly. I notice a pit bull behind the fence eyeing us with a disquieting low-frequency sound coming from his throat.

Looking back at the driver, I ask, "Is he friendly?"

The driver says, "Yeah, friendly. Well, someone messed with that little guy a couple of weeks ago. He took a shovel with a maple handle and leaned on the fence, teasing the dog with the handle. The dog bit the handle in half with one chomp. Do you have any idea how hard it is to bite a maple shovel handle in half? It could take you five minutes to saw through it."

I had the feeling he was pulling our chains, but after everything else we witnessed that night, I was not interested in putting it to the test.

Sly's next gig was in Philadelphia. Andy's many attempts to get together with the band and rehearse proved futile. Sly and the Family Stone were notorious for not showing up for gigs or having individual band members not show up, so that added to Andy's discomfort and

94

frustration. The band had been mired in internal disagreements, excessive drug use, and had become dysfunctional to the point where the only reason they were still together was to support their drug-fueled lifestyle. The Philadelphia date came around, and the first time Andy played with them was that evening when he walked out onto the stage. Larry Graham, Sly's bass player, became Andy's ally and friend, so he maintained eye contact during the show, telegraphing the song endings so Andy would know what was coming. Andy lasted with them for about a year and a half. With Sly and the Family Stone on his resume, he began a long career as one of the most in-demand studio drummers in the world, with clients like John Lennon, George Harrison, Roxy Music, Cat Stevens, Pink Floyd, Rod Stewart, Sting, Laura Nyro and so many more. Oh yes, and of course, Carly Simon with Paul and me.

So if you're bored between shows and you have a couple of hours to kill, why not ring doorbells in Beverly Hills? You might just find someone looking for your skill who has an instrument in their bedroom on which you can audition and get them dancing on their waterbed. It worked for Andy.

Stoking the Star Making Machinery

Though The Critters no longer influenced my life, I hadn't quite given up on being a solo artist. I loved lightening my creative load as a backup guitarist, but I still had an itching to ride that parabola. I watched Carly's rise to fame, and some egoic little voice inside kept egging me on:" You can do that. Go on. Do it." Since that little voice persisted, I decided to take advantage of the moment. Jac Holzman, CEO of Elektra, and the person who signed Carly to her recording contract, was becoming a common presence in our lives. He was a fan, and there'd never be a better time to get his attention. One night at the Troubadour, I pulled him aside, reviewed my history of hits with The Critters and said, "I'm looking to do a solo career. Would you be interested in hearing a few songs?"

He replied, "Of course. Please call my secretary and make an appointment for this week while you're here in LA, and we'll sit down and chat."

I did, and we did. I brought my trusty Martin to his office. We sat in the middle of the room on his oriental rug, him with his chair reversed and leaning forward on the back, me sitting on another chair facing him. I played the first song I had prepared.

Jac said, "Ok, let's have another."

Not exactly a standing ovation, but at least he asked for more. I sang a second song.

Again, he responded, "Any others?"

No compliments yet. I played my last song, and he didn't immediately speak. When he did, his feedback smacked my ego pretty hard. Jac told me I had top-notch guitar playing skills. He didn't love my songs, but there are many talented songwriters dying to have new artists perform their work. No problem there. My voice is what killed the deal.

He said," Singing a song involves more than technique. You sang accurately, in tune, and on the beat, but I can't find Jimmy Ryan in the resulting sound. You don't sound confident or original. Competent, but not confident. Not much feel or emotion. Sorry, man."

Don Ciccone's words about conjuring up lost loves came racing back to haunt me, but it was too late - I had no more songs. The audition ended, but my career did not. Life as a post-Critters studio guitarist might not have been my first choice in those initial weeks with Carly, but I couldn't help but notice that things were going great. I kept myself busy making money, playing music, traveling the world - and more auditions were on the horizon.

Phil Kurnit facilitated my next attempt. One of his clients, Alan Bernard, managed The Carpenters, Herb Alpert, Randy Newman, and later, Jim Croce. Alan agreed to listen to me, and his reaction was the opposite of Jac's. He loved my music and agreed on the spot to manage me. Second try, was a buy! In the ensuing weeks, we signed contracts and our working relationship began... with me calling him to ask what he would be doing to further my career, and him neither taking nor returning my calls. In our first meeting when I auditioned, he suggested I work with Mark Lindsay of Paul Revere and the Raiders, but this match didn't seem practicable to me. Our music had little in common, and I didn't want to end up sounding like Raiders 2.0. Except for a brief meeting where Mr. Bernard attended a session I was producing in London, I never heard from him again. Phil honored my request to end the contract, and Alan did not protest.

My third prospect, Lou Adler, had super credits as producer and record company exec for The Mamas and the Papas, Carole King and many others. This connection thrilled me. I loved The Mamas and the Papas, and I loved Lou's production on their records. The fact that he also produced Carole's *Tapestry* closed the deal in my mind. Phil set up the meeting and off I went with my trusty Martin in hand.

Lou Adler was a pleasant, easy-going guy, and because of his relationship with Phil, he was happy to lend an ear. The audition setup was similar to Jac Holzman's - Lou's office, two chairs and an oriental rug. After a couple of songs, he stopped me and said:

"I really like what you're doing, and I have an idea that may interest you, maybe even more than a solo project. Scott McKenzie ['San Francisco'] and Don Everly [The Everly Brothers] are thinking of putting together a trio along the lines of Crosby, Stills & Nash. You would be the perfect third member."

I thought about it for a second. I loved singing Everly Brothers songs at beach parties, and I liked Scott's voice and songwriting, so why not? For the moment, I dropped the idea of going it on my own, and said, "Absolutely. I'm in. Please tell them I'll be happy to make myself available for a trial run."

That was the end of it - Lou dropped the ball. I asked Phil to follow up, but it became a dead end. There was talk that Don Everly was on the fence, Scott was busy touring, blah, blah, blah, zip. You don't make that follow-up call more than once or twice. If they were interested, they would have reached out. They didn't. Lou didn't. I dropped the idea of a solo career for the time being, and focused on my playing, practicing daily and perfecting my craft. That was what was paying the rent at the moment, and despite my bruised ego, I was enjoying myself.

I keep mentioning the pleasure and ease of getting out from under the solo artist's creative burden. After all, this book's theme is a life *behind* the stars. The spotlight wasn't the big problem. It's that trying to get on that elevator and ride it to the top was constant hard work, disappointment, dashed hopes, and more often than not, failure. Chalk it up to one of those life goals that no matter what I did in the present, it kept slipping into the future. The ego is a funny thing. It can often be a great cheerleader, and it can just as often be a liar. I had tremendous encouragement about my musical abilities growing up from friends and family, and it was always about me, not so much about my musical associates. That planted a little seed that never germinated, because it was never meant to. As I will continue to tell in the chapters to follow, every attempt to pursue a solo artist career, despite my hard work and proven abilities, crashed on the rocks, while almost every attempt to support the careers of others and work in the background has blossomed. You'd think I would have learned early on in the game. Ahh, that ego. Ok, on with the happy Carly years.

The Bitter End

How about a short, funny little story about Kris Kristofferson? On May 22nd, 1971, we took our show to the Bitter End in NYC, a kind of homecoming for me. Because the club employed several of my friends, I always rode free, so I practically lived there over the previous few years. I saw almost every show that came through, and the variety was mind boggling - Bob Dylan, Peter Paul & Mary, Tracy Chapman, The Everly Brothers, Spencer Davis, Exuma, La Belle, Curtis Mayfield, Jackson Browne and so many others. The Critters also played there several times, and a poster of one of those gigs is part of the Bitter End's permanent wallpaper. In fact, our Kenny Gorka became its owner and managed the club until the month he died.

For the Carly team, this week of shows was fun but uneventful. I don't recall any highlights other than a positive review by *The NY Times*. My story for this gig actually involves Kris Kristofferson, the headliner, not so much us. He was also Carly's love interest for about a month, but she tells that story much better than I could in *Boys In The Trees*. No need to cover it here.

Kris had one of the deepest voices I've ever heard, both speaking and singing, and his singing style? Low-key. Very low-key. Though his shows may not have shaken the rafters, Kris could certainly craft a song. He had an enormous hit with Janis Joplin's "Bobby McGee", and we recorded "I've Got To Have You" on Carly's second album, so kudos on his writing skill. He also had a successful acting career, but…

"Has anyone seen Kris?"

"Nope. Did you check the bar?"

"Duh."

Yeah… that's where he could be reliably found, and maybe not the best place to have been before an hour-long show. Think memory issues, bathroom issues, verbal stupidity issues and… staying awake issues.

During one show, prior to which he treated himself to a few doubles at the bar, he began singing "For The Good Times", a quiet, very slow song. About half-way through, his head began to droop, his lyrics became unintelligible, and BONK - his forehead hit the mike. The alcohol had sunk his boat. Because he was singing so quietly, the house mixer had his mike turned up to ten to compensate. The head thump to the mike caused a bonk through the sound system that sounded like someone hitting a car hood with a baseball bat. Fortunately, the impact, plus the jolt, woke him up, or he would have landed face down in the cheese dip on the table in the front row. He staggered slightly, caught his balance and just said, "God damn it, I fell asleep." The band never stopped playing, and Kris Kristofferson simply continued the song as if nothing had happened. Carly's interest in Kris, though strong going in, faded pretty quickly after the Bitter End gig, and both of them soon moved on.

Carnegie Hall

Carnegie Hall was a dud. It sucked. Let's backtrack so that those two statements make sense. I was hanging around my apartment in early May 1971, doing nothing in particular, and the phone rang. It was Carly.

"Hi Jimmy, are you sitting down?"

"Give me a minute to pull up a chair. Ok, what's up...?"

"We're playing Carnegie Hall with Cat Stevens on June 5th!"

This was it - the moment that any musician with ambition and a grasp of history longs for - the opportunity to perform in perhaps the most glorious, world-renowned concert hall in existence. Though the show was a month away, I proclaimed victory! I had made it. Hall of fame. I went downstairs to the local liquor store, bought an expensive bottle of champagne and placed it in my two-thirds-empty bachelor refrigerator. Then I pulled out my Martin acoustic and started practicing like the concert was the next night. I wasn't taking any chances. To bomb at this gig would be career suicide. At least that's what I thought.

In the ensuing weeks, we only rehearsed a couple of times. Carly's songs were fairly simple from our point of view, and there were no challenging solos. The onus was on her - if she was on, the show would be a winner. Because of her fear of performing, her musical focus on stage was always laser sharp. I never witnessed her having an off night. I don't know what kind of practice routine she had in our absence, but it must have been formidable. She always sang pitch perfect, and I don't recall her ever playing a wrong chord or bad note on guitar or piano. That's part of the joy of working with someone of her caliber. Once she made a decision, she didn't let her phobias get in the way. She took her job seriously, and in my twenty-one years with her, never let an audience down.

Showing up to Carnegie Hall was not like showing up to an outdoor festival. Carnegie is subtle. One doesn't pull up to the front entrance in a gangsta stretch limo to screaming fans with autograph books. This venue has showcased the highest level of musical expertise in history, from Rachmaninov to Bernstein, from Vladimir Horowitz to Chick Corea, the best of the best... and now... us! Also, the Carnegie audience is high-end, sophisticated and discriminating. They don't do overt fan worship. At least I've never seen it, having attended many concerts there. They express their worship with "Bravo!", extended applause and standing ovations. Then they go to the bar.

When playing Carnegie Hall, one shows up discreetly in whatever conveyance is convenient, not to the front entrance but to a stage door around the corner. I don't recall ever seeing fans at that door. Arlyne did not book us a limo. I came down the six flights of my apartment stairs with my guitars and bass, walked half a block over to Madison Avenue, and hailed a yellow cab. The hall is located in a busy section of Manhattan, two blocks south of Central Park at 57th St., and 7th Ave.

We pulled up to the stage door, I paid my fare, dragged my guitars out of the cab, and just stood there staring at the entrance. 161 W. 56th Street. In that moment I felt a little small, a lot humble. I laughed and thought I wouldn't be worthy to cut the toenails of most of the artists that entered through that door. Nonetheless, my day had come to walk this hallowed path. I reached for the handle, opened the door, and with butterflies in my stomach, entered the great Carnegie Hall. Well, actually I entered the backstage area, which is nice, but a bit industrial and worn compared to the gilded walls and velvet chairs of the hall proper.

Carly & me in the Carnegie Hall dressing room

As I climbed up the short flight of stairs to the stage, something occurred to me. I had stepped on to many stages in my life, some beautiful, some funky, and this was just another one. This evening, I would play my guitar like I always do, faithfully reproduce my riffs and harmonies from Carly's records, and bask in the glow of hers and Cat Stevens 'adoring audience. No more butterflies. Time to go to work.

These were the days of folk rock. Simpler times. Singers and their songs. Uncomplicated band setups, with mostly acoustic instruments and small amplifiers. Compare that to modern day stadium concerts with massive PA systems, wireless mikes, huge drum kits, rows of guitar and bass amps, epic light shows, video wall backdrops and all the fanfare and hype. On the vast Carnegie stage, which could support a ninety-piece orchestra, we looked like a postage stamp. I had a little Traynor fifteen-watt bass amp that I used for my electric guitar and bass, Carly and Paul used the house Steinway grand piano, and Andy brought his normal drum kit. It would seem impossible to fill this massive 3,671 seat space with our little setup. This is where Carnegie is in a class of its own. It is

100

an acoustic wonder. If you are sitting in the farthest row of the top balcony and someone speaks to you from the stage, you will hear them. Of course, we hired a sound reinforcement company to install a mid-size but powerful stage-mounted PA, because we weren't putting on a quiet classical concert. There had to be some oomph to get people's feet tapping. That being said, when we launched into our sound check, I felt a rush of excitement. We sounded wonderful and filled the hall with Carly's beautiful voice and music. This would be an evening for the books!

Countdown to the show. We found more bouquets and vases of flowers in our dressing rooms than a presidential funeral. A lot of people were treating this like a big deal. Carly was nervous, but not overly so, because we were the warm-up act. Cat Stevens headlined the show, and that actually made a difference to her. Not an enormous difference, but it took some responsibility off her shoulders. The show had sold out weeks ago, and through the dressing room walls we could hear the murmurs of thousands of excited fans. As a precautionary warm-up, we sang a verse or two of the more difficult songs in the dressing room. We wanted to kick the show off like it was the second set, fully warmed up and nerves left behind.

Time to go for it. A subdued and dignified announcement rang out into the hall:" Please give a warm welcome to Carly Simon." No garish carnival barker calling" New York's Own." Maybe a little too subdued. Whatever. We marched out, guitars in hand, and once again opened with the as yet unrecorded "Anticipation". Same reaction as Central Park. Huge cheers. By this point, I had completely forgotten that I was standing on the stage that vibrated to the music of the New York Philharmonic, George Gershwin, Pyotr Tchaikovsky and so many of the greats. It was us and our adoring audience, and Carly's uncomplicated yet beautiful music was bringing the house down. When I say uncomplicated, I don't mean to demean her. I say uncomplicated compared to Ravel or Stravinsky - music that carves a direct path to the heart. This is not an intellectual process. It is involuntary and magical, and she is a master of it.

The set was flawless. She even made a joke or two and turned this massive hall into her living room. When she finished with a standing ovation, we almost staggered back to the dressing room, exhausted from the tension and the grandeur of where we were and what we just did. Though Carly's sisters and brother greeted us with warm smiles and congratulations in the dressing room, I felt a little pang. Two weeks earlier, I had called my parents who lived about an hour away in NJ and invited them to the show. Thrilled and proud to be performing in this historical hall, I wanted them to be there to share the experience with me.

101

They declined. They said it was too far to drive. I would be performing in the most important concert of my life... and one hour was too long a drive. I stuffed it as best I could and wandered out to the audience to watch Cat Stevens 'set. This time he nailed it. The drums and keyboard made all the difference, and the full, rich sound of his voice was now well-supported by one of London's finest rhythm sections.

Now comes the reason for those two opening sentences. I felt alone after our show. Paul and Andy disappeared with their friends, and I didn't see them again that evening. The same happened with Cat and his band after their show. My brother and older sister lived in California, so they couldn't be there. My younger sister lived two-and-a-half hours north in Woodstock and she was not a Carly fan. My one-hour-away parents declined my invitation and spent the evening in front of their TV. I asked Carly if there would be an after-party or celebration. She shrugged. She had planned to spend some quiet time with her siblings. Nothing to do but go home. I packed my guitars, stepped out alone through the bronze and glass stage door onto 56th St. and hailed a cab back to my apartment. That old joke, "How do you get to Carnegie Hall?" No one from my family gave a shit.

Yep, pretty depressing, and for the record, I did not pop the cork on that expensive champagne. I put on a set of headphones, smoked a joint and listened to *Sergeant Pepper*. Therapy came to the rescue the following Monday, so dear reader, no worries. I told my story to my support group, and the love and compassion they gave me was overwhelming. Some admonished me for not telling them about the concert in time to get tickets. I said I didn't want to seem like I was bragging. They called bullshit, they were right, and we all had a good laugh. In the end, this event that should have been one for the books did not leave a damaging impression. Yes, I was sad and hurt that I could be part of such an important event, yet not important enough to have my family raise a finger. Early childhood memories flooded into my head while alone in my apartment that night, but eventually, with a little help from my friends, I forgave my family and chalked it up to karma. I had the rest of my life to make up for it, and I did. In spades. So, was Carnegie hall a dud? Did it suck? For a while, yes. But standing on that stage facing 3,671 smiling faces singing along and cheering? Priceless.

Proud Mary

Next up for us was the Schaefer Festival in Central Park, the same venue I played with Arthur Brown the year before. This time they called it "Good Vibrations In Central Park." The ride to the venue was particularly fun for me. Arlyne hired a limo for the short trip from Carly's apartment on East 35th St. to the Park, which begins at 59th St. Some believe that in show business, appearances are almost as important as talent. Arlyne, who had formerly worked as Hugh Hefner's entertainment director at Playboy International, knew this well. If you want to give the impression of being important, you don't drive through a gathering of fans in a Ford Fiesta. Picture this: We slowly approach in our limo, and the police open the barricades to let us in while moving the crowd of fans back. Think Moses parting the waters. We cruised into the off-limits area of Central Park like a President's motorcade. Carly was not yet a household name, but this went a long way towards giving the impression she was well on her way. From my side, I was still trying to heal depressing memories of being a Critter, playing lame senior proms at Long Island country clubs, setting up my own gear and driving myself in heavy Long Island traffic to and from the gigs. I don't mean to demean any of the musicians that do this kind of work. They are an essential component of so many important social gatherings, and I highly respect them for that. It only becomes an issue when your work diminishes from large festivals and concert tours to small catering halls. It's the downfall and feeling of failure that chafes. This little limo ride to a gig where we would be celebrated and filmed for TV in a historical venue was a very refreshing alternative.

Carly was the opening act for a killer roster of bands. The Beach Boys headlined the show, with Ike and Tina Turner and us in support. The Beach Boys had been my heroes since eleventh grade. "My buddies and me are getting real well known, yeah, the bad guys know us and they leave us alone!" That was our Westfield High School theme song in my senior year. I would ride around town with my "buddies," Larry Grant, Tom Brown and Steve Hipsley, in Steve's 1960 Ford Thunderbird convertible with the radio blasting "Be True To Your School". Tom Brown and I would head for the Jersey Shore, singing "Surfer Girl" and "Catch a Wave" all the way down the Garden State Parkway. Curiously, none of us ever surfed. We did occasionally sleep under the Seaside Heights boardwalk, though. Having been caught by a policeman with a flashlight, we were also forced to sleep on benches in the Seaside Heights courthouse.

Showtime was approaching. After a delicious catered dinner, we changed into our performance clothes and did our usual last minute tuning and preparations. Carly popped out of her dressing room barefoot in a burgundy leotard with scarves hanging around her waist. She looked super hot and caught me by surprise. I said, "Are you going out on stage in front of six thousand people dressed like that?" I regretted it the minute the words left my mouth. She looked like a goddess, and I sounded like her dad or a jealous lover. I was neither. Well, maybe a little jealous as I was pretty fond of her in those days. Don't ask. Anyway, she said, "Yes. Why? Don't you like it?" God bless her. She tossed me a 'get out of jail 'card to help me delete my prude-ass question. I responded, "No, I don't... I LOVE it!" Whew. Safe.

Carly & Me getting ready
to start the show

With that resolved, we shuffle upstairs to the right side of the stage and pause behind the curtain. The canned music fades, the crowd quiets down, and Ron Delsener's voice comes over the PA: "Good evening and welcome to Good Vibrations In The Park," followed by the usual, no flash cameras, no recording, etc. Then our cue, "Please give a warm welcome to New York's own - CARLY SIMON!!" And out we trot, grinning from ear to ear, gazing in wonder at the sea of six thousand cheering fans. Carly sits down on her stool, I help her adjust her mike while proudly sporting my clear plastic Dan Armstrong bass, and we launch into "Anticipation". You just know when a song is a hit. You see it in the expressions on the fans 'faces. You feel it as you blow through the chord changes, harmonies, verses, choruses and big endings. You just know it. Only those who attended our Carnegie Hall concert had heard "Anticipation" before, as we had not yet recorded it. No worries. It was catchy enough, and she performed it so well that everybody got the idea. They let us know with screams and cheers. By the time we got to "That's

The Way I've Always Heard It Should Be" she had them eating out of the palm of her hand. After a standing ovation, we left the stage feeling at the top of our game.

The fun continued backstage after the show. I received a few more unexpected introductions to put in my mental autograph book as Carly's VIP admirers waited for us in the wings. With bass in hand and still buzzing, I found myself standing face to face with George Harrison. He introduced himself and said he loved our show and particularly liked my clear plastic bass. My favorite Beatle wanted to know what it was and where I got it. I briefly told him the Dan Armstrong story, meeting Carly through Dan, etc. Then Mike Love stepped up and joined in the conversation, turning the unexpected into the unimaginable. And my guitar gently whispered, "Enjoy. This is just the beginning."

In these moments I describe, i.e., meeting my teenage heroes under these circumstances, I noticed a very satisfying dynamic that is absent when you are the fan. If a popular artist has just performed and you approach them at an autograph table or backstage, you'll soon realize it's all about them. They may or may not be listening to you. The impact of "you were great" fades quickly with each repetition from each new fan. They've heard it so many times, it goes right over their heads. You might even notice their eyes glaze over while you're talking. On the other hand, meeting these stars after you are the one who just brought the house down with an artist of Carly's caliber raises the bar quite a few notches. In this scenario, it's not about them; it's about you, or me, in this case. If I had met George Harrison after a Beatles show, I doubt if I would have gotten much more than a nod, and I wouldn't blame him. But after our show, he was attentive, respectful, asking thoughtful questions and holding my attention so much that it took me a moment to notice that standing next to him was his previous chat mate, Art Garfunkel. When George and I finished our bass talk, he introduced me to Art, who was equally complimentary. Mike couldn't resist, so he jumped in with "loved your show." Though I was a fan of them all, I noticed I didn't have to say or do much. The responsibility was not on me to be clever or try to keep their attention from wandering. This time, they were the fans, and the dynamic had been reversed. It's quite an experience when your idols become your admirers, even if it's only for a few moments! With this, I conclude my lab report. I logged time on both sides of the autograph table and respectfully submit my conclusions. Not hard to imagine I prefer the signing side.

Ike and Tina Turner were now walking on stage. You have to see Tina Turner perform to believe what a force of nature she is. Her voice is known the world over, but seeing her sing and dance live takes that energy to a whole new level. When she gets going with "Proud Mary", it is impossible to stay in your seat. Her leg gyrations and moves all over the stage are a cardio workout to challenge Olympians. Keep in mind

Ike and Tina Turner

that while she's doing her one lady decathlon, she's also singing in tune with plenty of breath to spare and as soulful as any R&B artist I've ever seen. On the other side of the stage, Ike was kind of... well, there. Perhaps he was the musical genius behind the show, but in the show itself, he was only the guitar player and occasional deep voice. Anyway, they certainly warmed up the audience for The Beach Boys.

Now when I say I'm a huge fan of The Beach Boys, that comes with a qualification. Brian Wilson's writing and production are the primary reason for The Beach Boys 'popularity. As the biographies tell us, though Brian frequently collaborated with Mike Love, Brian was the genius behind their songs, their singing style, their harmonies and their records... and Brian wasn't there that night. Bruce Johnson was his replacement. Brian was up to his eyeballs in demons and hadn't performed with the band for some time. Without him, things weren't

The Beach Boys

quite at their surfin 'best. Mike was his usual cocky self, MC'ing the show and singing his usual leads, "Do It Again"," Be True To Your School", "Fun Fun Fun", etc., but something was wrong. There was a weird vibe on the stage. It felt like discontent. I

don't mean to be unkind, but they sucked. During the group harmonies, they sang something, but I'm not sure what. Except for Mr. Love, they all sang off mike. I could barely hear the harmonies and when I did they

106

were often out of tune. I would say they were just having a bad night, but I've seen them a couple of times since, and it was the same. They didn't seem inspired and were just as the expression goes, "phoning it in." The thrill seemed to be gone. Did they even like each other? No evidence of it that night.

My opinion of their show is not meant to detract from their incredible recorded legacy. I love these guys, every one of them. They made those wonderful records, and they remain a magical part of rock 'n' roll history. Their recordings still sound inspired to this day. The Beach Boys had a long history of dissonance in their personal interactions, starting with Brian Wilson's drug problem and subsequent mental breakdown, horrible competitiveness between Mike Love and Dennis Wilson, Carl trying to cover for Brian, but not quite having the voice to do it, and Al getting to do only a handful of lead vocals, the most famous being "Help Me Rhonda". Despite the rancor, The Beach Boys are a hall of fame group, but a social experiment that went wrong like so many bands. If their music lives on in the decades to come, it won't be because of their live shows.

England Swings

Carnegie Hall wasn't just a big deal for Carly. It was just as big a deal for Cat Stevens, whose career was also on the rise. I was unaware at the time that Cat's producer, Paul Samwell Smith, flew over from England to see the entire show, not just Cat's but ours. Little did I know we were auditioning. Everyone loved Cat Stevens 'records, the pure, clear sound, the simplicity and the originality. Much of the credit for that goes to Paul Samwell Smith. Arlyne had been talking to him for a few weeks, hoping to interest him in producing Carly's next LP. She suggested that rather than judge Carly on her first album produced by Eddie Kramer (Jimi Hendrix's producer), he should come and see her live. Carly didn't want to record another album with Eddie Kramer for many reasons, and she was looking for a fresh start - a Paul Samwell Smith start. I'm glad she didn't let us in on her little ploy, as I would have been a lot more nervous. Her idea was to take us over to England and record the band the way we sounded on stage.

During the week after the Carnegie show, a conversation ensued between Arlyne, Paul and Elektra Records. They discussed time frame, budgets and personnel, and after a few day's negotiations, sealed the deal. That's when Carly broke the news. Paul was enthusiastic about working with her and was fine with including us! We were going to England in a few weeks and recording her second album with a man who was a founding member of the Yardbirds, and had worked with Jeff Beck, Jimmy Page, Eric Clapton and most recently, Cat Stevens. The idea that we would be flown to London to make an album with an international pop star was unthinkable a year before. But this was my new life. Not so much a star, but an integral part of the star making machinery. As this story developed, I found myself feeling more at home, more relieved to not be in the spotlight. I loved being part of the support team.

Fast forward, our English journey would be a night flight, this time from JFK International. We were packed, ready to go, and again picked up in a limo for our ride to the airport. In The Critters, the only limo I ever rode in was our clunky, beat-up Pontiac stretch. I know the excitement around limos sounds petty and maybe a little starry-eyed, but you have to remember, we were naïve twenty-five-year-olds swept up in a magical adventure. None of us came from wealth, and the big time seemed to be opening up right before our eyes. It looked mighty enticing.

Riding with this crowd was a massive upgrade from our previous lives and was the smoothest of sailing. Paul Samwell Smith traveled back with us to England and was in charge of our tickets. On the ride to the airport, he handed them out in envelopes from the travel agent. Everyone put them in their pockets or shoulder bags, but always being cautious and curious, I slit mine open to confirm that everything was in order. I couldn't help but notice the word "First" printed prominently in the boarding section of the ticket. Wow. The Critters never flew anywhere, leave alone first class. We drove everywhere, no matter how far (thirty days on the Dick Clark Greyhound), but since Carly was not a big fan of air travel, she insisted on first class. For her, flying over land was bad enough, but flying for almost seven hours over the open sea, where one could fall out of the sky, crash in the ocean and never be found, was a living horror movie. In her mind, if it was going to be a multi-hour fingernail chomp, accompanied by constant thoughts of aeronautical malfunction, ending with a terrifying plummet into eternity, it damn well better be comfortable. I loved that she always traveled with us. If she flew first class, we flew first class. We departed JFK at 9pm, and with London being six hours ahead of NY, we landed at Heathrow at 4:30am... wasted. Remember, I don't sleep well sitting up, and this was before British Airways had seats that turned into beds in first class trans-Atlantic flights. It didn't matter. We were young, had pulled all-nighters before, and were too excited to sleep. Movies, drinks and long philosophical conversations filled the six hours and fifty-five minutes, making the time pass quickly.

Though tired and bleary-eyed, getting through customs and immigration was a breeze. In those days the TSA didn't exist. There were no drug-sniffing dogs, and airline hijacking had not yet come into fashion, so we were on our way to London in no time. Our new homes for the next few weeks would be in the Regents Park area of London, around the corner from Primrose Hill. Instead of hotels, Elektra rented us apartments, one for Carly and one for the band.

Born To Be Wild

I'm not sure what possessed us, but in our first week, Paul Glanz and I decided to buy motorcycles. Paul bought a BSA, and I bought a similar Triumph Tiger. I had never owned a motorcycle before, and always wanted one, so why not? That was my warped, twenty-something brain weighing in. I had too little common sense, and too much confidence in London weather. A pair of unfortunate incidents occurred within a couple of weeks of my purchase. The first involved my ignorance as to why bikers wear Gore-Tex suits, those waterproof outer garments. As I rode down the Adelaide Road back to the apartment, it started to drizzle. My rain protection? Jeans and a jeans jacket with a T-shirt under it, perfectly fine attire for dry sunny weather. The drizzle quickly changed to a soaking rain. I still had about a seven-

My Triumph 650 Tiger

minute ride to the apartment, and the temperature was around 60°. My jacket and pants were starting to soak through, and the cold fabric against my skin was not good. The wind from riding in wet clothes at thirty-five mph caused rapid evaporation, wicking heat away from my body. To get an idea of the experience, imagine standing naked in a cold shower in front of a high-powered fan outdoors at 60°. Hypothermia was setting in. It is a feeling of illness like no other. You notice intense, freezing pain as your core temperature drops, dizziness takes over, and your decision-making processes deteriorate. I can honestly say, I have never been so cold in my entire life. I didn't think I was going to make it. I had to maneuver an unfamiliar, high powered two-wheel motor vehicle through traffic on slippery pavement in a state of intense pain and declining mental acuity. Chalk it up to good karma and the grace of the heavens that I didn't end up in a London hospital with a rearranged skeleton. I left the bike unlocked on the street in front of our house and staggered up the stairs to our apartment, throwing the front door open and announcing, "I have to have a hot bath immediately." Andy and Paul gave me that "what the hell happened and why are you soaked like you just climbed out of a swimming pool" look. I begged them to get out of my way, dashed into the bathroom, slammed the door and ran a bath. Without even waiting for it to fill, I tore my wet clothes off and hopped in, lowering myself down into the first inch of water. I just sat there shivering, knees to chest, arms around knees, waiting for the warm, soothing water to rise. Once the tub filled and the hot water surrounded me, it didn't take long for my core temperature to rise back to something more reasonable than a January swim in Alaska.

I must have been in that bath for two hours. Paul figured out what happened when he spotted my bike sitting out front in the pouring rain. He had owned bikes before and either wore slicks or didn't go out when it rained. He checked the weather and was smart enough to not venture out that day. When I emerged from the bathroom wrapped in towels, he said, "Why did you take your bike out today? Didn't you check the weather? It's London. It gets cold and rains a lot here." I wanted to punch him but then the towel would fall off causing further embarrassment.

The second ill-fated motorcycle event happened in central London near Hyde Park. I was out on a happy-go-lucky joy ride and found myself in some heavy traffic. A London taxi lumbered along in front of me, much slower than necessary, and I decided to pass him. Keep in mind, the British drive on the left side of the road, so passing someone on the left is their equivalent of our passing on the right - bad idea. Not being conscious of that in the moment, I did what Americans do - pass on the left where he couldn't see me. I downshifted, leaned left and hit the throttle.

London taxis are tall black vehicles, and if you're close to one and on a bike, seeing around them is quite difficult. A pedestrian stepped down onto the zebra crossing (British crosswalk) in front of the cab. Like many places in the world, a UK pedestrian has the right of way, and if they step onto the roadway, traffic must stop. The cab hit his brakes, and because I anticipated having more space to get around him, I made a critical error. My right hand gripped the handlebar throttle, and when I twisted it to accelerate, my thumb tucked under, then forward. As I attempted to maneuver around the now stopped taxi, my thumb and handle grip hit his taillight hard enough to shatter it. I do not practice karate, so it didn't go well for my thumb. It felt like I had punched a

110

brick wall. The bike and I parted company as it fell over, engine still running and rear wheel still in gear and spinning.

People quickly gathered around me saying, "You aw roight mate?" "Blimey, that was awful, you aw roight?" Nodding my head, I carefully peeled my glove off to reveal a lacerated thumb that now dripped blood onto the red plastic taillight shards all over the pavement. I wiggled my throbbing digit, and it still worked. No broken bones, as far as I could tell. In a slight daze, I said, "Yes, I'm fine, thank you. Aside from feeling stupid, it's nothing a bandage won't fix." At that point, something quite profound occurred to me. I use that thumb to play guitar.

The only reason Elektra paid to have me shipped first class to this beautiful country was to play guitar on their favorite artist's new album. The idea was to play well - not so easy with only one working thumb. We're talking about my right hand, my picking hand. Imagine trying to hold a pick without a thumb. What in God's name was I thinking, buying this five hundred pound, two-wheeled suicycle?

The accident was clearly my fault. I now had to face the cabbie and own my reckless driving. Fortunately, he saw I was frightened and contrite, and in a sympathetic gesture, made me an offer I couldn't refuse. Pay him twenty quid cash to fix his taillight and we'd call it even. Neither of us wanted to get the police involved, so I reached into my wallet, pulled out a twenty and handed it to him. We bid g'day, and my sore, bloody thumb and I rode back to the apartment, this time with great caution and care. Thankfully, it did not rain.

My blue 1971 Triumph Tiger had become a deadly liability, and it had to go. As soon as I got back to NY, I put the word out and eventually sold it to a friend - I didn't enjoy motorcycling enough to risk my life. Russ Kunkel, as you may recall, became available a month or two before, because his tour with James Taylor got postponed. James learned the musician/motorcycle lesson like me, the hard way.

Summer's Coming Around Again

Paul Glanz and I were huge fans of Brazilian music, so much so that I took it upon myself to learn the bossa nova style of guitar playing. I bought records by Antonio Carlos Jobim, João Gilberto, Sergio Mendez and others, and listened and practiced until I was able to play this style with confidence. While working out one of Gilberto's songs, I unconsciously created an original chord progression and melody. I kept playing it over and over as a practice exercise until I realized that with a few refinements, it could be the basis of a new song. The next time Paul and I were together, I pulled out the guitar and showed it to him. He liked it and said if we wrote a complementary bridge, the song would be complete, but for lyrics. He walked over to his keyboard and said maybe something like this, then wrote a bridge section on the spot. His new section worked great for me, and I declared the birth of an original, Brazilian-style song. After a bit of self-congratulations, we left his apartment and went out for a beer at a local Greenwich Village hangout called Nobody's. Interesting place. It was never clear who actually owned it.

Later that month we were sitting around at Morgan Studios in London enjoying our new life of the not quite rich nor famous, but hopeful.

Carly said, "Damn, I'm one song short for the album. Do you have anything I might like?"

I looked at Paul, then back to Carly, and said, "Well… Paul and I have been working on a kind of Brazilian thing that needs lyrics."

I picked up my guitar and started playing the chords and humming the melody of our bossa nova baby.

She said, "I love it. Can we throw some lyrics around, see if we can finish it? This could really work well with the other songs."

I replied with carefully subdued elation, "Of course!" not wanting to sound too excited and jinx the situation.

For the next few paragraphs, to avoid confusion, I'll refer to Paul Glanz as simply "Glanz," and Paul Samwell Smith as "Paul."

Songwriter rule #1. The best way to convince an artist to cover your song is to write the song with them!

Carly grabbed a pen and pad from her shoulder bag, and out of the blue, started singing random lyrics to my melody:

Here now, summer's coming around again,
Every year it seems to come in this way,
Before you know it, you've fallen in love,
But be sure it's love before you sail away!

And in a short time, a new song emerged. While we were still refining the lyrics, Mike Bobak, our engineer, quietly came over and miked up my guitar and Carly's voice. What a wonderful vote of confidence in our first collaboration with Ms. Simon. We started running down the song with Carly singing the new lyrics as I played. Glanz tiptoed over to the piano and started playing along. Andy, who had been monitoring our writing session from across the studio, wandered into the drum booth and started clicking his sticks to the beat, almost like a metronome. Good choice. An organic, minimalist song like this would have been absurdly overpowered by a full drum kit pounding away. Paul had been listening from upstairs in the control room. He pressed the talkback button and said, "This is beautiful. Let's record it right now while it's fresh!" Within a short time, "Summer's Coming Around Again" was done, and we loved it. This was a dream achievement. Not so much because Carly, Paul, and I had written a song together. She was a close friend, so I wasn't star struck in that way. The thrill was that I could be playing around with a hobby, i.e. learning how to play bossa nova style guitar, and within a few months, be recording an original bossa nova song, co-written by my friends, in the studio, like The Beatles used to do, and in record time.

Anticipation

We recorded Carly's second album in much the same way as modern songwriters and musicians do today - one instrument at a time. A major exception in the seventies made this process tedious and frustrating, though. When I record in my modern studio, I always start out with a simple programmed drum part. In modern DAWs (Digital Audio Workstations), there is a tempo correction algorithm called "quantization." In layman's terms, that just means you can be sloppy with your timing as you tap the software drum keys or pads, and the computer will correct your errors. It can also leave a little of the sloppiness in, so it sounds more like a human and less like a machine. When you start with this simple drum loop, it guarantees that everything you do after that, guitars, bass, keyboards, etc. will have a predictable beat reference with which to align. But we had no such tools in the 70s. Drum machines did not exist, no DAWs, and all timing had to come from the players. That's why skilled drummers were so much in demand. They formed the bedrock of all recordings, and if they sucked, the record sucked.

Our drum machine on this album was Carly. Paul believed the musical essence had to come from her, not the band. For most of the songs, he would start off recording her singing the song and playing her acoustic guitar or piano. On her own, it would sound great. Then the big problem would arise. We would have to memorize her timing fluctuations and play our parts, trying to stay locked to a random timing map. Carly had pretty good timing, but not perfect, and her fluctuations had poor Andy banging his head on the wall. There's an expectation in pop music that a song's tempo will remain constant, not speeding up, not slowing down. That's what makes you tap your feet or want to dance. But singer songwriters performing on their own often treat their songs like poetry, with a little ebb and flow. That doesn't work so well with drummers. Together, they tend to sound sloppy and off-beat. Nevertheless, that's how Cat Stevens did it, and that's how Carly and Paul wanted to do it, so our timing map was set by Carly - conform or collide. Unfortunately, when you have to focus on every beat, groove and feel tend to suffer. This didn't kill the record. It just made it frustrating to record. We glossed over the fluctuations as much as possible, and in the end, made it sound fine. I don't mean to single out Carly here. Almost any non-percussion-playing musician in her position would have the same issue, including me. That's why, before drum machines, great drummers were a must.

The one-instrument-at-a-time process wasn't always a bust. It worked well in songs like "The Garden"," Summer's Coming Around Again"," Julie Through The Glass" and any of the songs that didn't have drums. I played my guitar in such a way that I didn't emphasize beats but worked more or less in between them, playing sparsely. The queen of songs that gave us the most trouble was "Anticipation". Carly did several versions on her own on which we tried to overlay our parts, but they just didn't work. No matter what we did, it always sounded stilted, clumsy and off. This song had a strong rhythm component that needed to be consistent, and Carly wasn't able to create that on her own. After a concerted pressure campaign from us, she and Paul agreed to try the song with all of us playing together. It worked! Having played it so many times live, it just flowed in the studio.

Here's why I think it worked better this way. When musicians play together in an ensemble, something happens that is almost psychic. If

they're listening as they should be, they sense what their band mates are about to do. It is not a mental process like an arranger thinking out parts and writing them down on a scoresheet for an ensemble to perform later.

Carly & Paul Samwell Smith

That's the classical approach, and if the arranger is talented enough, musicians playing only the written page will produce music that's beautiful and inspiring. Pop music rarely works that way. During a performance, someone plays a phrase or rhythm, the others pick up on it, build on it, and before you know it, a recording emerges with its own personality, similar but usually more interesting than the bare song. With "Anticipation", Andy laid down a drum pattern, which Carly followed as she played. Her strumming hand locked on to Andy's drumsticks and a wonderful, bouncy rhythm emerged. The same with Glanz. I played bass on that song, so I locked on to Andy's kick drum. Also, if an infectious groove is emerging, it inspires the singer to perform with more commitment and energy than they would in a sterile, soundproof booth in front of a microphone by themselves. With our new ensemble approach to "Anticipation" the result was an infectious, "locked groove" and ultimately a hit record... not to mention a very successful ketchup commercial!

Other songs like "The Garden" wouldn't have worked at all if we had recorded them together. For that song and most of this album, Carly wouldn't even allow us to be in the building while she created the basic track. "The Garden" required tremendous vulnerability, and for that, she wanted to be alone in her fantasies, safe and unthreatened. Paul and Mike kept silent in the control room, one level above the studio and hanging over it. Carly sat downstairs on an oriental rug with vocal and guitar mikes. They dimmed the lights in the studio to give the impression of a beautiful evening just after sunset. And then she wove her magic...

Carly going over lyrics for "The Garden."

When I came in the following day to do my guitar parts on the song, I couldn't believe my ears. I hadn't heard the song before, nor had I ever heard her sing in such a breathy, subtle, sexy way. This one got the proverbial "WOW!" She and I thought very much alike about guitar parts, so complementing her performance was easy. I sat down, put on my headphones, picked up my guitar and turned my focus inward.

I let the song take me. There was nothing to figure out. The tape rolled, the music began, and my fingers started moving like they were being led by an unseen force. The sheer quiet intensity of her singing was like a hypnotic wave and out came my backup guitar parts. Once they were done, we went to work on my solo. Again, the notes just fell out of the guitar while I sat there, eyes closed, immersed in the imagery and being in the moment. It's a wonderful and rare experience when things flow this smoothly in a recording session. I wasn't the only one who was hypnotized by her song and her performance. Paul Samwell Smith fell in love with Carly during these sessions and ended up leaving his wife for her. Sadly, the relationship didn't last, but the friendship did. They remain close to this day, and we continued to work with Paul frequently over the years. "The Garden" remains one of my all-time favorites of Carly's songs.

I fell in love with England on this adventure. The many varied English accents were music to my ears. Funny how I'd listen to someone like John Lennon or George Harrison speak, and I'd say to myself, "That's an English accent." I learned after being there a while that The Beatles 'accent was of the Liverpool variety. A keen ear could listen to a few words and pinpoint a Brit's roots with ease. Liverpool has its own dialect and slang as do the Midlands, the various shires, Devon, Cornwall, Hertfordshire, etc., and of course

Carly & Paul

London with its vast range, due to a heterogeneous and international population. Ringo's accent is nothing like my ex-wife's, which was a Lincolnshire accent from the East, nor the Queen's, which is a proper English, upper-class accent. Hence its name, "The Queen's English." I made a hobby of listening and imitating these twists and variations until I could master a few of them. Of course, they've all merged in my mind now, and I'd sound like a right prat if I tried to imitate a cockney with London so many years in my past.

Despite being enamored with the country and people, one thing I never got used to was the way Brits consume alcohol. This may have changed with the international influences that flowed into England during the European Union years, but in the seventies, it was a strange world for me. When I was there, if you were to walk into a pub, step up to the bar and ask for a mixed drink like a Black Russian or a Vodka Gimlet, you would get a flat, "Nah mate, we don't do those Yank concoctions." For the British in those days, a mixed drink would be the pure liquor of choice plus ice... or water... or nothing. I never got used to that, but then I wasn't much of a drinker anyway, so no stress.

The other British alcohol anomaly was their beer tradition. I learned about this at Morgan Studios during a dinner break on one of our first sessions. They had a packaged junk food lady and a small bar in the studio lobby. We had been working hard for several hours and were about to enjoy a nice relaxing break, so I decided to order a beer. The bottles were lined up behind the barmaid on wooden shelves. Unfamiliar with English breweries, I looked at the colored labels, took a wild guess and said, "I'll have a John Courage." She reached up, took one off the shelf and handed it to me. I said, "Hmmm, could you grab one out of the fridge?" She said, "The fridge? Oh, love, we don't drink 'em cold here." God bless them, the British drink their beer warm. I cannot think of many things less appetizing after a hard day's work than a warm beer. I took a pass and just got some water. The Americans on our team were all in agreement on this one. No warm beers. Ever! If you want a cold beer in England, go to an Indian or Japanese restaurant. I haven't been back to the British Isles since the seventies, but I hope that when and if I do, they will have come to their senses on this one.

We returned from England in late September. My memories of this wonderful time in my life had planted a seed that would grow to when, in 1973, I would pull up my roots in NYC and move to London. I loved it there, but why would I turn my back on my country of origin and move to a strange place where I had neither friends nor family? It will all make sense as this story develops. For now, on to the next adventure!

Chapter Four
The Soaring 70s

You Don't Mess Around With Jim

B ack at Villanova in the 60s, I had a college mate who was a pretty decent singer/songwriter. In the summer of 1967, I took a short bus ride down the Lancaster Pike to Bryn Mawr to see him and his wife performing at The Main Point. They were wonderful, and I thoroughly enjoyed their show. I didn't get a chance to talk to them that night, but our paths crossed four years later.

Phil Kurnit represented two producers, Terry Cashman and Tommy West, and thinking we'd all enjoy meeting each other, he introduced us.

Tommy West & Terry Cashman

It turned out that Tommy also graduated from Villanova, and we had so much in common, we became immediate friends. In late 1971, they brought me in on a very special project.

Tommy called me and said, "Remember that Villanova singer/songwriter you mentioned you saw at The Main Point a few years ago? Well, Terry and I are going to be producing an album with him, and we'd like you to come in and play bass on the title track." The artist and mutual college mate? Jim Croce. What a thrill! I was going to be working with two fellow alums who, like me, ended up going pro and getting record deals. I couldn't wait for the date.

They booked the session at the famous Hit Factory in NYC, appropriately named having recorded the likes of John Lennon, Stevie Wonder, Paul Simon, The Rolling Stones and countless others. Coincidently, Jerry Ragovoy, The Critters' first producer, built and owned it at the time. When the morning of the session day rolled around, I practiced my butt off. I wanted to be up to scratch on the first count in. With bass in hand, I grabbed a cab and made my way through traffic to the studio, 421 W. 54th Street. It felt like coming to a jam with old friends. First, my old friend Gary Chester, on drums, who had also worked on several Critters records. Then, guitarist, Maury Muehleisen. I had recorded with him a while back on his *Gingerbread* album, also

118

produced by Cashman and West. This was getting better by the minute! I leaned my bass against the amp set up for me and wandered into the control room to check in.

Tommy and Terry greeted me and said, "Jimmy, you remember Jim from Villanova and gigging around Philly?"

Of course I said, "Yes," shook Jim Croce's hand and said, "Good to see you again and even better to be making music with you! I loved your show at The Main Point. Will we be recording any of the songs from that night?"

Maury Muehleisen & Jim Croce

He laughed and said, "That's all the old stuff. I'm no longer singing with my wife or doing that material. I'm now working with Maury [Muehleisen, the guitarist], so the songwriting has taken quite a turn since then."

An ironic note - Maury got his recording deal first, and Jim was his accompanist. While the resulting album, *Gingerbread*, received critical acclaim, it didn't sell, so eventually, they switched roles and Maury became Jim's accompanist.

Tommy was eager to get started, so we all wandered out to the studio and picked up our instruments, ready to learn the song. I expected Jim to play us something warm and folky about love, liberation and truck stops, but nope. He picked up his guitar, cleared his throat and began to play a muted "chunk chunk chunk chunk" on his guitar. This was no love song. This thumping blues shit kicker spun a grisly tale about bad people doing horrible things to even worse people. I tried not to laugh at his "tugging on Superman's cape" reference in the chorus, but it really was funny and clever, and I loved it. Kudos to the well-written lyrics, but I could only describe them as dark and violent as hell. They told a gruesome story about a big dumb dude named Jim Walker. He called it "You Don't Mess

119

Around With Jim". I had been used to the sweet harmonies and warm melodies and lyrics that I heard from Jim and Ingrid at The Main Point, but here's a sampling of what he sang to us that day:

Well a hush fell over the pool room
Jimmy come boppin' in off the street
And when the cuttin' were done
The only part that wasn't bloody
Was the soles of the big man's feet
Yeah he were cut in bout a hundred places
And he were shot in a couple more
And you better believe
They sung a different kind of story
When big Jim hit the floor

Aside from the storyline, recording this song was a cinch. It only had three chords and followed the standard blues progression. The chorus diverged slightly, but not enough to throw anyone. Jim played his chunky rhythm part, Maury played blues riffs on acoustic guitar, and Tommy played piano. Gary Chester stuck to bass drum and snare, and I don't think he ever hit a cymbal. I must admit, as strange and violent as the lyrics were, the song was infectious and irresistible. Who writes about pulling the mask off the old Lone Ranger in a pop song and gets away with it? Jim did. Also, the original lyric was "you don't piss into the wind," but all agreed that might get it banned from radio play, so Jim changed it to "spit into the wind."

This song cranked out three minutes and two seconds of pure foot stomping bliss. It was also an artist-establishing hit, and when all was said and done, it launched Jim Croce into the big time. With his songs and timeless stories about his life and the exotic and chaotic characters of his imagination, it's no mystery that he became one of the most beloved singer/songwriters of all time.

Jim and Maury's short three-year career, recording and touring together, abruptly ended on Sep 20, 1973. They had just performed at Northwestern State University in Natchitoches, LA. Jim's manager chartered a small Beechcraft E18S to fly them to the next gig in Sherman, TX. On that evening, their pilot, who had severe coronary artery disease, made the questionable decision to park his car and run some of the three miles from the motel to the airport to get a little exercise. The official report said the pilot may have had a heart attack during takeoff, causing him to lose control of the aircraft. They barely made it past the runway, crashing into a pecan tree and killing all on board.

Palm Springs

I won't go into a great deal of detail for subsequent Carly shows in the early 70s. Most were well received, but uneventful. I will, however, highlight a few of them for their sweet, bewildering and sometimes hilarious memories.

This next event marked one of the rare times we had to rush from one gig to another. Carly never scheduled more than one booking per week or two. Sometimes many weeks would pass without work. She hated traveling and performing with equal venom. On this occasion, we would be guests of honor at the Elektra sales convention, Jan 6-9, 1972. She resisted performing under the best of circumstances, but to travel cross-country and showcase for a bunch of salesmen? Our girl hit an all-time high for the number of excuses she conjured up to avoid this one. When Arlyne told her that these were the people promoting her records, the ones that get her airplay and TV exposure, with slumped shoulders, she caved. Begrudgingly acknowledging their importance, she agreed to go, and promised to charm them to death. We couldn't wait, knowing we'd once again be flying to an exotic destination to do what we loved best - play and lounge. Next stop: the beautiful Riviera Hotel in Palm Springs, CA, and a big convention showcase featuring The Doors, Harry Chapin, Bread and us. All recognized it as an opportunity to share the stage with world-class bands and boost credibility with the movers and shakers at Elektra.

When we arrived at Palm Springs airport, we did the usual: follow the signs to baggage claim, get our bags and look for a driver holding the sign "Carly Simon." We lined up to see the bags thumping onto the moving ramp, one crashing into another. As luggage rode around the conveyer, we each grabbed ours and waited. And waited... Carly's bag never arrived. After a lengthy inquiry in the baggage claim office, the agent dropped the bad news. The airline lost her bag. Stolen or left behind at LaGuardia? No one knew. Barcode scanning had not yet been invented, nor had email or texting, so any inquiry had to be done by phone using long bag tag numbers verbally exchanged between various agents and baggage handlers. No luck. The bag contained her wardrobe, cosmetics, underwear, boots, books, everything, gone. They never found it, so the airline offered her their current maximum for lost bags, $300. One of her outfits for stage cost double that, but the rules are the rules, and arguing proved futile. Once Carly accepted the disappointing news, our driver dropped us off at the hotel. She and Arlyne took the limo and drove into town in search of a new bag and everything else she needed to survive, thrive, and perform for the next three days.

Sales and distribution meetings were not our concern, so we had plenty of time to lounge by the pool, ride horses, enjoy gourmet food and relax on a four-day VIP holiday. Palm Springs boasts multiple climates, depending on your location. At its base, you'll find hot California desert weather. Then there's the upper region. On our first morning, we went full-out tourist and took a ride on the Palm Springs Aerial Tramway. This oversized dangling bus, the world's largest rotating tram car, travels 2.6 miles over the breathtaking cliffs of Chino Canyon and terminates at the

Mt. San Jacinto State Park. Pristine wilderness. Goodbye desert. When the tram doors opened, we stepped out onto patches of snow and a temperature of 36°. The ticket booth lady neglected to advise us that shorts and T-shirts were dumb-ass clothing for the Palm Springs tundra. We briefly admired the redwoods and fabulous mountain views, shrugged, turned around and took the tram back to the desert! I could have used a hot bath.

Saturday night arrived, and with it the big gala dinner. Once Jac Holzman (Elektra's founder and CEO) had made his speech, the artists gathered on the sidelines, ready to do their stuff. Harry Chapin opened

Harry Chapin

the show. I had never seen him, and to my surprise, found myself hanging on every word. His song "Taxi" depicted a chance encounter as a taxicab driver, where his rider turned out to be an ex-lover. The song brilliantly covered every emotion - nostalgia, angst, yearning and regret, a triumph of music, poetry and drama. What an amazing singer-songwriter.

Next, us. Despite her baggage debacle, Carly seemed in good spirits and ready to knock the socks off the Elektra salesmen and their wives. Our short set featured "Anticipation"," That's The Way I've Always Heard It Should Be" and a smattering of songs from the new album. It was a winner! The Elektra team fell in love with their new budding artist, Carly Simon, and were eager to hit the ground running with her new album!

After our show, we found a table, ordered drinks and sat back to watch and listen. Bread took the stage. This was the era of well written, melodic, easy listening songs, and that night, Bread reigned victorious, delivering hit after hit to the cheering convention crowd. "I Want To Make It With You"," Baby I'm-a Want You" and so many others.

Bread

The Doors closed the show. In those days, they rightfully claimed supergroup status, but the absence of their iconic lead singer, Jim Morrison, had the crowd on the edge of their seats, not knowing what to expect. It had only been six months since his untimely death, and Jac Holzman, a personal friend of Jim's, was still grieving his loss. Many of the Elektra team who had known Jim during the band's years at the company shared the sadness. Could the surviving members pull it off? All I can say is it felt odd and bittersweet. The band was struggling without Jim, no question. They kicked their set off with "Love Me Two Times", a great opener, with Ray Manzarek singing lead to cover for Jim. If you closed your eyes, you'd be certain you were listening to the authentic Doors.

The Doors without Jim Morrison

Nothing was missing from the sound. But if you opened your eyes, the visuals were another matter. There was a pervasive sadness about them. Fair enough, they had recently lost their brother, but they just played the songs, nothing else. Dull stage presence, no patter, no movement.

Without Jim Morrison revving up the audience with his crazy, psychedelic, screaming, drug-fueled vibe, the quintessential focal point of the band, it was almost like watching three quarters of a Doors tribute band. Close your eyes and it was magic. Open them, and "meh." It wasn't so much that Jim was the whole band. It's that the musicians' stoic, almost Addams Family persona framing Jim's loose cannon antics created a charismatic and seductive phenomenon. Remove either element, and the charisma collapses. That night the band lacked four crucial ingredients - sex appeal, mystery, unpredictability and acid-laced insanity. Without Jim Morrison, you knew what would happen next - the next song.

In my opinion, I doubt Jim would have done any better as a solo artist than the surviving Doors without him. Just as with Mick Jagger and The Stones, it's the entire picture, all the personalities meshed together that create the phenomenon.

The convention was a big success for Harry Chapin and Carly. Subsequently, both of their careers took off, and we ended up doing a couple of shows with Harry in the ensuing months. He was such a sweet, unassuming and humble guy, and a terrific storyteller. Our sales team debut was now over, and next up, the scramble. On Jan 14th we had to be in Chicago for a week's stay at a medium sized club in the Midwest - The Quiet Knight. We air-sprinted back to NY to do laundry, change strings, and repack for the next event.

The Quiet Knight

When we arrived in Chicago it was cold, really cold, as the winter usually is in Chicago. Andy and I decided to brave a local diner on one morning during our week in the Windy City. I remember nothing about the food - probably eggs. At diners, a breakfast of eggs is usually a safe choice. What I remember is something I hadn't seen in my twenty-something years. We had a window booth. I didn't take my coat off, being pretty chilled. While staring at the window, I realized I couldn't see anything but blurry light. Why, you ask. Grease? Dirt? No. Windows often steam up during frigid weather. But this was more than that. It was so cold, the window had an eighth-inch layer of ice - on the inside! Though the radiators and kitchen churned out plenty of heat, the cooking steam and people's breath froze to the window and created a literal sheet of ice. A hair dryer or fan heater under the table would have been nice, but nope. No such luck. With coats zipped up tight, we carved our names in the ice with butter knives, ate our eggs, and left.

Carly experienced a buildup of nerves that week. She often talked about her stage fright, and I did my best to soothe and encourage her, making sure she knew we were there to support her no matter what. It helped, but despite my efforts, she always had a hard time relaxing and enjoying the fact that people adored her. Carly Simon never wanted to be the on-stage focus. She asked that they place my mike stand even with

125

hers, front stage, to create the impression that she was just a member of the band. If we were the Starship, and she was Grace Slick, that might prove credible. But people paid to see Carly, not the Carly Simon Band. Rearranging mike stands served only to assuage her fears.

As most people know, electronic guitar tuners are common these days. You can get a good one for under fifteen bucks. What the cellphone generation may not understand is that they didn't exist in the 70s. How do you tune a guitar without a Korg PC-2, they ask? With your ears, dear friends, with your ears, the same way they did in Beethoven's time. This brings us to an odd and pain-in-the-ass quirk of The Quiet Knight. They insisted on keeping loud canned music going at all times when performers were not on stage. In steamy clubs, when the weather is cold outside, guitars don't stay in tune very well. That means if you tune guitars at sound check, then move them from stage to dressing room, the wood expands or contracts with the change in atmosphere and they go out of tune. Reliable tuning must take place immediately before the show. Here's where ears get the ultimate test. I climbed onstage, and while The Stones blared on the house sound system, tuned the guitars to the piano. Press E on the piano holding down the sustain pedal, then place my ear on the top of the guitar, pick the E string on the guitar, twist the tuning peg and try to match the piano note while my other ear gets blasted with "Paint It Black". I felt damn proud of myself for getting it right every night. It took time, patience, and ignoring my right ear, but I had no choice. Amazing what the brain can do under duress. Beyond that little annoying challenge, the shows went smoothly and were well-received.

We had a great time in Chicago. We were kids on the road, playing with a hot, up-and-coming artist and enjoying all the frills. In the end, I think Carly, too, found a way to make it a rewarding experience. Despite her nightly desire to crash through the stage door, out into the street, and grab the nearest taxi to anywhere else, she remained a trouper and powered through the rest of the week's shows. It paid off. Her reviews in the Chicago press were stellar. This was no longer an occasional gig for us. It was now our full-time job. Paul Glanz, Andy Newmark and me, formerly the ELP wannabes known as Ivory, were having the time of our lives in our new role as the Carly Simon A-Team!

Centerfold, Part I

Before we head to O'Hare airport, I have one more tantalizing story. Chicago was home to Hugh Hefner and his Playboy mansion. As I mentioned earlier, Arlyne, Carly's manager, used to head up the entertainment division of Playboy International. With that in mind, we begged her to finagle an invitation to Chicago's famous house of ill repute and epic parties. Again, I remind you we were in our twenties, the horny, peak-testosterone years, so the idea of an evening on the bunny planet seemed like a dream. Almost.

Arlyne came through. With the invitation secured, after one of our Quiet Knight shows Andy, Paul, Arlyne and I grabbed a taxi and headed to 1340 North State Parkway, The Playboy Mansion. Carly declined, having little interest in bunnies or Hefner. Disclaimer - I have never once felt the need to open the despicable conglomeration of pathetic nubile pseudo-porn that is *Playboy* magazine. Hahahahaha, right!

Ok, so the mansion is pretty impressive from the outside. We ring the doorbell, the grand entranceway door swings open and Shel Silverstein bids us welcome. You may remember Shel as the controversial poet/artist that sent parents scurrying for their lawyers with his book *A Light In The Attic*. Schools and libraries launched a concerted effort to ban this "children's book" because of the... what shall we call it? ... unabashed depiction of nasty, spoiled kids attempting and succeeding at suicide when their parents didn't give them what they wanted. Shel was one infamous dude as well as the cartoonist and often commentator in hundreds of *Playboy* issues over the years. He was also a lifelong friend of Hef's (Hugh Hefner's nickname) and a valued collaborator to the *Playboy* legacy of jokes and literature. I was disappointed that Hef had meetings in LA and couldn't be there for our visit. Nonetheless, Shel did his best to make us comfortable.

Most of the mansion was off limits for obvious reasons. Hef valued his privacy, so even Shel, a man at the top of the VIP list, had to honor certain boundaries. On the other hand, the entertainment areas were fair game. He showed us all around the ground floor with its many rooms, sumptuous sofas, beautiful decor and some captivating artwork, then invited us to sit for a chill and chat. After tossing around a few stories and getting acquainted, an attractive young woman entered the room offering to take our drink orders. I guess because of magazines, TV and legends we expected to see her dressed in a bunny outfit - to our disappointment as young lads, she looked like a conservative hostess at an expensive NY restaurant. Upon writing down our requests, she smiled and returned to her hidden bar, somewhere in the bowels of the Playboy Mansion.

Shel took a sip of his drink and asked, "Is anybody hungry? I know you guys have been working hard over at The Quiet Knight. Would you like something to eat?"

I said, "Uh, sure. Whadaya got?"

Shel says, "Anything you want."

I replied jokingly, "How about a filet mignon, with garlic mashed potatoes and creamed spinach?"

I was certain he would laugh and say, "Hmmm, maybe chips and dip?"

Instead, he replied, "How would you like your filet, medium? Rare?"

He wasn't kidding. The mansion sported a full-time chef and high-end restaurant kitchen, with a huge, fully stocked fridge and freezer.

Our drinks soon arrived, and shortly thereafter, trays of scrumptious food. Unlike me, Andy had read some of Shel's columns, so they struck up a fascinating conversation about art and literature. To avoid making a dumb comment on something I knew nothing about, I kept out of it and ate my filet. Shel pegged us as young, drooling fans of the whole Playboy thing, so next came a tour of the *play area*. He led us to an elevator, then down into a completely silent subterranean bar, with walls covered in soft, dark blue fabric, and thick, color-matched carpeting. Simple, comfortable furniture faced an enormous aquarium window that occupied an entire wall like a theater sized video screen. No fish, though. From this swimming pool viewing area, one could enjoy watching Hef's beautiful house mates and party guests swimming with or without bikinis from an unobstructed and comfortable vantage point. Sadly, for our frustrated young libidos, no frolicking mermaids were flapping about in the warm, still waters that evening. But ever the gracious host, Shel asked, "Would you guys care for a swim?"

Glancing at Andy and Paul, I replied, "We'd love to, but we didn't bring swimsuits."

Not sure what he had in mind. Skinny dipping for his and Arlyne's entertainment would be a little too *Boys Gone Wild* for my taste.

He laughed, "We have a full cache of swimwear in the next room. Everything you need is through there…"

He pointed to a door on the wall adjacent to the she-quarium window. The door led to a cabana style dressing room. We could access the main entrance to the pool from there. Oh, hell, why not? Our moment in pig heaven would make a great story for our kids… when they were over 21.

Upon entering, we found only one dressing area, not two, i.e., no separate men's and women's - U-ni-sex. Two columns of shelves stacked with swimsuits graced the opposite wall. The men's side contained the traditional, manly swim trunks in every imaginable size and color. The women's side contained a small selection of bikinis with about as much fabric as a container of dental floss. If the women ran out of swimwear, no worries, birthday suits were always in season at the Playboy Mansion. What we would have given at our ages for a micro-

128

swimsuit fashion show.

We took a splash around in the almost bathtub-warm pool, diving underwater with goggles and looking through the enormous window into the bar where Shel chatted with Arlyne, both waving to us. Also, the fabled grotto mentioned in Playboy legends did exist, though it was kind of Disney-faux. The architect did a decent job emulating a natural cave. Real rocks mixed in with sculpted concrete and dim lighting made for a fun, nature-themed swim. The waterfall was a remote-controlled plumbing job - not quite Kauai, but warm and nice.

After our pool romp, we dried off, threw our suits and towels in the laundry bin, got dressed and rejoined the others in the blue bar. Another round of drinks arrived while lounging on the velvet sofas, and after about twenty more minutes of conversation, we decided to call it a night.

I'd finish the Playboy Mansion story here but would be remiss if I didn't mention the part that made this visit not the most wonderful experience in my short life. I had so hoped to meet a real live bunny, and though our time here was ending, my wish almost got fulfilled. I know this sounds like a school trip to a freak themed safari park hoping to see a two-headed giraffe, but read on…

Back upstairs, while Arlyne continued her conversation with Shel, Andy, Paul and I wandered around looking at the artwork on the walls. While admiring a watercolor nude, I heard footsteps and instinctively looked over my shoulder. Two beautiful young women were approaching. This was the moment. This was the dream. Fire. OMG, gorgeous and bodies like… well… centerfolds, as one would expect here in Babes-R-Us. I mentioned they were approaching us. That is, I thought they were approaching… *us*. Nope… They were headed somewhere else, and we were about as interesting to them as roadkill. Why did this feel full-on creepy? When I say they ignored us, I don't mean they gave us disinterested half smiles as they passed. We offered them our best Joey Tribbiani from *Friends*, "how YOU doing?" and it was as if we were talking to ourselves. They looked straight ahead, no response, no glance, no smile, just an almost ghostly pass-by. Andy and I looked at each other with a mutual WTF? Talk about a mind-scrambling experience. If we were in the mansion, were we not VIPs? Had they no idea who we at least thought we were? We watched them retreat in disbelief, swaying their butts like Victoria's Secret runway models, as they disappeared down an off-limits hall. It was as if they were never there, an apparition of an unfulfilled fantasy. I'm reminded of the hotel hallway scene with the Grady daughters, the twin ghost girls in Steven King's *The Shining*.

I had to summon Shel and get his take on it. After we described the brush-off, he let out a nervous chuckle and said, "House rules."

Apparently, there is an unwritten Playboy Mansion edict - unless there's a formal party under way, with a house full of the rich and famous, Hef's beautiful little angels are under strict orders - they may not interact with any unsanctioned male guests - Hef's property, Hef's rules. A Google search will reveal many confessions and autobiographies from ex-Hefner ladies that bear out the truth of our non-interaction and their sequestered life in the mansion. Transactional objectification might be an apt name for it. While I was grateful for the hospitality and experience, I left 1340 North State Parkway with a slightly sick feeling in my stomach and a strong desire to take a shower.

No Secrets

This short period, late summer of 1972, is the line of demarcation where things started taking off for both Carly and me. The *Anticipation* album only had one hit single, the title song. Time to move on! Carly was thrilled with the way her career was going and started writing songs in every minute of her spare time. Elektra was aware of this, had heard some of them and was strongly encouraging her to get going on a third album. They made a suggestion she initially rejected. Paul Samwell Smith had done a fine job on *Anticipation*, but Jac Holzman wanted a producer with AM/FM hit experience for the next LP. He suggested Richard Perry. I remembered Richard from my Kama Sutra days - from time to time, he'd pop in on Critters sessions and chat with Artie Ripp. I had great confidence in his abilities. During one of our rehearsals for the new songs, Carly asked me what I thought of him. I responded I thought he was an insightful producer but couldn't say whether she and he would be a good match. In the end, Jac won the argument, and Carly said she'd give him a shot.

Me, 1971

Richard and Carly both loved England, so they planned to record this third album in London. Trident was the studio of choice and had quite the reputation. The Beatles recorded many of their hits there. More importantly, Richard had produced Harry Nilsson's famous hit "Without You" there with a young and talented engineer, Robin Cable, who had agreed to work with Carly. We were walking into a situation with a hit producer, a hit engineer, and a studio that had recorded "Hey Jude", David Bowie's "Space Oddity", Elton John's "Your Song" as well as artists including Frank Zappa, Genesis, Queen, Lou Reed, Black Sabbath, The Rolling Stones, Ace, Peter Gabriel, Rush and James Taylor, to name a few. Talk about a jump start! This studio was so good, you could go in with a kazoo and a coffee can and leave with a hit. Ok, slight exaggeration.

I remember the first day at Trident. "The Right Thing To Do" was the song on the docket, but a bass player had not yet been chosen. I found an old Fender Squire bass leaning against the wall in the drum booth. We had rehearsed the song back in NY with me playing bass, as there was no guitar envisioned for it. I asked Richard if I could take a stab at it. He said fine, so we started the ball rolling. This cheap Squire bass had been modified, and to my amazement, sounded like the best Fender I had ever played. Richard and Carly loved the sound, so we went with it. The musicians on the track would be Andy Newmark on drums, Carly on piano, and the famous percussionist Ray Cooper on congas. We would overdub the backup singers and strings on a later session. The song didn't take long to record, so we broke for lunch early. That's when I learned about basic British sandwiches. Robin directed me to a small deli downstairs, so I gave it a try. Imagine coming from a brown rice, sprouts and wheatgrass world back in NYC to this:

I came out of the studio onto St. Anne's Court and there, across the street, I see the tiny storefront with a sliding window. I walk up to the window, and a smiling old lady with some teeth left says, "Hello, luv. What kin we gitcha?"

Me: "Could I have a tuna on whole wheat with a pickle on the side."

Her: "Ay?"

Me: "Tuna? Whole wheat? Pickle?"

Her: "Oh, no luv. We got nuffin like 'at 'ere. Ow 'bout tomah'o and cheese on white, or just cheese? Marmite? 'At's oh we got today."

OMG a Marmite sandwich? On white? I didn't want to laugh and be the ugly American. I also didn't want an involuntary gastric cleanse, so I thanked her and politely declined her delicious offerings. This "food" hut made any back road Louisiana truck stop seem like the Cafe Des Artistes. Thankfully, I noticed a Chinese takeout halfway down the street that seemed safe. The menu had been Britishified, but I chose what I thought would hold me over until we could find a decent place from which to order. I can't imagine The Beatles would have suffered this level of cuisine during the "Hey Jude" sessions. Anyway, I enjoyed my sweet and sour gerbil, and there were leftovers for the next day.

Back to the recording. Carly had not included Paul Glanz on this project. For reasons unknown to this day, she and Paul did not mix well. On the other hand, she encouraged bringing in the best musicians England had to offer, and I didn't complain. Making the cut and spending another summer month in London worked just fine for me. Though I missed my old friend and bandmate, Paul, I'd be playing with some of the most renowned studio musicians in the world.

Some initial adjustments to our recording schedule needed to be made, though. Richard Perry liked to be late. Chronically late. His range of lateness spanned about an hour to an hour and a half. Every session. Every day. Carly tired of this very early on, so we worked out a ploy. We would secretly book the session for 11am and tell Richard 10. When he would still show up a half hour later than our faux time, we extended the difference by another half hour. Like clockwork, Richard would show up an hour and a half late for the faux booking, and right on time for the real one. Everyone got what they wanted. He got to jerk Carly around in his mind, and Carly got to not be jerked around and not have to pay for an hour and a half of unused studio time. She let him in on the ploy towards the end of the project, but as I will show later, nothing changed. Late people are late people. God help them if they do the Landmark Forum (formerly EST)! Google it.

Let's get to the good part - "You're So Vain." As I mentioned earlier, I believe the genesis of this song was my interaction with Warren Beatty at the Troubadour, which Carly has neither denied nor affirmed. When I listened to the song for the first time in the studio, I agreed with Richard - it had the potential to be a monster hit. We began the recording with Andy Bown on bass and Andy Newmark on drums. It didn't go well. We started over the next day. Andy Bown recommended his friend, a well know London studio drummer named Barry DeSousa. Barry played well, but again, his style didn't suit Carly's and Richard's vision for the song. Out of the blue, Richard got a call from a legendary LA session drummer, Jim Gordon, who at the time was on a break from his band. Jim's resume comprised about ten pages in small print, including Crosby, Stills & Nash, Steely Dan, The Beach Boys, Linda Ronstadt and Leon Russell just to name a few. Andy Newmark didn't feel the least bit slighted. He held it as an opportunity to watch one of his idols at work. Jim knew Richard from the LA scene and called him on a hunch that he might get some work to fill the tour's down time. Of course, Richard asked him to join us, but he made another change. Andy Bown was out; Klaus Voorman was in.

Klaus brought in two instruments on his first day with us: The usual Fender bass and something else. As we sat around chatting, I noticed the large case behind his chair and asked, "What on earth is in that huge case?"

He said, "It's a guitarrón," and began to explain the history of the instrument while taking it out of the case. It's a very large Mexican acoustic bass guitar. He picked it up and started playing, but not like a bass. He played it like a flamenco guitar. Klaus is also a classical guitarist and absentmindedly played an impressive finger style classical arpeggio on the guitarrón as he talked. He used all the fingers on his right hand to rapidly and individually pick each note in the sequence of an A minor chord. Richard spoke into the talkback that we needed to get started, so Klaus put down the guitarrón and picked up his Fender bass. While waiting for the rundown to start, he played the same arpeggio on the Fender that he had shown us a minute ago. Richard hit the talkback and said:

"Klaus! What is that? What are you playing?"

Klaus said, "Sorry, I was just fooling around."

Richard responded, "NO, keep doing it. I love it. That's how we should start the song!"

Carly wholeheartedly agreed, and that, dear reader, was the birth of the strange bass part that opens "You're So Vain", where Carly whispers, "Son-of-a-gun."

The next revelation took place during the playback of one of our takes. Jim Gordon and I wandered up to the control room while the others stayed downstairs in the studio. While a separate discussion ensued between Richard, Carly and Robin, I struck up a conversation with Jim:

"Hey Jim, I loved your playing on this. It really brought the song to life. I'm Jimmy Ryan, the guitarist that you probably couldn't see behind the sound baffle."

We shook hands and exchanged a few pleasantries.

I then said, "So what brings you to England? I know from Richard you're an LA player."

Jim said, "I'm on break from a tour with my band, Derek and the Dominos."

To be clear, Eric Clapton's Derek and the Dominos, whose album was on rotation at my apartment, and whose drummer was currently standing in front of me.

I said, "Wait... you played on 'Layla'?"

He replied, "I did. I also co-wrote it with Eric."

Not to embarrass myself by doing the *Wayne's World* prostration, "I am not worthy," I toned it down and said, "Wow, cool. That's one of my favorite albums. It's a great pleasure to meet you!"

He smiled and thanked me for the compliment, humble and unassuming.

As I wrote this, another piece of info appeared in my research. The piano section at the end of "Layla" was not entirely Jim Gordon's work as he claimed. According to Rita Coolidge's Memoir, *Delta Lady*, she and Jim collaborated on the piece. They played their complete version of the song, words and music, for Eric Clapton, and he passed on it. Imagine her surprise when the instrumental version of the song appeared at the end of the final version of Layla without any credit for her. Jim Gordon and Eric Clapton kept all the royalties of this million seller. Oh, you nasty boys.

Jim Gordon

Here's what none of us could have known in 1972, including Jim - I brought his name up many years later on another Carly session back in NY. During a dinner break at Right Track Recording Studios, I just dropped, "Hey, anybody in touch with Jim Gordon? No one's mentioned him lately, at least not after the 'You're So Vain' sessions."

The entire room became silent, and all eyes locked on me and my sandwich, which abruptly stopped on its way to my mouth with the sudden silence.

I said, "What? Did he piss somebody off? Not show up for one of your sessions?"

Carly replies, "You're joking, right?"

Me: "Um... no. What happened?"

Carly looked around the room." Who's going to tell him?"

During the mid seventies, Jim developed a condition that prevented him from sleeping and eating. He was misdiagnosed with alcohol addiction and treated incorrectly. In fact, the recreational drugs he had been enjoying over the years had taken their toll, and he developed acute schizophrenia. On June 3, 1983, he suffered a psychotic break, and obeying instructions from voices in his head, brutally murdered his mother and cut her up into small pieces. Her head turned up in a hat box on his coffee table, discovered by a visiting friend who, out of curiosity, tipped the lid. In answer to the "where is he" question, he is in permanent lockup at the California Medical Facility in Vacaville and still plays drums, currently with a prison band. Jim has been denied parole on at least two occasions. According to his doctors, his condition has not improved. He is still a considerable danger to others if he doesn't take his meds. Jim's story has been written up in many articles, except for the hat box detail. That comes from a friend of Jim's whose name I will protect for obvious reasons.

To be sitting on a studio chair and hear this story while trying to eat my sandwich… imagine Freddy Krueger on drums playing "Layla". My sandwich wasn't all that attractive to me after this. The hairs standing up on the back of my neck kind of put me off my food.

Ok, now that we've completed the *Nightmare On Elm Street* detour, let's move on to lighter subjects. We did several more sessions to complete "You're So Vain". Carly came up with an idea for some string parts, so she asked that Paul Buckmaster of Elton John fame be brought in to arrange and conduct them. As always, Carly did her lead vocal in an empty studio with only Richard and Robin at the console, after which she and I had an amusing interaction. She brought back a cassette of the day's work and called me over to her apartment to to get my opinion. She inserted it into the cassette machine, cranked the volume and hit play. So far, so good. When we got to the chorus, something bothered me. After letting the song complete, I said, "I love it. Great job but for one thing."

"Mmm, what?"

"The chorus - you sound like Mick Jagger on the chorus."

"No. Really? You think so??"

"Yes, I really do. Why would you want to do that? Your voice is so good. Everybody loves it, and all over the world it's… blah, blah, blah."

In being complimentary and encouraging, I hoped she'd hear me, but damn, this was not the time in her ascent up that parabola to be imitating a Rolling Stone.

I told her, "People should be imitating you!"

Carly was now sporting a very non-defensive grin. She gave me that half smiling, fake questioning look and said, "Hmmm. I actually sound like Mick Jagger to you? Y'know... you may be right. It's probably because Mick came in the studio this afternoon and I asked him to sing the chorus with me."

Damn! The friggin 'who's who of British rock just kept showing up for her.

She said, "The Stones had a session next door at Air London. Mick wandered in while I was singing and started flirting with me. It made me angry, because Bianca was next door at the Stones' session. I doubt he told her he was coming to my session, or she would have wanted to come. He showed bad faith to her and acted like a jerk. I ignored his BS, and told him to make himself useful, and come out and help me sing this chorus."

Carly could do that. When it came to men, she had no problem flaunting her power and charm, laying it on as thick as necessary. Mick happily agreed to sing with her. It was a brilliant distraction and killed two birds with one stone. She didn't have to issue an embarrassing rejection, and she persuaded a world-class artist to sing on what would become her biggest hit of all time.

I performed on the basic track of "You're So Vain" with my electric guitar, the Gibson 335, but Richard felt an acoustic guitar might also be helpful. That session was uneventful, but for the fact that after Klaus's flamenco bass intro, that Martin D-28 I secured back in my Dan Armstrong days is the first instrument you hear. I know it's kind of nerdy to keep mentioning guitar model numbers and techie details, but some readers like having that info. Here's to us nerdy techies!

Carly had always planned a guitar solo for this song. Robin gave me a rough mix on cassette a few days prior, so when I came in that evening with my Gibson ES-335 and a little 1953 Fender Vibrolux Amp, I was ready to go. I plugged in, he miked up my amp, and they rolled the tape. The solo comprised a section with my normal left-hand fingering and a section with a bottleneck I kept on my baby finger. When I finished playing what I had rehearsed back at the apartment, they stopped the tape.

I said into the microphone, "That's the idea. Let's run it a couple more times and hopefully it will improve. Is there any particular part that sticks out for you?"

Richard said, "No. You're done. That's it. Come in. It's perfect."

I said, "Are you sure? I can probably do it better with a couple of more tries."

Richard: "No need. We love it. Come on in."

This was a first for me. I had my mind on dinner and just knocked out what I rehearsed while craving Chinese food. My solos usually take a bit more time, since they have to please three people, the artist, the producer and me. This was like a bowling spare. All three pins went down in one shot. That was how it happened, and that one pass solo is what ended up on the record.

"It Was So Easy Then" was another song that had me scheming. I felt strongly that the song would benefit from a guitar solo. Carly and Richard weren't sure, so I took matters into my own hands. When you record a song live with other musicians, generally you start with a basic track. That might consist of drums, bass, guitar and keyboard. That was our lineup for this song, minus the piano. They called in Paul Keough to play acoustic guitar, Klaus Voorman on bass, Andy on drums, and Carly also on acoustic. I played electric. Normally I wouldn't play a solo on the basic track because that can create problems later - you may not like what you played and risk it bleeding onto other live mikes in the room.

Paul Keough, Carly, Klaus Voorman

Then you end up with unwanted notes whispering in the background behind your new, overdubbed solo. I was young and headstrong back then, and on the first take, when the open section came up, instead of continuing my rhythm guitar, I just started playing a solo. As usual, Richard recorded multiple takes to get the song exactly the way he wanted but didn't say a word about my minor infraction. Next take, I did the same thing. And again. And again. When he finally got a recording he liked, I kept my mouth shut. By the time we got to that last take, I had perfected the solo and performed it with no string buzzes or mistakes. The session ended, and no questions were asked. I sure as hell didn't bring it up, and that live solo that shouldn't have been included on the basic track made it all the way to the final album release. I've never done that before without permission, and never attempted to do it again, because solos usually require some thought and feedback. On this song, I knew what it needed, I didn't want to risk them spoiling it with something contrived or a different instrument after we recorded the basic track, and I took matters into my own hands. My only criticism is that in the mix, they put the solo through a phaser. This gave it an unfocused, wishy-washy sound that I didn't love. It was ok, but I was going for a pedal steel guitar sound. Ha, maybe that was their way of getting me back for my pushy move! I never complained. I was grateful and happy it made the cut.

"Waited So Long" was the next parade of superstars. There's not much to say about the actual recording process. No super exciting moments. But… the musicians on that track were ridiculous and famous in their own right. The Stones came into the picture again at this point. Richard brought in the British keyboard wonder who had done many Stones records, Nicky Hopkins. On drums, Jim Keltner of George Harrison fame, Klaus on bass, James Taylor on backup vocals; on organ was Bill Payne of Little Feat, and the legendary Lowell George, also of

Doris, Carly, Richard, Sir Paul, Bonnie
and Me (on the right)

Little Feat, performed the bottleneck solo. When I thought back to The Vibra-Tones and the high school sock hops and realized how far I had come and who I was sitting with in this studio, it made me smile. It wasn't like being famous. It was more like being valued and appreciated. That's an incredible feeling.

Now the big one. We recorded a basic track on "Night Owl," a James Taylor song. Richard brought back Jim Keltner to play drums, Klaus on bass, Nicky Hopkins on piano, Ray Cooper on congas, and a new addition, The Stones' own Bobby Keys on tenor sax. But the highlight of this song was a surprise guest that none of us had anticipated. He appeared during the backup vocals. Carly had wanted a soulful chorus for this one, so she called in Bonnie Bramlett of Delaney and Bonnie, Doris Troy who had her own hits in the early sixties, me, and herself. We were standing around the mike trying to come up with background parts, and it wasn't going as well as she had hoped. Richard kept coaching us, "Not quite. Try again. Let's try something different," etc. Frustration was starting to build because we knew he was right. Then, after another take, there was a pause. Richard didn't say anything. Had we finally gotten it right? Still more silence. I poked my head around the baffle and saw that Richard wasn't even paying attention. He was talking to someone who had entered the control room. Who was it? Wait... WTF? It was Paul McCartney. What was it about Richard and Carly that these superstars just kept casually dropping by? In this case, we were working at Air London, George Martin's complex of studios, and Paul was recording in the main studio down the hall. He was on a break, curious, and just thought he'd go exploring. Apparently, in their conversation, Richard shared our dilemma with him. Paul pressed the talkback button - in our headphones and in that unmistakable Liverpool accent, he said, "Richard tells me you're in a bit of a pickle with the backing vocals. If you like, I could come out there and maybe throw some ideas around."

The Beatles were my number one heroes in high school and college. No one could play, sing, and write like they did. I learned every single one of their songs and played many of them in The Vibra-Tones and Critters shows. And now, here I was in London, at George Martin's studios, with a Beatle asking if he could help out with our song. "I don't know, Paul. We got this. Thanks anyway," said no person in the universe, ever. Paul came out, Robin fitted him up with a set of headphones, we all uncovered one ear, and Richard played the track for us. When the chorus came up, Paul sang what he thought might work as we listened and took notice where he placed the notes. The tape stopped, and Paul said, "Doris, you sing this, Bonnie, this, Carly and Jimmy, double up on this part, and I'll sing this." Richard hit play, and again the chorus came around. We sang Paul's suggestions, and all agreed, the new parts worked perfectly.

After we completed the backing vocals, Bonnie and Doris left the studio. Linda McCartney had wandered in while we were recording, so now there was only Paul, Linda, Carly, Richard, Robin and me. Paul just casually dropped that he had been called to write the new James Bond theme. He wasn't sure if it was any good, so he asked if he could play it for us to see what we thought. The idea that he would think something he wrote might not be any good was a stretch, but hey, he's human. I'll give him the benefit of the doubt. He sat down at the Air London, nine-foot Steinway grand piano and played us "Live and Let Die". No one but him, Wings, George Martin and Cubby Broccoli the movie's producer had heard it yet. We got to witness the private premiere of what was to become a legendary movie theme and a two-time hit, first with Wings, and later with Guns 'N Roses.

What a thrilling three minutes and twelve seconds. Of course, we were all effusive after the final chord, but it didn't end there. We were at Air the following day, as were Wings with a full orchestra. Paul invited us to drop in if we had a free moment. We did. Carly and I wanted to be discreet, so we quietly snuck into Studio A. The control room of Air Studio A, like Trident and Morgan, was again one story above the studio floor. The orchestra had gone home, so it was just Paul, George Martin and an engineer. Paul was trying to convince George to make the French horns louder in the orchestra mix. George just leaned back in his producer's chair, arms folded, and responded, "No Paul, that simply won't work." Only George would have the balls to kill a Paul McCartney idea without even trying it. In my opinion, George was an incredibly talented arranger and producer, and his track record of umpteen hit albums with The Beatles gave him the right of refusal. Paul acquiesced, and the engineer played back what they had recorded. It was pretty much what ended up on the record and in the movie.

We didn't stay long. One doesn't want to intrude on such private emotional exchanges, and we had already heard the song in its infant stage. Nothing more could be gained by hanging around, so Carly and I took our leave, thrilled and fulfilled.

Centerfold, Part II

I would be remiss if I didn't mention our second encounter with the Playboy franchise. During the making of *No Secrets*, Arlyne announced that there was going to be a big party in town and asked if we would like to attend. Of course we said yes. Our social life was non-existent in London, considering our limited stay with few friends and connections. I had to ask, "Who's having the party?" - a silly formality, as I would have gone to any party at that point.

"Victor Lownes," Arlyne said, with an odd smirk.

The name meant nothing to me. She continued, "Hugh Hefner's London partner? Head of Playboy Club International?"

I replied, "Oh, THAT Victor Lownes!"

Andy and I were stoked. This party would be teeming with VIPs and playmates, who under these circumstances would be more than happy to talk with us. Also, Arlyne wanted to expose Carly to a wealthy and influential audience outside her normal fan base. Everything about this party looked good. Nothing was planned that day, so Carly and I got together and rehearsed a potential setlist. I didn't bring any dressy clothes to London, though. Should I have been worried? If the dress code was anything like what we saw on Hef's TV series, *Playboy After Dark*,

I'd look like the dishwasher. I pictured gentlemen in tuxedos smoking pipes with scorching hot babes slinking around in low-cut gowns and everyone sipping martinis. Arlyne assured me that as musicians, no one would expect us to show up in formal attire.

8pm, Saturday evening - time to assemble at Carly's London house, where we would be picked up by a town car and taken to the party. Andy and I were at our apartment, and he knocked on my open door with a mischievous expression on his face.

I said, "What's up?"

"Are you feeling adventurous?" he replied.

"Uh... sure. What did you have in mind?"

"I scored some LSD and have enough for two hits. Care to join me?"

Though I'd steered clear of psychedelics in the past, this was a special night.

I was a pushover." Sure, why not?"

Andy pulled out two little pieces of paper with blue dots on them, much like those candy strips from the 50s. He handed me one, and we both licked them off the paper. It would be about thirty minutes until the mind warp kicked in, or roughly ten minutes into the party. With the ball now in motion, we walked over to Carly's, hopped in the waiting car, and set a course for the Victor Lownes party. I had no clue how the acid would affect me, so as a precaution, I told Carly and Arlyne what we had done. They shrugged their shoulders and resumed their previous conversation with little concern. So far, so good.

We arrived fashionably late, making our grand entrance into a house full of happy, casually dressed people. No worries about that dress code. And more beautiful women than I had ever seen in my entire life. Normally, I would walk around and strike up conversations, but tonight would be different - the acid was already starting to interfere with my cognitive functioning. I felt disoriented, a little dizzy, and everyday things were beginning to look unfamiliar. Fortunately, in *this* Playboy Mansion, the women seemed friendly. No zombies yet. Victor had hand picked them from the swaths of bunnies and centerfolds under his employ, hoping to impress his business and movie star friends. Would the bunnies know who was who? No name tags on this lot, so maybe a humble, almost famous musician could have a shot, especially since tonight, the "Hef Rule" had been suspended.

By now I must have looked about as relaxed as an alien abductee heading for outer space... But then a beautiful, partially dressed woman caught my eye. I had to talk to someone, so I wandered over, despite feeling confused and disoriented. I did my best to hold it together.

After greeting me with a big, "Are you rich and famous?" smile, she leaned in, "Hi. Where are you from? How do you know Victor?" etc.,

etc.

We slogged through the usual small talk until I couldn't contain my weirdness any longer. I said to her, "Listen - I'm feeling a little uncomfortable here. I think that before I embarrass myself and say something stupid..."

Then I dropped the bad news:

"I took some LSD just before the party, and my head is kind of spinning."

Remember that incident with those women at the Playboy Mansion finding us about as interesting as roadkill? Deja vu, only worse. Her smile instantly changed from "Hi, baby," to "Oh my God, how do I get away from this creep." The look of horror on her face was almost comical. She didn't even try to hide it or make an excuse, like needing the bathroom or a drink refresh. Without a word, she turned around and walked away, leaving me standing there holding my scrambled thoughts. I took no insult. She reminded me of a cartoon bunny out of *Watership Down*, running for her life into the safety of the warren. As I scanned the room, I realized why my scary revelation took her by surprise - this was an old school party, a Hugh Hefner booze-in, not a Timothy Leary be-in. That poor, shocked woman may have been my age, but not my generation.

With communication skills offline for a while, I surrendered to the situation and assumed the role of observer. The nearest corner looked like a safe spot, so I parked there with my cranberry juice and just took in the flirting, flaunting and slowly drooping eyelids as the martinis flowed. Then Carly signaled to me from across the room - our host wanted us to perform. I looked at her and mouthed the words:

"Perform? What are you talking about?"

My deer-in-the-headlights expression must have raised a red flag. She slipped through the crowd, easing up to my side, and whispered, "Don't worry. Just get your guitar and come upstairs. Everything will be fine. We'll play a couple of songs, and it will be over."

I said, with peaking paranoia, "Upstairs? What do you mean? Why are we going upstairs? What's up there?"

I found out soon enough. We would be performing in Victor's bedroom, sitting on the side of his bed. Maybe I'd be more comfortable in an intimate setting. We climbed the stairs and were greeted by Victor in a smoking jacket, silk pajamas, and a crazy number of people stuffed into this small space. Yeah, it was definitely intimate - like a three-person sleeping bag. I crab-walked sideways, squeezing my way into the crowded room, taking out my guitar and looking at it... suspended at the end of my arm. The body had a familiar appearance, but the neck, strings, frets and dot markers seemed alien and confusing. Despite years of practice and study, I had serious doubts I could play this unfamiliar instrument.

Again, Mama Carly zoomed in and whispered, "Let's do 'Anticipation'. I'll start it out."

Thank God I tuned the guitars before we left - God help me if I tried now.

She started, "We... can never know about the days to come..."

Muscle memory took over and while I observed myself from an imaginary distance, my hands started moving, pressing on strings, strumming, picking and actually making music. It was a bloody miracle.

LSD can cause unpredictable, sometimes dangerous, occasionally wonderful but often terrifying experiences. Dumb luck saved me from the dangerous ones, as I had no desire to jump through a window. On the other hand, nothing wonderful came of this LSD romp. An out-of-body experience now gripped me - not quite the "hovering above the operating table" kind - more like the minimal command of my motor functions kind. How my arms, hands, fingers and voice could be making music without me, I'll never know.

We received a wild round of applause for "Anticipation" from our raucous bedmates. I'd estimate fifty people had crammed into that room. They climbed on top of each other, stood against the walls, hung in the closets, perched on the furniture and spread out on the bed. But Victor Lownes 'bedroom was not the best place for my current sensibilities. Andy sat cross-legged on the floor clicking drumsticks on the legs of the lamp table in about the same condition as me. Carly remained calm and sober as a judge. She suggested we do "One More Time" from her first album and again started the song by herself. As my hands began the guitar part, I heard a ruckus behind me. An obnoxious partier was yelling over us, going on and on about Britt Ekland. Little did I know, Britt Ekland was sitting behind Carly on the bed. I was tripping my brains out, so even sitting up was an issue, leave alone trying to sing, play and have any audience awareness. Then the same drunken jerk leaned on me from behind, reaching around my head, and tried to shove a small burning object into my open singing mouth. Fair enough, he was attempting to pass me a joint, but I didn't know that. He almost pushed me off the bed. In my delusional state I thought I was being attacked by a crazed, fire-wielding monster, so I panicked. My arm flew up to block the insertion, and I thrust my back into Mr. Godzilla, sending him tumbling backwards into the fifteen others on the bed. Who knows where the joint went? The bed didn't catch fire, so we'll assume someone rescued the reefer. Everyone thought it was all good fun, laughing and shouting over our song like shit-faced patrons in a Paddington pub.

Just to drop some names here, my joint wielding aggressor? Roman Polanski. He came to the party with Britt Ekland, the former James Bond actress from *The Man With The Golden Gun*. Roman Polanski gained world fame for his films *Rosemary's Baby* and *Chinatown* and was well

Roman Polanski

Britt Ekland

known for his marriage to Sharon Tate, the actress murdered in 1969 by members of Charles Manson's cult. As of the writing of this book, Mr. Polanski is a fugitive from the US criminal justice system. He fled the country while awaiting sentencing on five criminal charges, including rape. Cool guy.

I regret having dropped acid that night. It would have been fascinating to meet and talk with some of these people straight, but the past is the past, no redos. One last event in the LSD story and we'll move on. While wandering around Victor Lownes 'townhouse, I became aware of a recurring theme to the artwork. While Hugh Hefner's collection favored the erotic but tasteful, Victor's favored porn. Not just any cheap porn, mind you. An erotic painting by Pablo Picasso actually graced one of his walls. His collection included many well-known artists, with every piece masterfully done if you don't mind the subject matter. Some exceptions to the sex theme did exist though. I found a landscape painting in a beautiful ornate gold frame hanging over a cabinet near where I stood. But even this beautiful pastoral image had a grotesque twist. Perched on the right lower edge of the frame was a leprechaun. I stared at it for a while, trying to figure out whether the artist placed him there as a joke to distract the viewer, or Victor added it when he had the painting framed. Whatever, it was a very lifelike carving with highly detailed face and beard, colorful clothes, and those silly little pointy-toed boots that these Keebler characters always wear.

While enjoying my painted porn art walk, I spotted Andy across the room and decided to go talk to him. We hadn't seen each other after I decked Roman Polanski, so I thought we'd catch up and have a laugh about it all. Now that our sentient abilities were coming back online, I described the odd painting with the leprechaun. He had not yet seen it, so I said, "Come on, I'll show you." We approached the painting and before I could say, "See?" I stopped dead in my tracks. Goosebumps. Chills. WTF?? The leprechaun had vanished. Before us, on the wall, hung an ordinary landscape painting. Fear and anxiety gripped me as I looked back and forth between Andy and the painting. Did I hallucinate that little bugger? Serious question - when we hallucinate, do our minds deceive us with three dimensional nonsensical visions like dreams? Or are hallucinations dimensional rifts through which we peer into other planes of existence? Damned if I know, and in that moment, damned if I wanted to find out.

Suffering a full-on anxiety attack, I excused myself and left the party. There was a park about a block away, and I wandered into it, walking to nowhere, anywhere, hoping to find some peace of mind but still buzzing from that blasted brain-altering lysergic acid diethylamide. A young woman was passing through, and I hailed her, hoping to strike up a conversation. She stopped long enough for me to describe my compromised state of mind.

I said, "Would you be kind enough to just sit with me for a few minutes and talk me down? I'm not doing so well on my own."

She had a comforting and humane reaction, unlike Alice in Bunnyland from three hours ago.

"Ok," she said with a smile. "I've got a few minutes." Obviously, I was a little short on decision making ability, so she said, "Let's go sit on that bench."

She got what was going on, felt no threat, and agreed to be my temporary social worker. How lucky was I to stumble upon this wonderful, attentive listener in my hour of nuttso? I recounted, to her amusement, the adventure that had just taken place. After listening and thinking about the situation, she came up with a remedy for my nerves. While talking to me in a soothing voice, she rolled a joint in her lap. I questioned her logic - getting higher was the last thing I needed. She assured me that this would calm me down and diffuse some of the effects of the LSD. We lit up, and after a few tokes I began to feel my normal senses coming back online, perhaps in a slightly stoned fashion, but much better than the disconnected, hallucination-laced stupor I was enduring an hour ago. We sat and talked for about fifteen minutes. Then she smiled and said she had to go. I thanked her profusely, but like an idiot, didn't ask for her number. On the other hand, if she had any desire to hook up with this freaked-out acid-head musician, I'm sure she would have offered it.

145

Chapter Five
England

She's Leaving Home

Once I returned to New York, I had a sense that it was no longer my home. I had fallen in love with England over the two summers I spent there with Carly, and though it was pretty radical to walk away from a flourishing NY/LA session musician career, I made a decision - London was calling, and it was time to go. I transferred the lease for my beautiful Murray Hill loft to my friends, Bob and Bonnie, who, as a going away present, bought all my furniture. After packing guitars, stereo, tape recorder, two guitar amps, and clothes, I called my travel agent and booked a one-way ticket. Despite my fears, I had to reclaim my life from the hornets 'nest of insecurity and indecision that had marked my previous twenty-odd years.

My exodus timing was not random. On my previous visits to London, I looked up Dan Armstrong, who was now living there. We rekindled our old friendship, and I now had at least one friend in this wonderful land I would soon call home. Dan was one of my greatest mentors, so to be around him for this adventure was a true bonus. I also had a job. Richard T Bear, a great singer songwriter and one of Carly's former roadies, was also in England, and turned me on to a job opportunity that had crossed his sights. A New Zealand band called Bitch was looking for a producer. Experience aside, I applied. After vetting my credentials, the band and their record label believed our musical styles matched and gave me a shot. I now had free lodging and a gig!

Exit day arrived. Bob and Bonnie helped me haul my gear and suitcases down the six flights of stairs in my building and onto the 38th St. curb. We hailed a cab, loaded everything into the trunk and back seat, hugged and said our last goodbyes. In forty minutes, I arrived at JFK, checked in my mountain of gear and luggage and made my way to the gate. No one would describe me as calm as I sat twitching in my seat waiting to board. There's an interesting oscillation between fear and excitement when you extract yourself from an untenable situation and dive into the unknown. I'm glad I only did this once.

Time to board. The jetway can be intimidating when it's a portal to God knows what. I found my heart racing and a deep sadness rising in my chest. I was saying goodbye to my country of origin, my family, my friends and any recording work I might have enjoyed there, for what? No answer. I found my row and slid over to the window seat. Deep breaths. Jet engines revving. Mind racing. Is this insane? My logical self had an immediate answer, "No, not insane. Staying in NY with no long-term purpose, remaining in a casual relationship with no future, holding on to a family who I believed never loved me? That would be insane."

A book and a movie helped me survive the long trans-ocean flight between JFK and Heathrow. But once we were safely on the ground in London, things got dicey. Upon arrival in a country other than your own, your first stop is Customs and Immigration. Despite my fears, Immigration was a breeze. I assumed Customs would be painless too. This was my stuff, and I already paid tax on it in the US, so I headed down the "Nothing To Declare" aisle. Silly me. Here's how it went:

I roll up with a cart full of guitars, amps and suitcases, smiling while I hand in the filled out and signed customs declaration card.

"Nothing to declare, sir?"

"Nope."

"Musician, are you?"

"Yup."

Since I would be in England for an extended visit, my overflowing cart was an object of interest. I don't know why - my guitars were many years old. After a quick, open and close look at them, he moved on to my camera bag. I had a five-year-old Nikon F, but my wide angle and zoom lenses were new. The agent, who reminded me of Eric Idle from Monty Python, pulled out two lenses.

"All this lot's over three years old, ay?"

"Yup" (fingers crossed).

"You sure, mate?"

"Yup" (fingers still crossed). I wasn't a British citizen, and I wasn't about to pay import duty on my own damn lenses that I would take back to the US one day.

"So, it's your official declaration that these two lenses (holding them up and examining them) are over three years old?"

"Um, yeah, I think so" (fingers unraveling and now shaking).

"Right. You can leave your belongings here, they'll be safe. Please follow me."

Shit, I say to myself.

We were now leaving the customs inspection area and heading for a grey door, the other side of which couldn't be good. He opened the door to reveal another gentleman behind a desk who offered, "Well, what have we here?"

"We have some questions that need to be answered about a pair of Nikkor lenses. Please have a seat, Mr... [looks at my passport] Ryan. Now, you say these two lenses are over three years old. Is that your

147

declaration?"

He kept using legal words. This was not going well.

"Well, yes, I mean, I think so. I bought them from someone and didn't ask."

"Well, Mr. Ryan, we have a little problem with your declaration. You see these tiny numbers along the rim - they're called serial numbers. Would you be kind enough to read me the first two digits on this one?"

He held the wide-angle lens close to my face. I leaned in and squinted." 72."

"And are you familiar with Nikkor lens serial numbering?"

"Uh... well... no actually. Can't say I pay much attention to them after I send in the warranty."

(Damn, which I wouldn't have done if I bought them from "someone" who would have already sent in the warranty which would be void, because I am not the original owner. Which in fact I was. Arrrrrgggghhh).

"Well, here at Her Majesty's Customs and Excise, we make it a practice to familiarize ourselves with this sort of thing. You know, helps us do our job, ay? So, would you be interested in knowing what that '72 ' means?"

He was enjoying every bloody minute of this.

"Ok, sure, I'll bite. What does it mean?"

"It means that these lenses were manufactured in 1972."

I can not believe his obnoxious imitation of a B-movie inspector. He leans back and asks his fellow agent for a calendar. The other agent smiles and hands him a small desk calendar. They've done this routine before. For the record, the UK has no problem if the items are a few years old. Less than one year old? Extended stay in England? Problem.

"Mr. Ryan, would you be kind enough to read me the number at the top of this calendar?"

"Fine. Yes, it's 1973. You got me. Bloody hell. Happy?"

"Elated. Thank you. These lenses are now the property of the Crown. You may apply to purchase them back in three months."

He dictates to the desk agent, "Please note for the record, Mr. Ryan has confessed to violating section 24B-18906Z-9947312 subchapter zed of HM Customs and Excise."

He continues, "And I quote our detainee:' Fine. Yes, It's 1973. YOU GOT ME [his emphasis]."

He repeats my words with a smirk, "Bloody hell. Happy?" Agent two scribbles down my annoyed yet sad confession.

With that, he stood up. The other agent filled out a form and handed it to me. It was a receipt for the lenses and an application for getting them back. The price I would have to pay to have them returned was the exact price I paid for them in NY, plus twenty quid shipping and handling.

I was free to go. We left the interrogation center and walked back to customs entry to find my guitars, suitcases, and amps piled up in a corner. As I loaded them onto the cart, he smiled, "Have a nice day, Mr. Ryan," and returned to his station, leaving me with evil thoughts I will not describe here.

I had come to England to produce an album with the band Bitch, and I wasn't going to let this unfortunate incident spoil the joy I felt now living in this amazing foreign country. Producing Bitch was fun and a great education, plus it was the kick in the butt that got me to move to England, a change of environment I sorely needed at the time. Unfortunately, it did not produce any hits, so I'll end that part of the story here.

Dan Armstrong introduced me to a nice couple, Maggie and Tucker Finlayson, who had a large house in London and rented out rooms to people like me. As I had nowhere to stay yet, I jumped on it. And so began my new adventure in London, England, away from almost everything I knew in my previous lifetime in New York City. Was I worried? Hell no - I was beside myself with excitement about all the possibilities awaiting me in my new life!

Tucker Finlayson was a bass player and spent most of his time on the road with his band, The Acker Bilk Jazz Band (No. 1 hit, "Stranger on the Shore"). His absence from Maggie's life while on tour caused no end of consternation and loneliness for her. Because of my proximity, i.e. living in her house, she and I became good friends and talked endlessly about life, our concerns, our likes, dislikes and her unhappiness with her situation. In 1973, she pulled the plug on her marriage and declared herself a free spirit. By that time, I no longer lived in their house, so when she gave me the news, I invited her out for a drink to cry on my shoulder. She didn't cry. She had a twinkle in her eye, and I'll leave it at that. Fast forward, on April 30, 1976, Maggie became my first wife!

When The Music's Over, Turn Out The Lights

I bid farewell to the English countryside where I had been staying with Bitch and made the two-hour drive north to my new studio apartment at 34 Hillfield Road, West Hampstead. After moving in, I got straight to work calling record companies and making my presence known. I'm allergic to unemployment, so there was no time to waste. Jonathan Clyde, an exec at WEA, was at the top of my list, so having just produced one of his bands, and having been the soloist on "You're So

Vain", he was eager to sit and chat with me. He agreed to pass my number around and make the artist relations departments aware that I was now a permanent fixture in the London session scene.

My second call went to Richard Perry, Carly's producer. Though he was an LA resident, he had recorded most of his recent projects in London and was there at the time of my call. Nothing could have prepared me for our conversation that day.

He said, "A certain supergroup are looking for a bass player, and they're rehearsing here in London. I know you're busy, and you probably won't be interested, but would you like their number just in case you have some free time?"

I was laughing into the phone because we both knew I wasn't busy. I said, "Well, it depends on how super they are. Are they really super or just somewhat super?"

"They're really super, and you opened for them recently in Palm Springs."

"What, you mean Harry Chapin?"

"No, bigger."

"Bread?"

"Nope, bigger..."

"Holy crap, are you talking about The Doors? The Doors are looking for a bass player?"

"Yes, but I don't want to trouble you. There are a couple of other bass players I could call if you're busy..."

"NO!! I'm in. What do I do to make it happen?"

Out-of-my-mind excited would be an understatement. I loved The Doors. Opportunities like this are rare, and I didn't waste a second. Their drummer, John Densmore, would be my contact. I called him, relating my conversation with Richard, and he invited me to join them the following day for a jam. Robbie Krieger, The Doors 'guitarist, was staying about ten minutes from me, so I was to pick him up at 1pm and drive to a central London rehearsal studio.

As Robbie and I talked in the car and he described his ideas for the band, I woke up from my doting Doors stupor. Jim Morrison was dead, and if all went to plan, I would be joining what was left of The Doors. Ray Manzarek, their keyboardist, could recreate Jim's vocals with chilling accuracy. But for me, that wasn't enough. At the Elektra Convention in Palm Springs, they looked and sounded like a Doors tribute band. Jim was a magic charm. He was the iconic, mysterious force that kept fans riveted with his antics and stage presence, but his death robbed the band of its heart and soul.

We rehearsed two or three times that week, and though we sounded good together, my interest was waning. Then, to my astonishment, they told me they were dropping the name, Doors. Going forward, we'd be the Butts Band, with a new lead singer, Jess Roden. Jess was an excellent singer, but this made no sense. For all intents and purposes, they were starting from scratch.

The following week, we recorded one song at Olympic Studios with The Doors' producer, Bruce Botnick. It was lackluster. This new combination had none of The Doors 'originality, none of Jim's poetry and charisma, and with Jess Roden, none of Jim's sound. The Butts Band was a funk/blues band, not a psychedelic supergroup, and not my taste. I don't recall what excuse I used, but backing out was the right move. Ray Manzarek quit soon after me, and the band continued with a new bass player, a new keyboardist, and a second drummer. They released a pair of albums, but after two unsuccessful years, called it a day.

Despite the unfortunate outcome, I consider my time with The Doors a valuable experience. I enjoyed meeting them, hanging out and exchanging life stories, and I enjoyed playing with them, even without Jim Morrison. They were talented musicians, good people, and had been world leaders in the music of their generation. But the original Doors were four people, not three. Ray, Robbie and John knew that, which led them to try something new. To be a Hall of Famer though, you need to create a total experience - ears, eyes, mind, heart, and yes, feet! The Doors with Jim Morrison had it all and were an unstoppable force. The Butts Band were not. I wished them well and moved on.

MacArthur Park

My experiences being bullied as a kid with thick glasses kept me hiding in the shadows for a good part of my life. My fear of rejection would often rule situations that would have gone so much better if I was willing to take some risk. But now that I was on my own in a strange country, survival was in play - I had to take action. Indulging my shyness would be fatal to my career and fatal to my social life, not to mention survival itself. I loved when my phone rang, but I hated the dial (no keypad or touch-tone in those days). Nonetheless, I was determined to take my success with Carly and use it to build a session musician career

Jimmy Webb

in London. Yep, that required using the dial - often and regularly. It went well with Jonathan Clyde and Richard Perry, so why not keep it going.

I made another call, this time to Robin Cable, our engineer from the *No Secrets* album. I was always a little surprised when people were glad to hear from me, and Robin was no exception. My timing was perfect. He had been hired to produce a new album with famed composer Jimmy Webb and invited me to play guitar on the sessions. Jim had written some huge hits, including "MacArthur Park"," Up Up And Away"," Wichita Lineman"," Galveston"," By The Time I Get To Phoenix" and many more.

For the most part, this was a routine recording experience. I was thrilled to be called in to work on it, but most of the time, it was just reading charts, playing the chord sheets, getting feedback and recording take after take to get it right. There was one experience, however, that did stand out in my memory, and that was our first session. All the musicians showed up at Trident Studios and sat around, chatting while we waited for the inimitable Jimmy Web to show up. When he walked through the door, everybody greeted him:" So amazing to meet you," "I'm a huge fan," you know, the usual. Then, not being shy for a moment and throwing caution to the wind, I took a shot. Jimmy sat at the piano and was about to show us the first song we'd be recording, and I said:

"Wait. I know this might be an odd request, but could you play us 'MacArthur Park'?"

The band chimed in:" Yeah!" "Wow, cool." "That would be so great!"

He couldn't resist. Out came the famous piano riff that opened the song, and he was off and running. When he finished, we cheered, and another musician requested a second song, "Galveston". Again, Jimmy launched into the intro and sang his heart out. This went on for over an hour until we'd exhausted every Jimmy Webb song anyone could remember. It was a fun night, and his performance put us all in the mood to make some great music.

The ensuing album, *Land's End*, featured an all-star cast of musicians, including Ringo Starr on drums, Tom Scott on sax, and members of Elton John's band. But even with this massive firepower, Jim faced a similar problem to The Doors. He was a writer, arranger and producer - essentially a background artist. When the spotlight came on, he did not yet have the voice or personality of those who turned his songs into unforgettable hits, i.e. Art Garfunkel, Glen Campbell, Donna Summer, Richard Harris, The Fifth Dimension and so many others. *Land's End* did not move his solo career forward. He never gave up though, and between then and now, he has continued to compose for every medium from film to commercials, pop to classical, and has won

152

almost every distinguished award there is for his excellent work over the years. For me, playing with musicians of this caliber and an artist with so much writing talent was a memorable experience and a valuable lesson about sticking to what I do best - playing guitar, writing and bringing out the best in others. I kept getting these little reminders about the Peter Principle, i.e., rising to your level of incompetence. The desire to stand center stage, bathed in light with an average singing voice was losing traction fast!

By 1974, I had pretty much given up on the idea of being a solo artist. My experience with Jimmy Webb taught me it's ok to be the beacon that lights the path for others. The two work hand in hand - one cannot survive without the other. There are advantages to both, and there are also disadvantages. A superstar makes a lot more money than their support people. On the other hand, the support people don't need bodyguards, they need not live-in fortresses, they can go to public places without disguises, they are not plagued by paparazzi and don't have to spend their lives generating an often-fake persona to please the fans. Also, as I mentioned earlier, when an artist's career hits the rocks, their support people have the option to move on to another artist. What is not present in the background artist's lives is adulation, and high finance. Could I live without that? So far, so good. I believe the Universe supports you when you're in the right place doing the right thing and doesn't when you're not. I never thought I had a superstar singing voice. With singers like Joe Cocker, Elvis Presley, Bruce Springsteen, Cat Stevens, Huey Lewis, Rod Stewart and Mick Jagger, I was outgunned by a wide margin. In the sixties, when lighter, pop male voices were popular, I did ok. I had a couple of hits. Once the seventies and eighties came along, the bar moved up quite a few notches. But there was no crushing failure in letting go of my solo ambitions. I had plenty of work then and plenty now, doing what I do best. Opportunities to work with artists of the above caliber kept falling in my lap, so why fight the tide?

Keep in mind that much of the work in the studio production world never sees the light of day. There are so many artists that get signed to recording contracts, but fate kicks them back out onto the street. Either they don't have a breakthrough song, they don't perform well live, or suffer a long list of setbacks that finish their careers in short order. Though I've performed with some very successful artists, most of my work has been with unknown artists. Unless there are entertaining stories associated with them, I'll skip the ones that didn't make it.

153

A Whiter Shade of Pale

Ialways admired classical music, so the band Procol Harum was one of my favorites. I must have listened to "A Whiter Shade of Pale" hundreds of times; *A Salty Dog* is one of my all-time favorites, with all its orchestral shades and nuances. It strongly influenced my third Critters album and especially our song "Wooden Soldiers". Why do I mention this? Read on.

As I sat around my Hampstead apartment playing my guitar one summer day in 1974, the phone rang. I thought I'd let the answering service get it and check back later, but as a self-employed musician, that felt dumb and irresponsible. Putting the guitar down, I got my lazy butt up off the Turkish pillow on which I sat and trotted into the study to grab the phone before it stopped its British double ring. In the UK, one ring isn't enough. A double ring says, "Urgent! Drop what you're doing and answer that call from the Indian cat food telemarketer." Anyway, I answered, and someone with a very thick British Accent said, "Is this Jim Ryan?"

"Yes," I replied.

"I'd like to hire you," he said, cryptically.

He wanted to hire me. Ok. Since he didn't identify himself, I couldn't be sure he had the right number. Did he want me to clean his gutters?

I asked, "Hire me for what?"

He paused before answering." To play bass, of course!"

"Oh… Ok. Well... might I know who's calling?"

"Matthew Fisher."

The name seemed familiar, but I couldn't quite place it.

He said, "I'm finally getting 'round to my solo album and you were recommended by a colleague."

I inquired about the "finally getting 'round" part. "Were you busy with other projects?" asked the memory challenged ignoramus on my end of the phone.

He said, "Well, yes, actually. I've been on tour with my band, Procol Harum, for years and taking some time off to do my own album."

Procol. Harum. OMG - slapping palm to face. This was the gentleman who wrote and performed the famous organ part that opened and defined "Whiter Shade of Pale" and he wanted to hire me! And I answered the phone acting like he was looking for a plumber. I let out a nervous laugh and told him, "Of course I now remember you. So sorry for not recognizing your name."

He seemed distant, formal - the apology went right over his head.

"Yes, well, we'd like to start fairly soon. Are you available for rehearsals?"

I said, "I am. Where and when?"

He gave me dates for the following week and a rehearsal studio address, then abruptly ended the conversation with:" We'll be recording in Rome. Make sure your passport is current."

This was fabulous news delivered like a traffic ticket. Rome intrigued me, but Matthew's distant manner sucked most of the excitement out of it. Over time, I learned he was not a bad guy - just quiet, self-conscious, business-like and averse to small talk. But Procol Harum. Jesus.

It got weirder. I met Matthew's manager, Ronnie Lyons, at the first rehearsal. He was American. He liked cash. This would be a cash deal. No one ever paid me cash on a professional recording session. Financial negotiations usually took place between managers, agents and record companies, and our fees were usually paid thirty days (or months) later. Nevertheless, I loved this idea. We would be leaving every session with a pocket full of money. Instant gratification. It did have a slight gangsta vibe to it, though. Each night when we finished, he would summon us into the studio lounge, pull out a wad of twenties and dole them out into stacks on the coffee table. It felt like we had just robbed a grocery store. We'd each claim our little pile of cash, thank him, and be on our way.

Matthew Fisher

Ronnie Lyons was also an annoying watchdog, constantly reminding Matthew and us that time was money and to pick up the pace. We hated it, and it was not helpful to the creative process. But he persisted despite our complaints and kept it up for two weeks. Anxiety and haste marred our days, during both the recording and Rome in general.

I'm not going to be a snob or an ugly American and say that Italians are a little high strung, but two things do come to mind - 1) The taxi ride from the airport in which my life passed before me several times as our driver approached roundabouts at 70 mph and blasted through them at almost full speed in a screeching four wheel drift, and 2) In those days Italians tuned their pianos to A-445, at least in our studio. The rest of the world tunes to A-440. They tune their pianos higher. "High strung," literally. Now, since Hammond

155

organs (Matthew's instrument with Procol Harum) leave the factory hard-tuned to A-440, at least two instruments will be permanently out of tune with each other - the organ and the piano. In those days of tape recording, if you recorded with the high-strung piano first, and you wanted to add an organ (or celeste, vibraphone, tubular bells, Fender Rhodes, Wurlitzer, etc.), you would have to lower the speed of the tape recorder slightly to match the tuning of the recorded piano with the tuning of the organ. Instead of tuning the piano normally, you would have to tune the tape recorder, and along with it, the entire band. How did this start? Why does this weird practice continue? No one could tell me. Do they believe music is more exciting or "brighter" pitched slightly higher? Was it a tribute, honoring an ancient decree from Marcus Aurelius? After a Wikipedia search, I learned that since the 1700s, this has been an ongoing debate. I'll leave it at that.

Our engineer wasn't fazed. Adjust the tape speed to correct the pitch and move on. For me, though, that subtle little shift was an annoying assault on the ears. Imagine working all day in one tuning reference, then setting up for an overdub that's at a very slightly different pitch. Fingernails on a blackboard. Thankfully, they did this in my absence.

We finished the instrumental tracks quickly, much to the pleasure of Ronnie Lyons, and with the final track complete, he was on the phone booking our flight back to London. Just like that. Pack your bags immediately and go to the airport. Not one minute extra did we stay in Rome because, you know, money. We never heard vocals, we never heard mixes, and our input was neither required nor requested. It was play, pay and go away.

For Matthew's sake, I apologize for this mixed review. Until the writing of this book, I had no knowledge of what became of this album. No one ever contacted us about its release, nor did I ever hear from him or anyone in his entourage again. My first listening to a finished track was today, forty-seven years later. I queried YouTube and Google to research this chapter and was pleased to see the album had been released in 1974, the year we created it. I also saw on Spotify that Matthew continues to make a wide range of music to this day and finally won his case for a writer's credit on "Whiter Shade of Pale". Yes, his organ part was probably what you remember most from the song, yet he did not get songwriting credit, nor did he share in the songwriting royalties, which were substantial. He sued Gary Brooker, Procol Harum's lead singer, the song's composer, and eventually won. If you Google him and select images, you'll see an assortment of grim looking pictures of him from the sixties, then a picture of him obviously older in a suit, tie and overcoat, looking like he just came out of court. He has an uncharacteristic grin on his face. That's how you look when you win a huge royalty case on an international smash hit! That's also how you look when someone tries to screw you out of what's rightfully yours, and you kick their ass in court!

Some Guys Have All The Luck

England had now been my home for two years, and business was good. Through friends, I met a producer named Jimmy Horowitz who ended up hiring me for a lot of the session work I did in those days, mostly with his wife, Lesley Duncan. Through Jimmy and Lesley, I landed work with two of the biggest stars of the day. I'll tell you about Lesley in a minute, but first, I'll talk about an adventure with one of those famous or, if you like, infamous artists.

(ring ring... ring ring...)

"Hello?"

"Hey, it's Jimmy Horowitz."

"Hi Jimmy. Wazzup?"

"Nothing much, you?"

"Not much. Just sippin' a cup o' tea and listening to Stevie Wonder."

"Nice. So I'm calling you about a session."

"Cool. What are we doing?"

"Well, actually I won't be producing this one. The artist likes to produce himself, but I recommended you for acoustic guitar."

"Wow, thanks! Where and when?"

"Tomorrow at Air London 3. Starts at 2:30pm."

"Great. I'm free. Who's the artist?

"Roderick David Stewart..."

"Cool. Is he any good?"

"Jim... Roderick David Stewart!"

"Uh... not familiar... should I recognize that name?

"Jesus, Jim. ROD STEWART!!"

"Wait... what? That's his real name? Roderick? Duh. Ok, hell yeah! I'm in. Thanks!!"

We both laughed at my profound density, and after a brief chat about the prospective session, he closed with, "Good luck, Jim. I think you're going to enjoy this one!" I thanked him again, and we hung up.

Jimmy Horowitz was a partner and staff producer at the Billy Gaff company, and Billy managed Rod Stewart. I was aware of that but never pushed Jimmy for an intro. Rod had his own band that toured and recorded with him, so normally, he didn't use studio musicians. I welcomed this exception. We'd be doing demos of old standards - songs by Cole Porter, George Gershwin, etc. Not an expert on that period, I had

157

to rely on reading chord charts. No problem. My reading was up to scratch.

I showed up a few minutes early, and was surprised to see Rod sober, friendly and chipper. I knew little about him personally, only that he was an amazing singer, a party animal, and enjoyed getting wasted. He also had a reputation for percussive remodeling of hotels and studios, much like The Who and Van Halen. That Rod Stewart didn't show up this day. Instead, his gentlemanly alter ego met me in the control room, extended a friendly hand, seemed engaging, polite... and uncharacteristically sober. He also had a beautiful blond woman with him, whom he did not introduce. I assumed her to be Dee Harrington, a British model and his girlfriend at the time.

My bandmates on this session were Micky Waller on drums, Martin Quittenton on guitar and Ronnie Wood on bass, essentially the "Maggie May" crew. From the very first rundown, the songs all sounded like "Maggie May" with different chord changes. Not necessarily a bad thing. This band had such a distinct and recognizable style, I had to tread lightly, musically speaking. It would have been rude and ill-advised to impose my musical persona on such a classic ensemble.

So I just followed the chord sheets, keeping it simple. Rod is a rocker. The complex jazz inversions of the original chords would have taken him way out of his comfort zone. We rehearsed the songs among ourselves for about a half hour, then Rod stepped out into the studio and took a seat on a stool placed near the control room window. He sat opposite me. A microphone had been set up with a pair of headphones lying on the stool. Placing them over his ears, he made a few vocalizations, asked the engineer to turn him up a tad and put a little reverb on his voice... and we began.

Rod Stewart

I don't believe Cole Porter had ever envisioned "Every Time We Say Goodbye" to be performed like we did it that day. It had a distinctly rough edge, from the band's rock roots to Rod's classic scratchy voice, but it worked. You could admire it in the same way you'd admire a flowering cactus. Then Rod treated me to a big surprise. During the rundowns, I was having a little trouble hearing him. I didn't want to bother the engineer to adjust the mix in my headphones - you know, new guy? Don't make waves? Instead, when there was a pause in my guitar part, I slid one side of my headphones back, uncovering my right ear. That way I could hear Rod and the live band in the studio, without the iffy headphone mix. If you listen to Rod's records, he sounds like he's screaming. When you watch him in a live show, which I have done several times, again, he looks and sounds like he's screaming. He's not. That day, he was singing so quietly I had to strain to hear him... and he was only six feet away. Rod Stewart seems to create his scratchy vocal sound in his throat, not through power and force but through skillful control - quietly. It was crazy. His vocals had all the intensity of his records without any volume or strain. He was born with this grainy voice and there was little effort. Rod is still singing today, and to my knowledge, he's rarely lost his voice or suffered laryngitis. If he had been screaming all these years, his vocal cords would look like a loofah.

People have asked him if it hurts when he sings like that. The answer is always unequivocally no. He said his singing voice is the same as his speaking voice. Most artists that sing with harsh intensity develop "nodes," a condition where painful polyps form on the vocal cords from stress and dubious technique. With time, rest and silence, the nodes may go away. Microsurgery is the quicker but more invasive option and can be dangerous - a surgical slip would end one's career. In my research, I found a YouTube vocal coach who believes Rod was born with natural, benign nodes, and that's how he gets his sound. Who knows? Rod's only voice related threat that I'm aware of was at age fifty-six, when he underwent an emergency surgery for throat cancer. It put him out of business for nine months, and he thought he'd never sing again. Luckily, the odds were in his favor - he made a complete recovery. Despite the throat cancer, he has had an astoundingly successful career. As far as the charts go, Rod Stewart has the golden touch. He scored ten number-one albums and thirty-one top ten singles in the UK, six of which landed at number one. He scored sixteen top ten singles in the US, four of which reached #1 on the Billboard top 100.

My recording session with him took place in 1975. It was an exploratory project, never intended for release. Rod wanted to stretch out and see if it was possible to blend his sound into a legit musical environment. The project moved to the back burner for twenty-seven years, and the final version wasn't released until October 2002. He called the album *It Had to Be You: The Great American Songbook*. It made it to #2 on the Billboard USA's top 200 chart. I had lost touch with him and Jimmy Horowitz by that time, so unfortunately, I did not participate in the final production. I have no regrets, though. It was an honor to record with an artist of this caliber. And to witness Rod quietly producing

159

that scratchy sound with so little effort was a game changer.

I had another indirect connection with him that year, again through Jimmy Horowitz. He was due to perform at a large outdoor festival with the Bay City Rollers and didn't want to bring his band. He was just doing a couple of cameo songs, so it wasn't worth the trouble and expense. He called on Jimmy to create backing tracks for the two songs he would perform at the event. Enter me and a handful of British studio musicians in Air London, recreating the Rod Stewart sound. What fun! We sat in the control room, listened to the two songs several times making notes, sketching out chord sheets and agreeing who should play what, where and when. It was an easy task because we didn't have to create anything - just reproduce the original recording. Since everyone in the room was a seasoned pro, it was quick and easy. Rod approved our work, hit the road for the North Country, sang to our pre-recorded tracks, and the Bay City Rollers fans cheered him like the rock star he was.

My last encounter with Rod "The Mod" took place at the infamous Studio 54, a large and loud NYC club where people could pose if they were stars, or gawk if they weren't. Some also came to dance. I'm not prone to fawning over glitterati, but boredom had gotten the best of me that night. A couple of friends and I decided to trek up to this 54th Street social zoo and treat it like a research project. It was 1979, so the venue had aged a bit. Gone were the days of Bianca and Mick Jagger, Andy Warhol, Lou Reed, Cher, Liza Minnelli, and the in-crowd that made it famous. By now it had devolved into "bridge and tunnel," a condescending term for twenty-somethings from Brooklyn, Queens and New Jersey. Anyway, I chose to just wander the club that night and take in the sights - conversation in the main room was almost impossible with the deafening sound system. To my surprise, as I passed by a small alcove, I saw Rod Stewart sitting on a bench - the other Rod, the infamous one I didn't meet at our recording session. Same guy, different personality, chugging on a bottle of something that did not look like Diet Coke, and from the looks of his eyes, blotto. I said, "Hey, Rod," but he didn't recognize me. Fair enough. The club was dimly lit, and we only worked together for one day, four years earlier. I tried to refresh his memory of our last encounter and asked if he had stayed in touch with Jimmy Horowitz. He began to answer when a six-foot-three, Dwayne Johnson wannabe came up behind me and grunted, "Move along."

I said, with a touch of 'tude, "Relax, man. I'm talking to my friend. I played on one of his records."

No response from the bleary-eyed Rod, upon which scary bouncer dude repeated, "I said move along!"

Before I could protest, he picked me up like a sack of potatoes and carried me fifty feet across the club, throwing me up against a railing.

Then, pressing his left forearm into my chest, he said, "You've been warned. I don't ask twice."

I didn't contest his humiliating threat, nor did I loop around for a second try at Rod. With his wasted non-response to my greeting, and my subsequent encounter with The Hulk, I was way beyond giving a fuck about Roderick David Stewart. The past had passed.

Love Song

In the last chapter, I mentioned Lesley Duncan, Jimmy Horowitz's wife. Though she wasn't a household name, any pop music fan who ever read album credits would be aware of her. Lesley wrote "Love Song", a beautiful acoustic piece that appeared on Elton John's second album, *Tumbleweed Connection*. She also sang with him on it and provided background vocals for that album as well as countless others in her career. I was still living in NY on East 38th St. when I first discovered "Love Song", one of my Elton John favorites. Four years later, through Jimmy, Lesley and I would meet, and enjoy a wonderful three-year working relationship. I will describe how and why it ended later. First, the nice bits.

When I met Lesley, I only knew of her connection to Elton John, and that was enough to pique my interest. In 1974 Jimmy invited me to record

Lesley Duncan & Bob Cohen

with her. It became one of those deep relationships that transcended work. We hung out together, had dinners together, and eventually toured together. As I got to know Lesley better, she began to reveal her past. She had been Dusty Springfield's backup singer for years, and during that period she became one of the most in-demand session singers in London. A credit that takes her to almost-hall-of-fame status was singing on Pink Floyd's *The Dark Side of the Moon*. Though unknown to the buying public, the industry so admired her that A-listers were more than happy to perform on her first album, *Sing Children Sing*. Elton John played piano, Terry Cox of Pentangle played drums and

Chris Spedding played guitar. Chris, one of the UK's most successful guitarists, worked with Elton John, The Pretenders, Roxy Music, Paul McCartney and too many others to mention.

Our first album working together, *Everything Changes*, had some lovely songs on it, but unfortunately her greatest asset was the way her voice blended with others. Though producers considered her a first-call singer, her voice was no match for the million sellers. The pop music fans voted, and the album was soon forgotten, not by her many fans, but by the world at large.

While we were cutting the tracks, we'd often take a few days off and do live performances. Most weren't memorable enough to include here, but one made it into my top ten best gigs ever. Lesley's manager booked us at London's Royal Albert Hall, opening for Don McLean. If you're not familiar with it, the Royal Albert Hall completed construction in 1871 and was named after Prince Albert, the late husband of Queen Victoria. One of the first artists to perform there was the famous classical composer, Richard Wagner. The hall is an architectural masterpiece and seats 5,272.

Don McLean's huge hit, "American Pie", helped sell our concert to almost capacity, and Lesley's friends, Elton John and Rod Stewart, showed up to cheer us on. Meeting them again and knowing they were watching us was both exhilarating and terrifying. As we walked out onto the stage, I recalled the irony that prior to 1971, I knew nothing of Lesley Duncan other than seeing her name on a few of my favorite records. And now I'm at the Royal Albert Hall, walking out into the spotlights with her to entertain thousands of cheering fans. And a couple of her superstar friends. Heady stuff.

Despite being the opener for Don McLean, Lesley was very well received. England loved and admired her, and they showed it that night. She and I had something in common - we both chose a career helping others become famous. Ironically, that night, she was being honored for it, but I remained in the supporting role. No complaints, no jealousy, just a mental note. I was fine with her taking responsibility for keeping this immense audience engaged.

I'll pause the Lesley Duncan story here. There's more about this friend and wonderful artist, but it comes later. In the meantime, read on for what actually came next.

Maybe I'm Amazed

The very first Hard Rock Cafe opened in London in 1971. It was my go-to hangout on nights off, and a networking utopia. Many successful bands and artists hung out there to feast on the best burgers in London. During my brief encounter with The Doors, Richard Perry called me to offer an invitation to an intimate concert by Paul McCartney's new band, Wings. It would take place at that same Hard Rock Cafe. This small venue suited Sir Paul's needs perfectly - a low key, industry-filled bar gig like the famed Cavern in Liverpool. It thrilled me to be invited. And... I met a cute French lady, Ivonne, the previous weekend at the Speakeasy and invited her, hoping she would be impressed with my cool friends... Nope. Little did I know Ivonne was not a Paul McCartney fan, nor did she enjoy pop music. She did, however, enjoy being a drag.

Aside from that, I had a fun and unusual night. Wings set up in the center of the room allowing the audience to surround them. We managed to get front row seats, five feet away, with an unobstructed view... of their backs. Hearing them was easy; we just couldn't see their faces. No problem with the sound though. With Paul McCartney's budget, it was impeccable. This was the original Wings with Denny Laine from the Moody Blues on rhythm guitar, Denny Seiwell, a NY player, on drums, Linda McCartney on keyboards and photography and a friend of mine on lead guitar, Henry McCullough. Henry, an Irishman, loved his ale and liked to celebrate when surrounded by friends doing exciting things. That night he celebrated big time, and like Kris Kristofferson, would have done better to celebrate after the show. He was now wasted and having trouble standing up. During a blues song, to my great surprise, he staggered over to me, and in a slushy Irish accent said, "Jimmeh, take me guitah. Ahm tiu drunk t 'play."

I stood up in astonishment as he handed me his Les Paul, then collapsed in the chair I had vacated, next to the now even more grumpy Ivonne. How to grasp what was happening and what fate dealt me? I didn't resist; I jumped in, both feet. Paul didn't even notice the personnel change until the song ended. At first, he gave me a WTF look, but then recognizing me from our meeting on the Carly "Night Owl" session, and realizing that I handled the part fine, shrugged and smiled. Hard to screw up a blues song. He glanced back at Henry who, with a brief rest, was slowly returning to the living.

Not wanting to push my luck, I approached Henry and asked,

"Feeling better?" He was tough and used to functioning on less than six cylinders, so he pushed himself up out of the chair, took his guitar back, and gave Paul an "I'm OK" wink. Henry struggled through the final song, doing the best he could under the circumstances. On the other hand, I was kvelling, having once again performed with one of my teen heroes.

After the show, I thanked Henry for letting me sit in. With him still pretty wasted, I had to accept a wink and a nod as acknowledgment for the favor. I then wandered over and thanked Paul for letting me pinch-hit. He was surrounded by fans and industry people, so again, the wink and the nod. Good enough. I spent the next half-hour chatting with friends and finally took my leave. Note to self - keep up your practicing. You never know when you might be called into action to play with a Rock God, without the opportunity to warm up. I also keep a pocket full of guitar picks, just in case. As for my French date, Ivonne? I dropped her off with little flair. We both knew she would not be the mother of my children.

Western Union

This was not my only fun story from the London Hard Rock. One night while sitting at the bar enjoying a burger and a beer, I noticed a cute young lady sitting a few seats away. We glanced at each other a couple of times, not so much in a flirting fashion, but in a "Do we know each other?" kind of way. After a few minutes, she leaned towards me and said, "Are you Jimmy Ryan?"

I said, "Yes, do I know you?"

She said, "I'm Debbie Delzotti from Westfield."

Wow, talk about an unlikely connection in an unlikely place. We went to High School together.

Debbie was several years younger than me, but a friend and a fan of The Critters. I slid my place setting down the bar and parked next to her. She and I didn't know each other well in the day - more like distant admirers, so we combined getting acquainted with catching up. Over a couple of beers, she told me of her fascination with Victorian and film star dresses from the thirties, often collecting them from LA movie studios for next to nothing. With an eye towards travel and monetizing her hobby, she opened a shop on the King's Road called Jesse Mae & Co, selling her dresses as well as cowboy and Hawaiian shirts, Afghan jewelry and exotic fabrics. Her clients included Steve Winwood (Traffic, Spencer Davis Group) and Ronny Wood (Faces, Stones), as well as many of the British rock stars of the day, so it was a fun hobby turned into a successful store.

I mention all of this because our conversation aroused the curiosity of someone sitting nearby. He was a little shy and said nothing at the time. But on a subsequent evening at the bar, he approached me, curious about my conversation with Debbie, and interested in my work with Carly Simon.

Extending my hand, I said, "I'm Jimmy Ryan."

He responded, "I'm Chris Jagger. Nice to meet you."

I then asked the dumb question, "Any relation to Mick?" expecting a no.

His reply:" Yeah, he's my brother."

It was one of those moments. I realized Chris had probably been living in his brother's shadow since 1962. I got my confirmation with the tone in his reply. A voice in my head said, "Keep the Rolling Stones questions to a minimum."

He said, "We can talk about The Stones at some point, but I'd like to offer something that might be more interesting to both of us."

Chris Jagger was a drug-free vegetarian and shared little in common with what he called "that Stones vibe." And more importantly, he wasn't there to talk about Mick. He was there to hire me. He was a singer/songwriter with a recording contract and offered me a spot on his

Chris Jagger

upcoming album as his guitarist. We'd be recording at Rockfield, a studio/residence complex in the Wales countryside. The sessions would begin in two weeks, and he had assembled a band of renown. On drums, Pick Withers, the Rockfield house drummer, who would go on to be a member of Mark Knopfler's Dire Straits. Andy Bown on bass who had worked with me on Carly's *No Secrets* album, and finally, Jean Roussel, Cat Stevens 'keyboardist.

Because of my chance encounter with Debbie, I ended up on an album with the brother of one of my favorite singers, and a fine artist in his own right. While writing this, I contacted Debbie on Facebook. I never had the opportunity to tell her of her role in that meeting with Chris so long ago, and her only disappointment was not being there the second night to meet him herself. Without our conversation in the Hard Rock, would I have connected with

Chris and ended up on his album? With all the talented guitarists in London - not a chance. The album was called *Chris Jagger - The Adventures Of Valentine Vox, The Ventriloquist.* Not a big seller, but some great songs and a voice close enough to Mick's that it sounds immediately familiar.

Before we leave Chris Jagger, I wanted to give a shout out to Rockfield Studios. It's in Monmouthshire, Wales, and from the outside, it looks like an old brick warehouse or farm. Don't let that fool you. It's a state-of-the-art recording facility and the first ever live-in studio. A little while after we finished Chris 'album, another group came in. They spent weeks crafting a song that would combine rock and opera. The band was Queen, and the song was "Bohemian Rhapsody". That certainly put this farmhouse, off-the-grid studio into rock legend territory. Other artists that have recorded there are Rush, Oasis, Coldplay, Black Sabbath, Robert Plant, Simple Minds, Annie Lennox, George Michael, Julian Lennon, Dave Edmunds and Nick Lowe among many, many others. One other silly mention. Wales is also known for a town that some say has the longest name in the world. The town is called, and I'm not joking:

"Llanfairpwllgwyngyllgogerychwyrndrobwllllantysiliogogogoch"

Amoureuse

The surprises kept coming in during the early and mid-seventies. I met a gentleman named David Katz whose job title was "fixer." Not like the gangsters in movies or Michael Cohen from the Trump era. In England, a fixer is the agent who books musicians on recording sessions. David rang me up one afternoon and said he had a session for me with a new singer named Kiki Dee. Kiki had not become famous yet, so I knew nothing of her. I always asked David about the producers, first out of curiosity, and second, if I had worked with him/her in the past, I'd follow up with a call to thank them for the booking. David said the producer was Reggie Dwight. Great. A new producer. This should be fun. New producers are always a welcome call and present the possibility of expanding my network. I had no idea who Reggie Dwight was. I know. You've seen *Rocket Man*, so you already know the joke. Shhhh. Don't tell anyone.

Fast forward to the day of the session. I pulled into the studio parking lot next to a powder blue Rolls Royce. The song "Who could it be now?" comes to mind. It was a single studio at this location, so the owner had to be someone on our session. I wondered if Mick Jagger or David Bowie had shown up to sit in. Upon entering the studio, I also noticed two A-list musicians, Davey Johnstone and Nigel Olsen from Elton John's band. Kiki approached as I was opening my guitar case and introduced herself. I stood up to greet her, and said, "It's great to meet you Kiki, congrats on starting your new album."

I glanced over her shoulder and, to my surprise, saw Elton John through the control room window. That answered the "Whose Rolls is in the parking lot?" question.

I said, "It's an honor to be here with you and these amazing musicians. And wow, Reggie Dwight got Elton and half of his band to work with us today? This is really going to be fun!"

She cocked her head slightly sideways and gave me a half puzzled, half "are you putting me on?" look. By that point Elton had come out from the control room and was approaching.

He joined us and said, "Hi, Jim. Nice to meet you. I enjoyed hearing your work with my friend, Lesley Duncan, and thought you'd be great for Kiki's album."

I replied, "Thanks, Elton, I really appreciate that. You obviously must respect Reggie Dwight's work to be here on his session with Davey and Nigel. I look forward to meeting him too."

Kiki moved in and whispered, "Jim... he's standing right in front of you."

"Wait... what? Where? Ohh nooo. You're Reggie? Damn, I'm so sorry! I should have..."

He interrupted, "No worries. Not that many people know. It's become an inside joke."

Yep, bright red cheeks on me along with eye rolls and grins on everyone else. This was 1973.

To the best of my knowledge, Elton had not revealed his true name to the world, so unless you were his friend or worked with him, you wouldn't know it. The song "Rocket Man" was released in 1972, but it would be forty-nine years before the movie *Rocket Man* would tell the story of Reggie Dwight. So there I was. I laughed and did my usual, "Yeah, I knew that."

We recorded a beautiful song that day called "Amoureuse", written and previously recorded by a French singer/songwriter named Véronique Sanson. The song was Kiki's first major hit, initially in England in 1973 reaching #13, then a year later in Australia reaching #12, then re-released in 1976 in England as the B-side of "Loving And Free". Both songs made it to #13 as a double-sided hit and reached #4 in Ireland. "Amoureuse" was reissued again in 1984 and again made it up the English charts to #77. Not a bad run, and a memorable recording session for me, despite the embarrassing beginnings!

Regarding Elton's stage name from 1960 to 1967, Reginald Dwight was the keyboardist in a band called Bluesology. In 1966 they added Long John Baldry on lead vocals, and the saxophonist Elton Dean. When the band split up, Reggie reinvented himself as a studio musician and songwriter, borrowing Dean's and Baldry's first names, hence Elton John. Remember earlier I said Buddy Holly was a huge influence to more people than me? Though he had normal sight as a teenager, Elton started wearing horn-rimmed glasses to emulate Buddy Holly. And while we're on the subject of name changes, Kiki's original name? Pauline Matthews. It began as "Kinky Dee." From her 2019 interview with *Classic Pop* magazine:

"Being young and inexperienced, I kind of went along with it, except I said to my dad, 'I don't think I'll be singing in five years if my name's Kinky Dee, 'so we shortened it to Kiki."

Wild World

As I mentioned earlier in this book, my connection to Cat Stevens came through Carly Simon and began in 1970. Sometimes when you record with somebody like Carly, band members experience a separation or disassociation with their ex-lovers, i.e. I never got to play on any James Taylor records, despite often being around him and his band during his marriage to Carly. I did work with him often on Carly's records. Same with Kris Kristofferson. I wondered if his previous relationship with her made me seem radioactive to him. Was my musical style a bad fit with his? I'll probably never know, but Cat Stevens was the exception to that rule. I received a call from him in the winter of 1974 to come and play on his *Buddha and the Chocolate Box* album. Finally, I had broken the" friends of the ex-lover" curse, and I would get to work with another one of my heroes!

The sessions with Cat were interesting and unusual. He was a very non-technical kind of musician and insisted that we approach the music in a loose and organic way. He would sing the song a cappella and ask me to play from the heart. I wanted to sketch out a chord sheet, but he said no. My memory works better with reminders, but no one was watching the clock. We could take as long as we needed to get it right. If anyone forgot a chord, we'd ignore it and continue. He couldn't care less. I would have been fine learning the songs at his house or in a rehearsal room, but he preferred the studio. Cat insisted that the instant we had a reasonable grasp of the song, that was the time to hit record. He was afraid we might forget important nuances from a previous

Bruce Lynch, Me & Cat Stevens

rehearsal. And so we plodded through the day, learning, forgetting, re-learning and so on. I'm not complaining. I loved working with these people. Cat's methodology ultimately got the job done, and that's all that matters.

Though it only produced one hit single, "Oh Very Young", the album was an enormous success. It sold over a million units, was certified platinum, and reached the #2 spot in the US Billboard charts. Two memories come to mind when I recall that project. The first took place at Air London. We completed the instrumental track for one of the songs, so Cat scheduled vocals for the following day. Though they didn't need me for guitar anymore, I made a point to attend vocal sessions for entertainment and education. Unlike Carly, Cat had no problem with people hanging around while he sang. Paul Samwell-Smith had now rejoined the team, so Cat had a talented and much needed producer to guide him through the vocals and mixes. While the assistant set up a vocal mike, the engineer played back the music track to which Cat would be singing. Cat's keyboardist, Jean Roussel, was there, and we sat in the back of the control room chatting. When the engineer hit play, what I heard disappointed me. I didn't think our music track sounded very interesting, and Jean said, "Wait. When he sings, it will all come together." I don't always consider the voice an instrument, even though it absolutely is. I consider the instrumental tracks as one sound group and the vocal tracks as another. In this case, Cat's voice became the final instrument that completed the song. A few chord changes passed. Then he began to sing, and the transformation was mind-blowing. Suddenly hearing the deep richness of his voice, along with his unique expression and singing style, was like first looking at a stack of two-by-fours, then seeing the beautifully completed house. The voice in pop music is everything. A great instrumental covered by a mediocre singer rarely gets any serious attention from record buyers. On the other hand, a singer with a great voice can pick up a guitar and play badly but tear your heart out with a magical voice. Cat played guitar just well enough to get the job done. It never mattered. He sang brilliantly and was an extraordinarily brilliant songwriter. That's what cemented his place in the Rock and Roll Hall of Fame.

The other memory, which I still have mixed feelings about, came later that year. "Oh Very Young" was topping the charts and Cat decided to tour. I had just finished a series of albums that involved a lot of international travel, including Rome, London, New York and LA, and had reached the point of burnout. That week I was staying at my old apartment on E. 38th St. NYC with my friends, Bob and Bonnie, and Steve (Cat) called me.

He said, "Hi Jimmy, how are you? It's Cat Stevens."

"Hey Steve, nice to hear from you. To what do I owe the honor of this call?"

"*Buddha*'s turning out to be quite a hit, so Barry [Krost] and the record company want me to tour to support it. I'd like you to join us and be my guitarist. Are you available? We'll open next week in LA and do concerts in the US, Canada, Alaska, France, Italy, Denmark, Germany, Australia and Japan. It'll be great!"

"Steve, wow… thanks so much for asking, but I can't do it. I just got back from recording all over Europe and the US, and I'm completely fried. I really need to take some time off, or I'm not going to be ok."

"Are you serious? You're putting me on, right?

"No. I'm dead serious. I'm really sorry, and I'm honored that you're asking, but I have to stop for a while."

"Do you realize what you're turning down?"

"I do, and I'm really flattered, but I'm afraid I'd just be dead weight. I'm exhausted. I'd love to work with you in the future, and thanks so much for thinking of me, but I'm going to have to pass this time. Good luck! I'm sure it will be amazing."

He was angry, and with few words, hung up. Musicians rarely turn down opportunities like this, and for Cat Stevens, this was probably a first. As I sat there on the sofa, gazing out the window at the NY skyline in front of me, I felt rattled by the call but also empowered. I chose to take care of my sanity and health, over being a slave to money and career. Though my friends supported my decision, they were surprised I could walk away from what seemed like such an amazing opportunity. As time wore on, my resolve became a little shaky. I knew many of the people on the tour, and the words I kept hearing were "sold out," "fans going wild," "incredible countries and good times" - I had rejector's remorse. Once I was rested, which only took a few days, the second-guessing went into high gear. Was I an idiot? I could have slept on the planes. Oh wait… I can't sleep upright in chairs. Well then hotels, I could have slept in the hotels and rested up. I'm young. I snap back easily. What was I thinking?

After all the churning and perseverating, I found out I had only lost an exhausting travel experience and some money. The hype was coming from the press, not my friends on the tour. Turning down the tour would not affect my career, because Cat's career was heading downhill. He was bitter about the music business, and at the best of times not a very happy guy. My friend Jock McLain, his tour manager, used to laugh about how on tour, Cat would constantly say to him, "I don't like you." I'm guessing that sentiment was not just reserved for Jock. Despite its success, I doubt the tour was fun. None of the musicians discussed it much after they returned. Cat's disillusionment with his record company and the music business at large caused the anger and resentment to seep into his creative work. He produced two subsequent albums that weren't as inspired as his previous ones and were neither critical nor financial successes.

From Wikipedia: *"In 1976, Stevens nearly drowned off the coast of Malibu, California, United States, and said he shouted: 'Oh, God! If you save me, I will work for you.' He related that right afterwards, a wave appeared and carried him back to shore. This brush with death intensified his long-held quest for spiritual truth."*

After the almost drowning incident, he found his spiritual center, and in 1977, converted to Islam, changed his name to Yusuf Islam and retired. Though his career for the time being was on hold, his life and self-worth took a huge upswing. Islam worked for him, and he was finding some happiness and fulfillment at long last.

And then the reversal. After twenty-eight years of renouncing music as being "haram" or antithetical to his religion, Cat grew tired of retirement. He changed his name again, this time to Yusuf Cat Stevens. With his interest in music returning, he started recording again, and even made it into the Rock and Roll Hall of Fame, oddly inducted on the same night as Kiss! I've never had the opportunity to see or speak to Cat since that fateful night and have often regretted our last conversation. We were friends while it worked for us, and with one phone call, unfortunately that friendship ended. If I ran into him today, I'm sure we'd both laugh about it, and brush it off like it never happened. If he ever reads this, I truly wish him well.

My Generation

John Alcock is an English producer who guided the careers of Thin Lizzy, Alice Cooper, Commander Cody, The Earl Slick Band and The Runaways… and also some unknowns that remained unknown. My first experience with him involved an album he was producing with

John Alcock

a Canadian artist named Neil Sheppard. Neil hired me because of my Carly Simon connection, and I brought in Ace Follington from Bitch to play drums. The project was nuts. John and I both liked Neil's songs, but the album turned into a frustrating mess. Neil kept wanting to overdub more and more instruments until what started off as a nice singer/songwriter offering became a cacophony of over-production. No dis to Neil's writing talent. He was excellent writer and had plenty of credits to his name, but this album ended up a loss. I'm not even sure they ever released it. There's no sign of it on any streaming service, nor is it on YouTube.

Back to John. He and I had similar tastes in life and music and developed a nice friendship over the years. I even dragged him in on my own band, Cottonmouth, which also turned out to be a mess. John scored us some free time at Nova, a first-rate studio on Brianston St. in London, and we went to work recording about eight songs. On completion, we peddled them to every record company that would listen, but no nibbles. Not that we didn't play well. We did, but not well enough. We loved Jimmy Frank, our principal writer and lead singer, but remember what I said about great instrumental tracks with iffy singers? We fit that bill. As

172

studio musicians, we played our butts off, but without a great singer and great songs, it made no difference. One out of three ain't good.

That band fizzled, but my working relationship with John continued. He called me in the summer of 1975 and said he finally had a worthwhile project for me, ran my credits by the artist, and got approval. I thought, ran my credits by the artist? Got *approval*?

I asked, "Who is it we're talking about? The Duke of Edinburgh?"

And in a pompous English accent, he said, "Who, indeed."

"Huh?"

"Who, indeed."

"John, what the hell? Who's the artist?"

"Precisely."

"Will you stop! Who's the friggin 'artist already??"

"Spot on."

"WAIT… WHAT??? THE WHO??

"One of them."

"WHOAH, which one??"

"John Entwistle."

Ok, not the whole band, but damn, Entwistle was one of the greatest rock bassists ever. This news blew me away. The Who were a staple in my record collection. I was a huge fan and had attended several of their concerts. They had crazy energy and crushed it live. Daltrey sang great, Townsend spent half the time airborne and played like a power chord machine, Moon was just completely bonkers, and John Entwistle - the 250-pound anchor that held the band to the floor. In the concerts, they lived up to their reputation with Moon randomly tossing drums over his shoulders, Daltrey hurling his mike in the air then swinging it in circles from its cord on a ten-foot radius, and of course, the obligatory trashing of their instruments at the end of the show… all but Entwistle. Again, the anchor. Also the sane one.

Back at Nova for the recordings, John Entwistle played bass and sang lead vocals, Graham Deakin played drums, Tony Ashton of Ashton, Gardner and Dyke manned the piano, and I played acoustic and electric guitar. Both Johns wanted a small, self-contained band for this recording and that's what they got… sometimes. This was a drinking band that could usually hold their liquor, but not always. The troublemaker? Entwistle himself. His assistant would always follow him into the studio carrying a case of Remy Martin Champagne Cognac. A case, not a bottle. No, they never finished a case, but they damn well tried on several occasions. By then, yoga and meditation informed my choices, so I rarely took part in the libations. And never anything like Entwistle or Tony Ashton. We had to accomplish something in the first hour, because after that, Tony would be asleep on the control room sofa. John held his own pretty well, but sometimes he and Tony just couldn't keep it together. Then the sessions would deteriorate into silly pub jokes and even sillier jamming.

John Entwistle could be a little awkward - smart, thoughtful, a killer bass player, but very quiet. We didn't have much in common beyond music, so our conversations were minimal. I grew up in genteel US suburbs and played with soft rock artists like Carly, Cat, Croce and The Critters. He grew up in a tough neighborhood in West London, spent time as a tax inspector, and in 1976, his band, The Who, made the *Guinness Book of World Records*, recognized as the loudest band on the planet. At a London concert that year, their sound level reached 126 decibels. 110 dB marks the threshold of pain, and 130 dB is agonizing and can cause permanent hearing damage. So yeah, 126 dB. In the end they all had hearing loss, especially Pete Townshend. By contrast, at that time I was in the south of England training to be a TM teacher, spending much of my time in silent meditation. How did we end up in the same band?? Never mind, I loved this guy and loved his other band (The Who) and didn't care if we never discussed our inner existential consternations. Just playing with him was good enough for me. So, he and I kept the conversations to the music, and I sat by as these guys got wasted every night. I tried not to be judgmental, but just the fact that I rarely joined them could have caused some distance to grow between us.

John Entwistle

I had a funny interaction with him towards the end of the project. The Who were going to be playing in London. They'd be performing *Quadrophenia*. I didn't love this album, but having now worked with Entwistle, I thought it would be fun to see him back in his natural environment, thrilling his fans and shredding their eardrums. He gave my wife at the time, Maggie, and me prime-circle tickets and we showed up excited and armed with earplugs. The Who began their show with familiar material from the past, then broke into *Quadrophenia*. Again, neither Maggie's nor my favorite, so after about an hour of waiting for them to play something/anything we liked, at less than deafening volume, we bolted. So far, so good. We enjoyed the earlier part of the concert, and they were still an amazing band, despite *Quadrophenia*. We removed our earplugs and drove home, happy to have enjoyed a free concert by a world-famous band.

I saw John in the studio the following evening and complimented him on the show, especially his playing. He was flattered and thanked me, and I should have stopped there. But I didn't.

I said, "And I noticed Townsend didn't break his guitar!"

His smile turned to a frown. He looked at me with a bit of a knowing squint and said, "Course he did."

Insert foot in mouth. Pete Townshend breaks his guitars at the end of their concerts. We left before the end of the concert. I'm recording with John Entwistle of The Who, the man who personally gave me complementary tickets to see his band, one of the greatest rock bands in history, and now he knows I walked out on his concert. Bloody hell. This was almost a Darwin Award faux pas. What was I thinking? John was not the kind of person who would make a scene, but I will say that the vibes in the studio that night did not rise to warm and fuzzy. Fortunately no one else heard our conversation, or they would have called security and had me escorted out of the building.

That was our last session, not because of the *Quadrophenia* concert fiasco, but because the backing tracks were done. He no longer needed us. Time heals, and memories are short. I ran into him at Manny's Music Store in NYC in 2000, and it felt like a welcome back reunion. We chatted for about fifteen minutes, while Henry, the store owner, took our picture for his wall of stars. We laughed about the Remy Martin and Tony Ashton's snoring louder than the studio playback, and he actually asked what I had been up to. John was not the reserved person I had worked with twenty-five years earlier - he was very open and forthcoming, a pleasant surprise and affirmation that people can change. Sadly, we lost him on June 27, 2002, the day before The Who's scheduled first date of their 2002 tour. He died early in the morning of a heart attack. Cocaine was originally cited as the cause, but after an autopsy, they discovered he had three blocked arteries and was suffering from severe heart disease. The cocaine was minimal and not life threatening. The heart disease was deadly. RIP, my friend.

Hit The Road Jack

In 1975-1976, I took a six-month sabbatical to become a meditation teacher. The course was taught in residence at a beautiful estate called Royden Hall, in the heart of the English countryside. It was an amazing experience, but a story for another book. Suffice to say, I was refreshed and ready to get back to work when the course completed. After a few weeks of practice, I was back on top of my game, and Jimmy Horowitz topped my to-call list. I reached him at his home, and my timing was perfect. He had scheduled a four-week tour with Lesley Duncan and offered me the gig. GM, Lesley's record company, wanted to promote *Moonbathing*, our second album together, and they were willing to support a tour.

We rehearsed for about a week then hit the road on our fun and often strange tour. Though GM Records agreed to promote the *Moonbathing* album, the tour proved to be an uphill struggle. With Lesley being virtually unknown in the US, every gig became an exercise in winning over a yawning audience. In one case, we were the support act for Hall & Oates. On that night, H&O's roadies seemed to be suffering from delusional star complex, unwilling to move their equipment one inch to accommodate ours. They insisted we set up in an awkward downstage formation that neither looked nor felt good. To our anger and frustration, their sound engineer kept our volume lower than the talking crowd. He didn't want us to interrupt those important conversations filling the time until Daryl and John hit the

Jimmy Horowitz

stage. And when they did, the volume magically rose to wall shaking, concert volume, and all conversations deferred to the music. After our show, we had the idea of letting the air out of their equipment truck tires, or maybe spilling beer on the driver's seat. We didn't do it, but we enjoyed the thought.

Don McLean joined us for a second concert and reprised his

wonderful set from the Royal Albert Hall. With just his voice and acoustic guitar singing "American Pie"," And I Love You So" and "Vincent", he had the audience feeling like they were sitting around the fireplace in his living room. At one point he divided the audience into three sections, singing a round with words from Psalm 137, "By the waters of Babylon…". To hear a thousand voices overlapping on these biblical words with an enchanting melody accompanied by one acoustic guitar was a consciousness altering experience. It's a good thing we opened that show. Closing it would have not gone well. We held our own though. This was our kind of audience, and anyone who loved Elton John knew Lesley's "Love Song". Once we played it and the Elton connection was made, everything improved.

This brings up the subject of intelligent routing. When promoting an unknown artist, it is so important to pair them with similar groups. Hall & Oates and Lesley Duncan were an epic mismatch. Soft acoustic acts have no place in a loud pop concert. The agent's excuse is" It will give you exposure," i.e. you'll be seen with a famous act which can expose you to audiences that wouldn't normally see you, but it can often go badly. With the wrong headliner, you're singing to audiences who have no desire to see you, nor buy your records. We were about as appealing to Hall & Oates' audience as catchup on a root beer float.

On a better note, we played a couple of the venues that I had played with Carly, including The Quiet Knight in Chicago. Thankfully it was June, so no frozen diner windows, and this time we skipped the Playboy Mansion. This gig went very well, because *that* venue often features artists like Lesley, inexpensive tickets and audiences that are open to exploring new music.

We also played a country and western club near Estes Park, Colorado. Lesley's only country roots came from the Yorkshire Moors. What a bizarre experience! She looked good in her stage outfits, but you would not mistake her for a Victoria's Secret model. Lesley had a toned-down beauty with great intelligence and a dry British sense of humor. When she stepped on stage, we had one of those crazy WTF moments. The cowboys started yipping, whistling and shouting like they expected some kind of burlesque show. Undaunted, Lesley stepped up to the mike and said, "Do you mind if we play a little music before I take my clothes off?"

That single line won the house. This venue would normally start up the mechanical bull and turn their backs to the stage if they didn't like you. With that line delivered in a Yorkshire accent, she won these cowboys over, big time.

As I said earlier, in all the years I've been a musician, I find I remember more details from the personal interactions with band and studio mates than the recording sessions or concerts. Jimmy Horowitz was and probably still is an incredible chef, throwing dinner parties with food that rivaled world class restaurants. I remember him being a little shy but with a delightfully dark sense of humor, cracking me up on so many occasions. He is also a talented pianist and classical music historian as well as a super easy going record producer. With Lesley, I remember long, personal conversations about spirituality and self-development. Her songs were well-written personal confessions with deep insight, and our talks never wandered far from the heart and soul. I will remember her as a kind, deeply spiritual person who often had my back in moments of self-doubt. I returned to NY in 1976, and we lost touch after that. Lesley passed away in 2010. Sadly, I never got to tell her how much I enjoyed our brief time together. I stay in touch with Jimmy through Facebook and he's doing well, a cancer survivor, remarried and living in Austin, Texas.

Chapter Six
Back in The USSA

Is This A Cool World Or What?

In September 1981, I attended a party and noticed a familiar face, someone I didn't know but had seen on stage. It was Karla DeVito. I loved the band Meatloaf, and my old friend from The Critters, Paul Glanz, was Meat's keyboard player. Karla DeVito was one of his backup

Karla DeVito

singers, and I wanted to meet her. No one around her looked familiar, so who would introduce me? I would. I just strolled over and jumped in at the deep end. As I approached, she gave me a big welcoming smile, putting me at ease. I opened with: "I'm a huge fan of yours. My friend Paul Glanz played keyboards with you when you guys played the Garden State Arts Center. Man, Meatloaf had a set of lungs, and I loved your version of 'Paradise By The Dashboard Light'."

She said, "Thank you! How do you know Paul?"

I said, "Paul and I were members of The Critters, The Crazy World of Arthur Brown, and worked for several years with Carly Simon."

She then threw me a curve ball: "I'm heading out on tour for my first solo album soon, and we're auditioning players. Are you free? Would you be interested in auditioning?"

Boom! Unexpected and sorely needed. Maggie and I had just bought a vintage clothing boutique called The Good Old Days, where she had worked for a few years, and the owners had retired. We took out a whopper of a loan, with no guarantee of the store's success. For Karla to be offering me the possibility of a record company sponsored tour was a gift and a blessing.

I can't emphasize this enough. I have often networked and cold-called until my phone dialing finger was blistered and numb, with little success. On the other hand, fate always seemed to bring in many more gigs than my hustling attempts. It's almost as if need, combined with being open to new career twists, landed me in amazing but unexpected situations. Who knows if this is universal or just my "karma?" Just to review: I looked up my girlfriend's cousin when I moved to Westfield in 1962 and landed a gig with The Vibra-Tones, which led to The Critters, which led to three top forty hits before I turned twenty-one. My last Critters keyboardist, Paul, led me to a tour with Arthur Brown. When I needed money, I wasn't picky, I took a job at Dan Armstrong Guitars and met Carly Simon. The number of gigs that arose out of that meeting is staggering. I also met Charlie Brown, Dan's guitarist friend, who gave me the hottest play on Broadway, *Hair*, to be in and supplement my guitar store income. Now I'm hanging out at a party and see someone who I admired, walk up to her looking for nothing more than to express my admiration for her work, and she invites me to audition for her band. She gives me the details on a paper napkin, we shake hands and move on to other conversations.

A few days later, I showed up at the place on the napkin, SIR (Studio Instrument Rentals), the big rehearsal venue in NYC, and there was Jeff Southworth, an excellent guitarist, also auditioning. I thought this could be tough, but I gave it my best. After the audition, Karla and her manager, Sam Ellis, took me aside, and were complimentary but resolute. They thought Jeff's playing suited her style better. I asked if they needed a rhythm guitarist. They said they already had one, Russ Shirley, who had auditioned earlier.

Karla then said, "Didn't you play bass on some of Carly Simon's records?"

Of course I said, "Yes."

"Well, why don't you be our bass player? We won't even make you audition."

Ok, that works. The job was mine if I wanted it. I said, "Yes."

The next conversation involved salary negotiations with two managers, Winston Simone and Sam Ellis. They offered me $250/week. Not per show. Per week. Were they kidding? I wanted to pass, but couldn't. Maggie and I had a mortgage on our new store in the Village and rent on our apartment. My calendar was otherwise empty, so I took the gig.

I enjoyed performing with Karla and her band, but once again, the travel was brutal. With a low touring budget, financial decisions always favored lean and mean. We drove everywhere in an RV - not a tour bus, not a plane - an RV. Everyone on the tour rode in this RV except the two roadies, one of whom was her brother. They drove and managed the equipment rental truck. Talk about torture. Everyone in the band smoked except me. I had to spend the lengthy rides between gigs at a semi-open window to not constantly be inhaling secondhand smoke. It was winter, so sitting in a powerful draft for hours on end felt like downhill skiing in a T-shirt. It also created some acrimony. When asked to close the window, I'd respond, "Sure, as soon as everyone puts out their cigarettes." No one did. Stalemate. This rankled some members of the band, but I didn't care. To breathe smoke in a closed area for hours on end is a terrible idea, regardless of whether you smoke or not. It can damage your voice, and we had to sing - every gig.

We all got along pretty well, so other than the smoke/window issue, we had no social problems. We were also an excellent band with few musical disagreements. Karla, being a positive, cheerful person, was the light that kept everything running on a happy keel.

Perhaps the biggest problem with this tour was the album - no hit singles. She had somewhat of reputation for her tours with Meatloaf, and a starring role on Broadway in *Pirates of Penzance*, so that brought in the curious fans, but she didn't have that breakout hit like Meatloaf with "Bat Out of Hell". As such, we did ok, but we never killed it. We just busted our butts for very little money. Driving from NY to gigs throughout the Midwest felt like an even worse version of the *Where The Action Is* tour, where we had big stars with hit records, and it was summer.

Our tour included Boston, New Haven, Philly, Cleveland, Chicago and many points between, but the standout gig for me - New Year's Eve, 1981. Karla's record company and managers double booked us. With guaranteed crowds and proven promotional value, it made good sense. We would bounce between The Bottom Line in Greenwich Village, NY and the MTV New Year's party at the Hotel Diplomat on West 43rd Street. The crew outfitted two stages with duplicate sets of equipment, and we'd zip back and forth between venues, performing the same show four times for four different audiences. Imagine - a full show at The Bottom Line with an encore, rush into the dressing room, maybe change, probably not, pile into cars, whisk uptown and hit the stage at the Diplomat. Ninety minutes later, back to The Bottom Line and repeat. It was a literal sweat and adrenaline marathon. Oddly, it was also fun. These crowds were on a New Year's Eve bender and cheered us like we were Led Zeppelin. An air of excitement surrounded these gigs that topped all others on the tour. I don't think I slept much that night. All that adrenaline had me so wired I came home with my head throbbing and my body shaking.

John Belushi showed up that night at the MTV party. All the performing artists were in the large backstage area used for greeting and smaller events. That night we used it for a lounge/dressing room/meet and greet space. John staggered in, looking confused and ill at ease. I was a big fan, but from the look of him, I decided this wasn't the best time to introduce myself. You know, don't try to pet a snarling mountain lion with a thorn in its paw. I stood nearby and observed. Karla gave him a hug, smiled and said something pleasant. His response:" Shut the fuck up and get me some drugs."

She knew him well enough to not take offense and just laughed it off. They had a few words, and it's possible he was half-joking with her, but who knows? That was the kind of character he sometimes portrayed on *Saturday Night Live*, so I gave him the benefit of the doubt. That was it. We went back upstairs, did our show, and he was gone when we returned. He did finally find someone to get him some drugs. Three months later, on March 5, 1982, he ended his life, having taken an accidental overdose of cocaine and heroin.

Love at the Diner

In June 1982, I stumbled into what I would call a miracle. Fate, being in the right place at the right time, and dumb luck took my career through a fascinating twist and some of the most fun I can remember on any stage. I got a call from a friend - a former band mate and fellow studio singer, Holly Sherwood. Holly was one of Jim Steinman's favorite backup singers, having sung on "Total Eclipse of the Heart" and just about everything else Jim had written and produced for artists like Bonnie Tyler, Barbara Streisand, Barry Manilow and many others. I picked up the phone and the conversation went as follows: "Hey hon, there's a Broadway show in town holding auditions. The original cast landed a TV series, and they need replacements for the show. I'd like to give it a try. Do you have time tomorrow to meet me at the theater and back me up on guitar?"

My day was clear, and it seemed like a fun thing to do, so I agreed. The play was *Pump Boys and Dinettes*, a Broadway hit and Tony nominee.

I packed up my Martin and met Holly at the Princess Theatre. Broadway was familiar territory for both of us, me with *Hair*, and her having been a child star. Back in the day, she thrilled audiences with her performances in the Broadway revival of *Annie Get Your Gun*. Today, she felt confident and collected. We entered the theater and worked our way down the long aisle to be greeted by three gentlemen sitting in the fifth row. They welcomed us and invited Holly to climb up on the stage and do her stuff. We'd prepared a couple of songs in various styles, so I quickly tuned and hit the opening chords of the first one. She tried to sing but could only honk. They were not holding goose auditions that day, so eyebrows went up as they glanced at each other. Holly was recovering from bronchitis, and the recovery hadn't gotten very far. We tried again. I played a few chords to introduce another song, but it was futile. She could barely sing a note. With embarrassment and profound apologies, she left the stage. I kneeled down to put my guitar back in its case, but they halted me.

"Excuse me, what's your name?"

"Jimmy Ryan."

"Jimmy, before you go... we're also auditioning men. Do you sing?"

Holly glared at me, turned and left without a word.

I said, "Uh, yeah, I do..."

"Would you like to audition?"

"Well... sure. Ok. Why not? I don't have anything prepared, but what the hell. Let's see... How about this...?"

And I played a Moody Blues song.

They applauded and thanked me. One of them asked, "Can you do an old-time rocker? That would be more appropriate for our needs."

I chose the Chuck Berry song "Johnny B. Goode".

Again, applause. Then came the surprise that parted the clouds:

"Love it. Thanks so much for auditioning. Can you come down here

Me in front of the
Princess Theater, 1982

and give us your contact info? We'd like to have you back next Wednesday to read. Are you available?"

I would clear my calendar for this one. "Read" meant they wanted to audition my non-existent acting skills. Of course I agreed, feeling I had nothing to lose. I figured "reading" would end my charade, but it would be fun to try just for the experience. They also wanted me to perform two more songs so others on the team could weigh in the following week. I didn't have high hopes, but I did my homework. They gave me the script and highlighted my parts, so I practiced for hours each day in front of a mirror with Maggie as my acting coach. Wednesday arrived, I stood on that goose-honk stage of the previous week and read my lines well enough to have them once again applaud. Then came the request for the two new songs. *Pump Boys* had a country-rock theme, so I chose "A Rose and a Baby Ruth" by George Hamilton IV. It's a fifties ballad that I used to love. That day, they loved it too. They asked for a fifties rocker, so I screamed out "Long Tall Sally" by Little Richard. It closed the deal. I had passed the audition to join the cast of a Tony-nominated Broadway play, *Pump Boys and friggin 'Dinettes*.

What a hoot! I never even attempted to perform in a school play, and my first acting job would be a high-profile, award-winning Broadway show. I had to laugh at the absurdity and the dumb luck. Professional actors spend years perfecting their craft, and many get nowhere. I'm not surprised Holly didn't speak to me for a long time. She sourced this gig and would have been great but for a lethal dose of bad luck. I didn't deserve this, but when it fell into my lap, I took it very seriously. To say I studied my songs and my lines with earnest would be a broad understatement. I was terrified and treated the learning process like it was life and death.

As with *Hair*, the first step was to watch the play many times from the audience and absorb the character being played by John Foley, whom I would replace. I learned a lot in this process and not all about acting. Broadway was a world unto itself. The cast was like a family with all the family dynamics, good and not so good. There were four men and two women sharing one dressing room. Sometimes we got along, sometimes we didn't. More on that in a minute.

Broadway has rules. Break them at your peril. Broadway also has unions, and unions rule with an iron fist. My first mistake during a rehearsal was to put my hand on a mike stand. Don't do that. In this realm, the only person authorized to even touch a mike stand is a union audio worker. If you argue that point, you risk shutting down a production. These guys like their jobs and don't play around with the possibility of the world realizing that a chimpanzee can move a mike stand. Nonetheless, I touched a stand, and a shout came from the wings, "STOP!!"

A stagehand came rushing out, and said, "Sorry man, you can't move that stand. Union rules. Where would you like it?"

I said, "Wow, didn't realize that. Yes, would you be kind enough to raise it up an inch or two?"

He happily obliged. To clarify, I was allowed to touch anything I brought in with me, but theater property was off limits. Once I got used to the rules, it became fun. Who doesn't like people willingly waiting on you hand and foot?

Another more practical rule involves communication. Actors may not comment on each other's performances. There is a specific employee, the stage manager, whose principal job is to deliver all notes and comments. If one actor has an issue with another, they tell the stage manager. Then he or she conveys their thoughts and comments to the other actor, and the stage manager takes full responsibility for the note or suggestion. Performers aren't told who originated the comment, so hostility and resentment between them is kept to a minimum. Meanwhile, the show usually improves with the notes.

It works well until somebody does something so bone-headed, the chain of command breaks down. On New Year's Eve, 1982, we began the show as we normally would, with one slight glitch. Ronee Blakley was the female principal, and Louden Wainwright was her male counterpart. These two carried a lot of the dialog in the play and depended on each other for the flow and delivery of jokes. Before I continue, I'd like to say that Ronee and I were good friends. I had played in her band before this show and was thrilled when she joined the cast. This is not meant to be a deep dig on her. We all do stupid things sometimes... but this one was a doozy.

Ronee had her New Year's Eve dinner at a bar that night and got drunk before the show. Not only was she having a walking problem on stage, she was having a memory problem. She was a popular country singer and a movie star, having played the award-winning role of Barbara Jean in the 1975 film *Nashville*. That night, Ronee wandered onto the stage with alcohol-fueled confusion and wrote a new play on the spot. Louden would feed her a line, and she would respond with something that was off-script, from outer space and not funny. The rest of us tried to not show our horror and embarrassment. All we could do was jump to the next funny song at the nearest signal from Louden. She kept it up for the entire first act. Louden was brilliant. He took her drunken gibberish, turned it into jokes and continuously nudged the play back onto the rails, at which point we would all continue with our lines until she did it again... and again... and again.

During the intermission, backstage became a war zone. I heard Louden screaming at her, hurling an impressive volley of curse words. Mo, our stage manager, was so angry, she didn't even try to interfere. Ronee, wasted and wobbly, just stared at Louden while he shouted. Her blank face revealed nothing, so it wasn't clear how she was taking his verbal assault. Hopefully, she knew what she had done, but I saw no signs of remorse. I believe her response was something like, "Fuck you. Fine. I'll do my stupid lines." She dimly acknowledged that the show might go smoother with no further reading of her alternate play.

Here comes that union again. As an Actors Equity performer, you can only be fired for committing a crime, for example, killing another

185

actor with a prop. Unfortunately, killing a performance with drunken psychobabble doesn't qualify. Hence, Ronee could not be fired. The producers took her out of the play but had to pay her full salary until the end of her contract. Her punishment? She had to show up every night and just sit in the wings like a kid in a time-out. Fortunately, Cass Morgan, one of the original cast members, returned to replace Ronee, and remained until the show closed. Cass was a fantastic singer-actress, and also a co-writer of the play, so it was a huge relief she was available and willing to rejoin the cast. It was just a shame that it was under such unfortunate and avoidable circumstances.

Below is a group shot of everyone who performed in the Broadway and touring versions of *Pump Boys* in the 80s. Boy, did I enjoy working with this group of wonderful, talented folks

The Full Broadway and Touring Cast of Pump Boys and Dinettes. left to right from bottom: John Foley, Malcolm Ruhl, Jimmy Ryan (me), Richard Perrin. Rhonda Coullet, Frances Asher, Debra Monk, Cass Morgan, Shawn Colvin, Maria Muldaur, Ronee Blakely. Michael Garin, Mark Hardwick, George Clinton, Jim Wann, Tom Chapin, Loudon Wainwright III, Gary Bristol, Mike Sansonia, John Schimmel.

Roll The Cameras!

In May 1987, Carly Simon invited me to be part of an HBO special to be filmed on Martha's Vineyard. The production team built a stage on the water to look like a dock and hired a band made up of the best musicians New York had to offer. I'll name everybody, and my apologies if these people are unfamiliar to you. I guarantee you have loved all of them at one time or another as they played namelessly on your radios and TVs behind the hits of the time. Michael Brecker on sax, Rick Marotta on drums, Robby Kilgore and Robby Kondor on keyboards, T-Bone Wolk on bass, Hugh McCracken and me on guitars with backup vocals by Frank Simms, Lani Groves, and Kasey Cisyk.

Everything about this gig was fun. Well, almost. The weather on this little island off the coast of Massachusetts was unpredictable, and this was an outdoor shoot. The film company did their homework regarding rain, and we had none during our shoot, but temperature and wind were another story. Even though it was June, on one of our filming days the thermometer hovered in the fifties. We bought all the thermal underwear we could find on the island, but that was barely enough. If you watch the video, you can see

Me warming Carly's hands

our hair blowing horizontally, and this was not a lip sync. We actually sang and played live with the accompanying chills and cold hands. The picture above shows me helping Carly warm her icy little fingers with which she struggled to play piano and guitar. It felt like my old days in marching band enduring October shivers, just without my baritone sax. They planned to take the best of two days and inter-cut the videos, but this idea blew out the window when the second day hit the seventies. Our spring look with no wind was so different that no inter-cut was possible. They went with day one. Despite the chill factor, we sang and played better that day.

Here's a moment of truth - tricks of the trade exposed! Whenever

Me on the Martha's
Vineyard dock stage

concert shows are created, there is a multi-track recording made simultaneously. They don't record just a stereo soundtrack. The instruments and voices are examined, embellished and carefully mixed in the days after the shoot. You could call it cheating, but I maintain it is an absolute necessity on an expensive shoot like this. This practice saved the reputations of many an artist, and here's how: If someone makes a horrible mistake or sings a bad note, it can be and should be fixed later in a recording studio. People don't want to listen to clunkers. If it's an unrecorded, live show, that's different. You won't be hearing it again, and you might not even notice a mistake or flat note if your attention is elsewhere at that moment. But if you're a fan and the concert is on HBO, and you want to watch it multiple times, do you really want to hear that horrible mistake over and over? With the secondary multi-track, it gets repaired. If the lead guitar is too loud, it can be adjusted. If the background voices aren't loud enough, no problem, raise them in the mix. That being said, there is always an effort to preserve the original live performance as much as possible. But is it cheating to repair career-killing mistakes or out-of-tune vocals? In our case, the multi-track recording was a lifesaver. The Martha's Vineyard wind was blowing so hard across our vocal mikes you could barely hear our voices for the whooshing and rumbling. We had to re-sing everything, or the show would have been a dead loss. The result was wonderful, and no one who attended it live or watched it on TV ever complained.

Let The River Run

Another fun adventure during the late eighties was creating the soundtrack for the movie *Working Girl*. The director, Mike Nichols, a friend of Carly's, hired her to write the music. My part started with Carly and her producer Rob Mounsey calling me in to do a solo on the theme song, "Let The River Run". I brought in my Hamer electric, which has particularly powerful pickups, and went to

188

work. We threw some ideas around, and with Rob and Carly's skillful coaching, I finished the solo in about an hour. I also added a rhythm guitar, which completed my role on the theme. The next phase would be to compose the soundtrack. Over a couple of sessions, I came in to Rob's studio and just created what I would call guitar ambience. This film wanted a sparse score, so sometimes it sufficed to put an electric guitar through a few sound processors and play long notes fading in and out as well as fragments of the theme song. I hadn't seen the complete film, so for me it was just watching a scene, listening to Mike Nichols, Carly and Rob describe what they were thinking and coming up with a part that fulfilled their wishes. It was a productive team effort. Rob is a talented orchestrator, so once my job was done, he filled the remaining cues with lush orchestral arrangements.

Next came the video for "Let The River Run". Since the film took place in Manhattan with the principal characters coming from Staten Island, they rented a Staten Island Ferry for a day-long video shoot. My instructions were to make my way to the Whitehall Ferry Terminal with clothes that made me look like a business commuter. I would start off as

Filming "Let The River Run" on the Staten Island Ferry

an actor in the video and switch to being a musician. Rather than take a subway or taxi with my guitar and clothes, I decided to drive and pull my car right onto the lower automobile deck. The producer also hired average-looking people to fill out the seats and play ferry commuters. While Carly sang the song, I would sit with the other passengers reading a newspaper and bobbing my head to the music allegedly coming from the ferry sound system. When my solo came up in the song, I would throw down the newspaper revealing my guitar. Then I'd stand and do my best imitation of a rock star playing a searing solo with all the usual gyrations and facial grimacing. It would be lip/hand-synced, of course, as with almost all rock videos that aren't live

189

concert footage.

But let's backtrack an hour. I arrived with my guitar and a small suitcase with my stage clothes. I did not arrive wearing them - dumb move. When I asked a production assistant where I might find a dressing room, she laughed and said, "Dude, this is a ferryboat, not a concert hall. Change anywhere you can and be back for filming in fifteen." I tried the bathrooms, but all were repurposed for Carly's assistants and makeup people. It occurred to me - this is a chartered car ferry. Cars are down below with no one in them. Crew and actors will be on the upper decks. I'll just change in my car, a BMW 633, with two tight bucket seats in front and two tiny toddler seats in back. It was going to be a super-cramped, Houdini-level change attempt, but that was my only option. So I proceeded down two flights of stairs to the automobile deck and wandered around sideways between tightly spaced cars, guitar case in one hand, bag in the other, until I spotted my car. Winding my way to it, I unlocked the door and squeezed in, leaving my guitar outside by the front wheel. Next, I dragged my stage pants out of the bag, laid them out on the passenger seat and tried to bend/reach around the steering wheel to pull off my shoes, while not honking the horn with my face. No luck. I needed about six-inch longer arms to reach them. Even if I could get to my shoes, trying to change pants in this cramped space would be ridiculous and perfect for a *Wardrobe Fails* video. The only solution was to get out of the car and change in the open. Though it was cold out, no one was around, so why not? With the narrow spaces between cars, I could just about open the door, gently resting it against the adjacent car.

Here we go: Stepping out, I take off my shoes, push out of my jeans and stand on the ferry deck in my socks and underwear, planning my next maneuver. Through the gated ferry entrance ten cars down, I see the Manhattan skyline retreating over the water as the Statue of Liberty comes into view. I then realize while dreamily gazing at Lady Liberty, I left my stage pants on the passenger seat. Now I'm leaning back into the car, reaching for the trousers, half-naked butt in the air, sticking out of the driver's side, and I hear a soft woman's voice behind me.

"Excuse me, would you please close your door a little so we can squeeze by?"

Startled, I push myself backwards out of the car, banging my head on the door opening, and turn to face Melanie Griffith and Joan Cusack, the two stars of *Working Girl*. Melanie sees my humiliation and terror, and gives me an "Oh you poor fuck" smile. Or was it a grin? Either way, I was compromised. She and Joan were kind enough not to giggle as I stood before them with my pants on the deck. I said something idiotic like:

"I don't always ride ferries in my underwear, but when I do, I wear

Calvin Klein!"

Maybe they laughed or just rolled their eyes. Who remembers? Easing back into the driver's seat, I pulled the door closed as far as I could without crushing my ankles. I was such a mess, it didn't occur to me to pull my feet into the car so the door could fully close. They smiled, thanked me, and made their way to the stairs. What I should have noticed was the actors 'trailer parked three cars behind where they had been hanging out waiting for their camera call.

Though she was very pleasant to me, Melanie felt out of sorts for most of the shoot, having bouts of fatigue and nausea. She was pregnant with her daughter, the now famous star of *Fifty Shades of Grey*, Dakota Johnson. "Let The River Run" became one of Carly's best loved and most recognizable hits. It was a powerful anthem, reaching #11 on the Billboard Adult Contemporary charts, and winning her a Grammy, a Golden Globe, a British Academy Film Award, and the big one - in 1989 it was awarded the Oscar for best original song from a motion picture.

My Romance

In 1981, Carly Simon released an album that her record company never wanted, called *Torch*. It did surprisingly well considering it didn't contain any of her usual modern pop, and only one original song. The rest were covers of old standards. As a result of its success, she took a second crack at the world of legit music. She called me to say she'd landed another HBO special, featuring songs by the great composers of the 20th century, and she'd like me to be involved. There would be an album and a video shoot. Not sure why they called a rocker like me, but no complaints. Here goes the blarney - "Sure, Carly. I'm all in. I love this music. Damn, Cole Porter, Rogers & Hart, Sammy Cahn - my faves!" It was true, but I'd only had a brief, rock-influenced encounter with these composers on that Rod Stewart session back in the day. Time to cram. Plenty of recordings of these songs by Sinatra, Nat King Cole and others could be found at Tower Records so the store became my library. Luckily, the arranger, Marty Paich, sent me the sheet music, or I'd have been in trouble. I could read music fine, but this would be a few notches up from the three chord rock songs I normally deal with on sessions. What a godsend. I studied the charts carefully so I wouldn't show up at the sessions trying to sight read chords like Bbm7b5+13aug8thDim15.

The next fun task would be finding the right instrument for the job. I preferred my Martin, but Carly had other ideas. Her friend, Dirk Ziff, heir to the Ziff-Davis fortune, collected rare guitars. As a favor to her, he volunteered to pull out seven of his best vintage orchestral guitars and invited me to pick my favorite to use on the sessions. I took the subway to his Upper West Side apartment, meeting him for the first time. As he invited me in, I couldn't believe what I saw. Was I walking into a gallery at the Metropolitan Museum of Art? Dirk had seven of the finest vintage guitars I'd ever seen, lined up like toy soldiers on stands in his living room. I didn't think it was safe to touch them, but of course that was ridiculous. He laughed and said, "Go for it. They're meant to be played!" I set to work, moving my belt buckle to the side so as not to scratch their perfectly preserved and polished backs. Carefully picking them up, one by one, I inspected them for tone and playability. The two most prominent ones were a low serial number D'Angelico New Yorker, probably worth about $25k, and an equally valuable Stromberg. My enthusiasm faded as I played random jazz chords and scales on each. Disappointment set in, and I couldn't lie. I had become so used to the sound of my Martin that by comparison, these sounded flat and thin to me. No question, they were superb instruments created by two of the finest luthiers in history, but in playing them, I wasn't in love. The Stromberg was the best of the lot, so I said let's go with that one, thanking Dirk for his generosity.

He agreed on my choice and volunteered to be my roadie. Of course he did. He wasn't about to have me walk out the door with his $25k, coveted collector's beauty into the subway and accidentally drop it on the tracks while a train was approaching.

When I arrived at the studio the following week, there it sat on a guitar stand, polished and gleaming, with a mike set up to record its dulcet tones. Frank Filipetti, our engineer and producer, asked me to play while he crafted a sound for it. He made no comments as I played and played, leaving me in the dark. Finally, he pressed the talkback button and said, "I'm having a little problem in here. Can you move the mike to a different spot on the guitar? It's sounding a little thin."

I put the mike right in front of one of the f-holes and resumed playing like a 40s jazz guitarist.

Again, the talkback: "Jimmy - did you bring any other guitars? Carly tells me Dirk offered you a bunch to choose from."

I had a hunch this might happen and pulled a switcheroo. They'd put me in an isolation booth adjacent to the control room where only my head was visible. Having brought my Martin as a backup, I put the Stromberg down, picked up the Martin and said, "See if this sounds better."

I played the same chords, and within seconds Frank punched the button: "Wow, that's so much better! You found the sweet spot for the mike!"

I replied, "No, I found the sweet guitar. This is my Martin. The Stromberg is back in the case."

"No way! Damn, the Martin sounds so much better. We'll go with that one."

The moral of the story - just because a guitar is well-designed and constructed, vintage and worth a lot of money doesn't mean it will sound brilliant to you. Perhaps if you're a die-hard 40s fan and want to only hear the authentic sound of an instrument from that era, you'd make a different choice. But this was a modern record. We were not using fifty-year-old recording equipment, so why use fifty-year-old-sounding instruments that don't fit the profile of the recording? I will make a notable exception to that rule. Our concert master, David Nadien, played a Stradivarius violin from the 1700s, probably worth several million dollars, and it was magnificent. Its sound was spectacular, especially in the hands of a virtuoso like him. Violins created by eighteenth-century masters are only out of fashion if they're broken. And this is just Frank's and my opinion. Others may strongly disagree, but for this record, the Martin D-28 Dreadnought I bought at Dan Armstrong Guitars for $395 won the day.

Just a little story from one of these sessions - Marty Paich was famous in his own right as a first call Hollywood arranger. Also, his equally talented son is David Paich, keyboardist for Toto, who wrote "Africa"," Hold The Line" and "Rosanna". Marty Paich knew how to take charge of an orchestra. We had around thirty string players on the sessions, and I got to witness a scary display of what happens when a player snoozes on Marty's watch. During a run through of "He Was Too Good For Me" Marty shouted out:

"Stop!!"

We did.

"Second violin. Miss... [she mumbles her name]... I don't give a fuck what your name is. Are you bored?"

Violinist, looking like a wide-eyed panicked rabbit, "No, sir."

"Then why were you looking sideways and not playing your part?"

"I was just..."

"I don't give a fuck what you were doing or why. Get your shit together. Play the page with the rest of us, or get the fuck out. Clear?"

"Yes, sir. SO sorry."

Then in the calmest voice, Marty Paich says to us:

"Ok, folks. Sorry Ms. Second Violin wasted our time. Let's take it from the chorus, letter B, bar 24. Ah-one, two, three..."

And the session continued like nothing had happened. To see some players with faint grins on their faces was both puzzling and amusing. I couldn't quite decide if it was schadenfreude or relief that Marty hadn't shredded them. The subsequent attention to Marty's every word and gesture was so crisp, one could almost feel the crackle in the room. In the past, I had worked extensively with David Nadien, the violinist I mentioned a minute ago. He was a virtuoso and the honored concert master for the New York Philharmonic under Leonard Bernstein. To my great joy, David loved to play on my jingles because they paid more than the most famous orchestra in the USA. He was sitting in the front row when Marty levied the verbal assault on his violinist friend (who David had hired for the date). I asked him if he thought Marty had gone too far with her. David replied, "Oh no. Marty's a pussycat. You should see Leonard Bernstein on a bad day!" Haha, no thanks.

The recording of this album went quickly because we did all the tracks live. The entire orchestra including the rhythm section (drums, bass, guitar and piano) were in the studio, together with the string players, so we rarely spent more than an hour on any track. As I recall, we didn't even need to record any overdubs or fix any mistakes. Frank recorded *My Romance* like a Frank Sinatra concert at the Copa - everything at once, straight through each song. To create a feeling of live realism, Carly sang with us, and the entire recording took three days. By contrast, Roger Nichols, who famously engineered Steely Dan's *Aja*, said they once spent two days getting a sound on a bass drum.

HBO Go!

On to the *My Romance* HBO special. Carly and her director, Kathy Dougherty, chose the Apollo Theater in uptown Manhattan as the venue. With the help of New York's finest stage designers, they turned this iconic theater into a 40s nightclub. Also, they hired the entire orchestra from the album sessions to be the house band. To up the box office potential, they included Harry Connick Jr., a camera-friendly and talented jazz artist with many recording and movie credits of his own, including a Grammy for the soundtrack of *When Harry Met Sally*. Carly and Harry put on a show that many regard as one of their best all-time performances. The songs were classics, we all looked great in our formal wear, and Carly was gorgeous in her 40s evening gown. Regarding the tech, they did not video tape this show. They filmed it like a movie, so it had a soft and dreamy look, perfect for the romantic music. One interesting point - unlike video recorders of then and now which can record for over an hour, film movie cameras require more frequent changeovers. The large, cumbersome reels can only hold about fifteen minutes 'worth of film. So we'd break at those fifteen-minute intervals, inviting everyone to get up and stretch, use the bathrooms, get drinks, and let the crew reload the cameras.

Time, once again, to peek behind the scenes. Harry Connick Jr., twenty-three, already famous and a little cocky, had a self-awareness lapse. On a break, with everyone standing around the set relaxing and chatting, he made a short, tasteless gay comment... on mike, loud enough for all to hear. Did he think it would make people laugh? Did he have an issue with someone on set? We'll never know, but everything came to a stop. Complete silence. You could hear a cockroach sneeze. Many of those present were gay theater professionals. Someone whispered," Oh no, he did not just say that!"

Murmurs began: "Seriously?"

Another:" I'm outa here."

His friend:" Fuck this, I don't have to take this crap."

Stage setup dude:" Either he goes or we go."

Harry initiated a seismic disaster, and the crew, reaching for their coats and hats, were ready to walk off the set. Kathy and Carly had to do light-speed damage control. Kathy gathered the disgruntled crew as quickly as possible, downplaying the comment, saying she was certain he didn't mean it, adding any additional excuses she could muster. Carly tended to Harry. She can be very convincing in a quiet but intense way and laid into him with impressive finesse. Harry, somewhat befuddled, said if he thought a little joking comment like that would unleash such a shitstorm, he never would have opened his mouth. Too late. Because of his words, a crew walk-out was brewing, which could potentially bring the shoot to an end. He had the proverbial blood on his hands and panicked. As the situation escalated, Harry Connick Jr. rushed up to the mike and apologized profusely, admitting to being thoughtless, tasteless and completely out of line. He begged the crew to let it go and come back to work. Between Kathy's coaxing and Harry's apology, the crew calmed down. All realized that a walk out would cost them a great deal of money and lose them a show credit. It could even get them in trouble for contract violation, so they agreed to take their coats off and get back on the job. Thankfully, this didn't put a pall on the affair. The repurposed theater was idyllic, the lighting fantastic, the music beautiful, and within a short time, we were back to preparing for the evening's shoot.

With rehearsal finished and dinner complete, it was show time. In any concert situation, everything changes when the doors open and the audience files in and takes their seats. A kind of magical transformation takes place, and a humming industrial environment morphs into a musical fantasy world. Our fans were in high spirits, laughing and chatting, enjoying an open bar and looking forward to a very special evening. The excitement was not just seeing Carly and Harry live. It was the thrill of being part of a concert that would air on HBO, YouTube (once it was invented!) and internet streaming services for years to come.

For most of the show, I sat with the orchestra. The placement was a little odd, though. They sat me in front of Steve Gadd's drum riser. That put his bass drum level with my head. Fortunately, the music was so low-key, he barely tapped it, saving me a headache and the sound engineer from having to deal with a ton of bass drum in my acoustic guitar mike. I was lucky enough to do a closeup with Carly on the song "No Secrets". She performed it Brazilian style, so I played like Antonio Carlos Jobim. I came out and sat on the edge of the stage while she sang, and the orchestra tapped their laps and snapped their fingers to simulate Brazilian percussion. You can find the video of that song on YouTube.

You're The Love Of My Life

I met Nora Ephron in 1991. Though not necessarily a household name to the average person, her movie making success was formidable. *Sleepless In Seattle, When Harry Met Sally, Heartburn* and *Silkwood* are some of the better ones. She was also married to Carl Bernstein from 1976 to 1980. You may remember Carl as the *Washington Post* reporter who, along with Bob Woodward, exposed the Nixon scandals, which led to the President's resignation. Nora tapped Carly to write the score for her new movie, *This Is My Life*. Carly accepted and got straight to work brainstorming. After experimenting with some ideas, she recalled her Uncle Peter used to sing songs to her when she was a little girl, accompanying himself with a ukulele. She and Nora decided a folksy score based on ukulele would be a wonderful background for this family movie. That's where I came in. She called me and asked if I played the ukulele. Oh, the blarney. "Uh, yeah, of course, sure, definitely. Why do you ask?" She told me about the score, sent me a cassette of her uncle Peter and said the score would be in that vein.

Back to school for me. I picked up a uke at Carroll Rentals and began learning the eccentricities of the instrument. It's tuned similarly to a guitar, but with four strings, not six. I tuned mine with the lowest string, like the guitar's fourth, a D, but tuned up an octave. Otherwise, the fingering is the same. Piece of cake. It took me less than an hour to be comfortable on it, listening to Carly's uncle and various other uke players I could find on old albums. With my experience on guitar, I could do things on a uke that most uke players wouldn't think to do, like throwing in jazz chords here and there and playing melodies on it like a classical guitar.

By the way, I've used the term "blarney" a few times in the book. Not to seem dishonest or disingenuous, I had been playing and studying

196

music for a long time. As such, to be competent in a new style or a similar musical instrument is not a big deal. To turn down a job because you had not yet mastered that style or instrument would be ridiculous if you were confident, you could get the job done in the amount of time allotted. So, blarney? Only if I couldn't do it. Turns out I could, and I did. I hereby self-pardon.

We started the groundwork on the score almost immediately. The core of the project comprised Carly, her keyboardist Teese Gohl, and me. We eventually added other musicians, but it was up to us to knock out the basics. Carly suggested Teese and I come up to her estate on Martha's Vineyard so we might rehearse in a relaxed and unpressured setting. We'd memorize the general structure of the cues to be better prepared for recording with additional musicians. And so up to the Vineyard we flew. Everything proceeded as planned until August 19th, when Hurricane Bob came knocking at our door. Bob hit Martha's Vineyard with sustained winds of 115 mph and gusts of 130. This uninvited monster put a little kink in our rehearsal schedule - a batshit crazy kink. I had never seen nature's fury hit this level of intensity, nor had Carly, Teese, or Jim Hart, Carly's husband. I volunteered that my

Jim Hart & Carly

9th grade science teacher, Mr. Shapiro, said you should open the windows about one inch so pressure will equalize inside and outside of the house, preventing the glass from being sucked out into the yard or blown in to your children or cat. No one believed me, but we tried anyway, and it worked - no windows broke - a lucky coincidence, because after doing some research, I discovered this practice to be junk science. Opening windows does nothing more than allow rain, debris and small rodents to enter your house. The other possibility from my misinformed reasoning - if the wind pushed the pressure in the house high enough, it could lift the roof off. Mr. Shapiro gets a zero.

Jim had a great idea that saved at least some of the day. The driveway in front of Carly's entrance was where visitors parked. A huge, old elm tree grew next to it and provided shade for cars. Jim suggested it might be smart to get the cars out from under the tree just in case it fell, and park them in the open field nearby. While we sat in Carly's living room that evening with the wind howling outside, we heard a great crash and the sound of breaking glass. Carly shrieked, and the rest of us leapt to the windows looking for an exploding airplane. As Jim had predicted, the poor old elm tree was no match for the wind. It came crashing down on the entranceway, smashing through the stained-glass ceiling. If the cars had been in their previous location, the tree would have crushed them. Instead, the entranceway was the only casualty.

The Martha's Vineyard power authority shut off electricity early to avoid fires and electrocution from downed cables, so that ended any notion of recording or use of electric instruments. It's difficult to describe the feeling of being in a large house with no electricity and a 115-mph wind screaming outside for eight hours. You might call it a combination of fear and wonder. Carly skipped wonder and moved directly to fear. None of us knew if her house could withstand the assault. Upon the storm's inception, I was my usual, "Nature is so awesome!" idiotic hippie self and just thought it was the coolest experience. That didn't last long. About mid afternoon the wind stopped dead. We must have been in the eye, as a patch of clear sky appeared directly overhead. Thinking it was over, I stepped outside to assess the damage. In the snap of a finger, the gale force resumed, and a tiny airborne twig struck my face. It stung like a bullwhip and drew blood. After that, I gave the storm the respect it deserved - my wonder and recklessness morphed into "OMG, STFU and stay inside!"

Then came the next farce - our attempt to hook up Carly's very small generator to her very large house. 1) The generator was in a shed or garage outside the house. Someone would have to brave the storm and fetch it. After being twig-slapped, it would not be me. 2) Someone would have to locate the breaker panel, and 3) know how to connect a generator to it without frying the circuits or themself. I remembered most houses carry both 110-volt lines for average appliances but also 220-volt lines for dryers, and heavy-duty equipment. Which would be which on the panel we had not yet found? What about polarity? Grounding? Our little Home Depot generator only put out 110 volts. Any hookup mistakes could produce unpredictable results... like electrifying a refrigerator door handle. In a moment of foolish bravery, Jim dashed out into the wind and rain and got the generator, solving issue #1. As Jim had told us, it resembled a small lawn mower, and would be barely powerful enough to manage a couple of lights and the fridge. Also, none of us realized that before you connect a generator, you must shut off the master power switch to the house. Otherwise, you'll be pumping 110 volts into the grid, lighting up the downed wires and potentially starting fires. You might also electrocute a lineman working on the telephone polls. No danger from us techno-dolts. We never found the breaker panel or the master switch, wouldn't know what to do with it if we had, and... our sad little generator was out of gas. 0 for 3. Candles and prayers for us. Such a lovely, romantic setting with hell's fury raging outside.

We survived the hurricane and got a little work done, using acoustic piano and ukulele, so at least we accomplished something. Nice, playing music by candlelight if you don't mind working with the roaring sound of wind, roughly equivalent to a Boeing 747 revving its engines in the front yard. And... let's not forget, Vineyard water is pressurized by electric pumps. No electricity, no water pressure. Now, think about those toilets. Sit, poop, flush. Poop gone. Silence. No toilet tank refill. Unflushed pee - no problem. Unflushed poo - problem. Carly said there was an old-fashioned hand pump outside by the well. We could take turns going out into the storm carrying the only two buckets she had and hand pump water for toilet tank refills. Or just let things pile up until the electricity returned. Might be a fascinating social experiment. None of us were members of the Paleolithic Cave Dwellers Club, so that idea got voted down. It was the bucket brigade or poo in the garden like rabbits. We chose the bucket brigade, keeping a full bucket by each toilet. Handy for those middle of the night surprises you wouldn't want to leave for your housemates. And... refilling the buckets was the responsibility of the current user. The good news was the storm ended late evening, so pump visits were no longer life threatening. On the other hand, the power outage lasted five days.

Getting home was an issue. We flew to Martha's Vineyard, but due to the extended power outage necessary for line repairs, the airport had shut down. Carly, being a considerate and generous soul, rose to the cause and hired a limousine to drive us back to New York City. You know I love a good limo ride, but here's a little-known fact - limos are designed to look great and be impressive. They are not designed to be sleeper cars and can be quite uncomfortable for long rides. The back seat isn't so bad, but those little jump seats you pull up from the floor for extra passengers? Brutal. The eight-hour ride including the Martha's Vineyard ferry was a killer. My back hurt, my ass hurt, and I was exhausted from getting very little sleep the night before, thanks to Hurricane Bob. My infatuation with limousines ended that day.

After returning to NY, we set to work at Right Track Studios, recording the soundtrack for *This Is My Life*. I enjoyed being a uke player and loved how this unusual instrument livened up the tracks to songs like "Back The Way It Used To Be". As a change of pace from Right Track, Carly booked Eddie Murphy's home studio for one of the basic tracks.

The studio was located deep underground beneath Eddie's estate in Englewood, NJ on the Hudson River. Though state-of-the-art, the studio was like a doomsday bunker, four stories down and decorated in early zebra. Descending to the studio in a small elevator felt like being a hostage in a James Bond movie. I'm not sure how anyone would get out if the elevator broke or there was a power outage. I did not see any stairs. Eddie must have decided the value of the equipment merited an expensive deterrent scheme for robbers. Of course the elevator was key and code operated, so there was a pretty good chance his gear was safe. It was also brilliant for soundproofing. A silent crypt-like environment like this might be good for recording, but for claustrophobics or those with nightmares of being buried alive, Le Studio Murphy might not be the best choice. The thought of earthquake vs in-ground elevators also comes to mind. Anyway, fun to hang at a house that one of my favorite comedians built. The recording quality was first rate, and in the end, no earthquakes, no power outages or elevator breakdowns, so, uneventful.

Now, for that one last little incident - an encounter that took place the day I met Nora Ephron. It was a bold awakening to how a small, seemingly ordinary clause in a contract can become lethal. In Carly's composer agreement with Nora's production company, there were two budgets. One, if everything went to plan, and the other larger budget if things went awry. Things did go awry, and I got to witness Nora telling Carly she was holding her to the smaller budget. Who knows how she rationalized her decision under the circumstances, but she probably failed to recognize a hurricane and a few other unforeseen expenses as fulfilling the definition of "awry." If she held Carly to the smaller budget, the soundtrack would go into the red and Carly would lose money. This nefarious maneuver was attempted via a surprise visit to the studio, hence my presence during the interaction. Nora advised Carly and Frank that she was going to enforce the lower budget. Arguments ensued, tempers flared, and then she directed a thinly veiled threat to Carly if she didn't comply. Frank Filipetti is a formidable six foot two, and with Nora's veiled threat, stood up, stretching his height to about seven feet. Out of his mouth came the roar, "Don't you ever threaten my artist. How dare you?" Nora, being a somewhat frail middle-aged lady, looked like her life was passing before her, and Frank, leaning into her with clenched fists, did not back down. Nora, realizing the situation could impact her physical health, reversed course with words like, "I never meant..." and, "Oh no, please, I think you misunderstood..." You know that sound trucks make when they're backing up? "Beep, beep, beep!" That was the end of the argument, and Nora conveniently remembered an urgent appointment. She hit the exit like Road Runner. A few days later, once lawyers got involved, she approved the appropriate, larger budget, and all was forgiven. It was quite an experience to witness this intense interaction… a little scary.

Indian Fields Ranch

Just a personal note here: Maggie and I split up in early October 1986. We had a good, ten-year run but we both knew our marriage had exceeded its "best by" date, and it was time to move on. I spent about three months licking my wounds and hanging at bars with buddies, but my bachelor days were numbered. That same year, I met my second wife, Avery, at a Christmas party we both crashed that took place at the Mudd Club, a punk-rock hangout in the Tribeca neighborhood of Lower Manhattan in New York City. Can you say "rebound"? Yep. But hey, that marriage lasted twenty years. It fell apart because over the years we grew incompatible, and one other little issue - she discovered she was a lesbian. Two down, one to go.

Ok, back to the main thread! I heard via the rumor mill that Billy Joel would be doing a benefit concert on August 8th, 1991, for the farmers out on the East End of Long Island, and that he'd invited Carly to take part. He would be holding it at Indian Fields Ranch in Montauk, Long Island, and there would be some top bands performing. I couldn't resist. She hadn't called me, because it was a charity, and she didn't want to impose.

When I asked her about it, she said, "There's no money in this, no hotels, no meals, nothing. Are you sure you want to do this?"

I said, "Absolutely. And don't worry about lodging and meals. Avery and I own a vacation house in East Hampton, a few miles from the concert site, so you can even stay with us and avoid having to deal with an expensive hotel."

She said, "Wonderful! Billy invited me to stay at his place, so I'm good for lodging, but thanks! I'm so happy you want to do this!"

She actually felt some relief having Teese Gohl and me along to teach her songs to Billy's band. Also, with her performing fears, she liked the idea of having familiar faces up there with her.

I would have paid for a ticket once I heard which bands were playing. The lineup was The Cars, Marc Cohn, Paul Simon, Don Henley, Foreigner, Billy Joel headlining and his special guests, us! Actress Kathleen Turner would MC the evening. Nick & Toni's, one of the most exclusive restaurants in East Hampton, would be catering the affair, donating a lavish spread of gourmet, French-influenced cuisine and a sumptuous table of every kind of dessert imaginable. Who would want to miss this affair? Hamptons and Montauk residents loved the cause, and every penny outside of production and rentals would be donated to that cause. I was more than happy to contribute my time.

For me, it was a thrill to play with Billy's band during the Carly guest spot, but the equal thrill was seeing all these bands together in one concert. Also, short sets meant no musical filler, no experimental songs, and no boring album cuts. Billy divided the performances into half hour time slots, so each band only played their biggest hits. To hear The Cars perform "You Might Think," "Drive," "Shake It Up" and "Just What I Needed" reminded me of what an impressive legacy they built over the years. Likewise, Don Henley performing "Last Worthless Evening", "The Boys Of Summer"," The End Of The Innocence" and closing with "Hotel California" had people on their feet. Paul Simon sang too many hits to mention, as did Foreigner. Kathleen Turner delivered a moving talk about the fate of East End farmers and the encroaching tourist and vacation crowd that was overtaking one of the oldest and most successful farming communities on the East Coast. She, Paul Simon, Ric Ocasek of the Cars, Mick Jones of Foreigner, and Billy Joel all owned vacation houses in the area, which made it easy and convenient to recruit their bands for the benefit. It also made the plea about encroaching vacationers a bit of a stretch coming from an encroaching vacation house owner.

Of course, there are always a few silly moments behind these events. I noticed a fan approach Paul Simon backstage, gushing about his incredible career, how she loved his voice, his writing, his stage presence, on and on. Either drunk, stoned or blind, she failed to realize she was talking to Paul's brother, Eddy, not Paul. When he identified himself and told her his brother Paul had not yet arrived, she turned the color of a "Red Rubber Ball," apologized and took her leave, tail between her legs. There's a strong family resemblance between Eddy and Paul, so I'm sure this has been an ongoing annoyance to them for decades.

Next, a reporter approached Don Henley as he walked to the artist's trailer after his show.

"Don! Can I ask you a couple of questions?"

Sweaty and barely slowing down, Don replied, "Ok, what?"

"Thank you, yes, ok, so when you're up there singing those beautiful songs, do you think about past lovers to get that incredible feeling into your performances?"

Don, grinning: "Are you kidding? The only thing I'm thinking about is what the hell is the next line in the song!"

He wasn't in a chatty mood, so with that answer he left the reporter standing with his little Sony Walkman and returned to his trailer. He had no interest in further questions.

When Carly, Teese and I finished our cameo during Billy's set, I left my guitar onstage. I didn't know if we'd be called back, so it seemed logical. As I stood in the wings watching, I noticed a woman standing near me, sharply dressed in a cowboy hat and designer everything. Out of the corner of my eye, I noticed she was bopping to Billy's music and was incredibly beautiful, but I didn't want to stare. Where had I seen her before? Oh yeah, now I remember - on the cover of *Sports Illustrated*! It was Christie Brinkley. And of course, she was Billy's wife. That was a fun sighting, but back to Billy. He killed it. Again, too many hits to list here, but a fabulous finale to one of the most entertaining evenings I can remember.

Time to pack up. I hopped onstage as the crowd was dispersing, grabbed my Paul Reed Smith guitar and walked over to where I'd left my case to put it away. The case was gone. I looked everywhere, thinking it had been moved. Backstage access was strictly policed, so there was no chance it had been stolen, and who would steal a guitar case anyway? I approached one of Billy's roadies and asked if he had seen it. He had. They thought it belonged to David Brown, Billy's guitarist, and tossed it into the band truck, way up front. It was now unreachable. He said he would drop everything off at Billy's later, and to call Billy the next day (he gave me the number) to go pick it up at his ocean front estate. Ok, this was getting better by the minute. I gently placed the guitar on a towel in my trunk.

Billy was having an after-show party, which I really wanted to attend, but couldn't convince Teese and his fiancee who were staying with us to join me. I gave up. We all retired back to my house and called it a night. I was disappointed, feeling it might be a great opportunity to network, but Carly told me later that I didn't miss anything. Everyone was tired, and it broke up soon after it started.

The following day, I called Billy to ask where he lived and when it would be convenient to come by and get my guitar case. He gave me his address and said we could come over now. I was hoping to see Carly, but she had already left. A friend of hers had a Lear Jet and whisked her back to Martha's Vineyard early that morning. It was just my wife Avery, me, Billy and Christie Brinkley. Billy couldn't have been more welcoming. He invited us in, introduced us to Christie, and brought us drinks. Then came a modified tour of the mansion. Billy had a nine-foot Steinway "D" piano in the den, which was so polished and clean, it looked like it had just rolled off the production line. Leonard Bernstein had been the honorary endorsee for Steinway Pianos for many years, and when he died, they passed the endorsement on to Billy as Leonard's successor. They gave him the brand new, $150,000 piano that now had a couple of my greasy fingerprints on its otherwise impeccable lacquer finish. He didn't offer to play, but we were fine with that.

Billy and I met a long time ago in the sixties. When The Critters played on Long Island during our "Younger Girl" days, Billy's band opened for us. They called themselves The Hassles. He remembered, and we laughed about the smoke-filled dives where we played prior to our more successful years. Our reminiscing about challenging times we shared in the past was going well. Then I took my size-twelve foot and inserted it in my mouth so far you could barely see the heel. In the early years of his career, Billy, like me, had signed a death-grip contract with Artie Ripp, whom I mentioned in The Critters section of this book. Artie produced Billy's first album, *Cold Spring Harbor*, and that contract gave Artie a percentage of Billy's royalties for ten albums. Considering the fact that Artie only produced one of the ten, a commercially unsuccessful one, this was insane. Most contracts like this have an end point of a year or two, maybe three. Billy's lawyer should have been disbarred for letting him sign this.

So here I go - "Hey, by the way, we have somebody in common!"

"Oh? Who's that?"

"Artie Ripp."

That bright, smiling face Billy had been wearing for the previous half hour fell into a dark, glum horror of a scowl. This was not his favorite subject.

"What's your connection with him?" he asked.

Trying desperately to get my foot out of my mouth so I could speak, I gulped and said, "Uh… He produced my two hits, 'Younger Girl 'and 'Mr. Dieingly Sad'."

While Billy recognized the songs, I can't say my success with Artie Ripp alleviated the dark mood I had caused. Avery sat quietly on a chair behind us, face palming.

I said, "He's not still collecting from you, is he?"

He looked down." We're almost done with the situation."

The release from the royalty rob was eventually granted, but at great emotional and financial cost to Billy. I couldn't have known that, but I shouldn't have even brought up the subject.

Billy didn't offer much more than the "almost done" comment. And though I tried to steer the conversation elsewhere and lighten things up, the stink bomb had exploded, and I held the detonator. He was polite enough, but I knew our welcome had expired.

Exit time. I said, "Hey, we have friends coming over, so we should be on our way. Thanks for inviting us in - it was really nice chatting with you!"

He said, "Oh no, please stay for lunch. We have fresh crab and a Mediterranean salad that Christie just whipped up!"

Hahahaha like hell. He actually said, "Yeah, sure man, your guitar case is by the front door."

We walked back to the entranceway where my case was leaning next to the umbrella stand. I grabbed it, shook his hand, wishing him well, and we were on our way. On the drive home, Avery opened up a can of "What the actual fuck were you thinking??"

I've spent many years in the self-examination chair. I'm happy to discuss my failures, heartbreaks and disappointments openly, but I have found most people are just the opposite. Billy was no exception. I had no intention of spoiling his good mood, but if I had any forethought in that moment, I'd have kept my mouth shut. There was nothing to gain by linking myself to the most controversial person in his life. Will he think favorably about me if my name ever comes up? I have two friends in his band, so that's not such a remote possibility. With my level of musicianship and experience, I'd be very comfortable playing his gig, and we have lots of common ground. But just that little incident in the back of his mind could kill any possibility of ever working with him. If his guitar player left and the position opened up, it is unlikely I'd get the call. Live and learn.

My Baby Just Sent Me A Letter

Here's where gossip can get you in trouble. First the good part. Carly threw a party at her estate on the Vineyard. She invited Teese and me up to have a fun jam and meet the celebs. She was willing to fly us up in a private plane, and we were more than happy to accept her invitation. We booked our flight and left from Long Island MacArthur Airport, the nearest one to both of us. But a problem arose when we boarded our twin-engine Beechcraft. Teese's keyboard and my guitar amp put us over the weight limit, and they would have to be left behind. We protested to the pilot that we needed the equipment to perform on a most important Carly Simon gig. It ended with him telling us that it wasn't that we'd use too much fuel. With the extra weight, we wouldn't gain enough altitude to take off safely, clearing the houses and trees nearby. He didn't use the word "crash," but the implication slapped us back into reality. With the keyboard and amp stowed at the airport, we set off for Martha's Vineyard and a fab party.

Carly housed Teese in a quaint little bungalow on the estate and me in a beautifully decorated guest room in the main house. The previous year, she built a big barn-like structure on her property with a full-size stage and PA, designed for this kind of occasion. After we unpacked and enjoyed a cup of tea, she summoned her sound mixer, and we did a brief sound check. With no keyboard, I would be her sole accompanist for the planned handful of songs. It wasn't the full sound we had hoped for without Teese's keyboard, so we treated it like a fireside, folksy sing along. No one complained.

When evening arrived and guests started filing in, I asked Carly who would be coming. She mentioned Carolyn Kennedy and her husband, a few local politicians, a few local entertainers and... Jacqueline Kennedy Onassis. I begged her to introduce me to Jackie. It's not that I was such a big fan. It's just the history surrounding her was so rich, it would be super-fascinating to talk to her. Carly remained noncommittal. She said Jackie valued her privacy these days, and it might be awkward. I agreed and let it go.

Carly decorated the interior of the barn like a nightclub, setting up multiple tables and chairs for guests to sit, relax, and chat while various musicians entertained. The party also extended out onto the lawn and pool, so there was abundant space to accommodate her many guests. I tuned my guitar, leaving it on the stage, and found a seat at a random table to enjoy a drink and some snacks. There was someone to my left with whom I started a conversation, but while answering one of his questions, I noticed he kept glancing over my shoulder. Then I heard Carly's voice behind me softly saying to someone, "This is (so and so), and you remember (so and so) from New York..." She was introducing people, and my conversation mate got a little distracted by her. And then she sat the person being introduced right next to me at our table. "Jackie, this is my friend and guitarist, Jimmy Ryan..." And Jacqueline Kennedy Onassis extended her hand:" Nice to meet you, Jimmy, and fascinating that you're a musician. Have you played on many of Carly's albums?"

Here I sat, talking with JFK's ex-wife, a woman who had survived his tragic assassination and who later married one of the richest men in the world, Aristotle Onassis. Where to start? "Hi, I wet the bed 'til I was eight and like to play superhero video games! I also like radios and my pet tarantula." Seriously, how does one start a conversation with such an extraordinary woman? I feared nothing in my life would be of the vaguest interest to this woman, but I was wrong. She kept the conversation going for what seemed like ages and never talked about herself. The minute I answered a question, she had another one ready, and constantly reflected the following amazing trait: I've often found that famous people scan the room while they talk. It's either disinterest in you or insecurity. They want to be sure people are looking at them or they're not missing a better conversation elsewhere. Not Jackie. She never turned her head and never avoided eye contact for one second. Her gaze was soft and appreciative, and she seemed genuinely interested in our conversation. I'll give Jackie Kennedy an eleven out of ten for being one of the coolest, most sincere women I have ever met.

Let's leave the party there. Nothing else that happened that night could match this wonderful interaction. Just a fun fact - Jackie came to the party because she was Carly's close friend and editor. Carly wrote several books and worked hand in hand with Jackie over the years. The Clintons were supposed to be at the party too, but their schedules intervened. I believe he was campaigning for the presidency at the time. Imagine Bill sitting in on tenor sax with us. Oh well, we'll leave that for another party.

Now to the troubling gossip part. I'm almost embarrassed to tell this story, because I should have known better. When Teese and I were in the plane on our way to the Vineyard, we had a brief conversation about the Billy Joel Montauk gig. Carly, in a cranky moment, told me she thought Billy was a cheapskate. He put her up in a beautiful guest house on his estate, but left no food in it - no fruit, no milk, no coffee, no juice, no snacks, nothing. Since she flew in, she also didn't have a car to shop for supplies. I'm guessing with the weighty responsibility of organizing the concert at the Ranch, Billy had so much on his plate, he dropped the ball - a harmless oversight, an innocent faux pas. For Carly, being the modern incarnation of Emily Post, it was just rude. I had no dog in that race, so who knows why I mentioned it to Teese? Just idle talk, I guess. Teese was thinking about taking flying lessons, and in the moment his attention was divided between the pilot and me. As he was distracted, he only heard half of my statement - the cheapskate part, not who said it.

Fast forward. Carly is no longer taking my calls. It's been a couple of years since we've spoken, and I can't reach her. She changed her number, and this incident predated text and emails. What to do? Her manager scheduled her for a signing at my local Barnes & Noble for her new children's book. If I couldn't reach her by phone, I would show up at the signing, confront her and learn firsthand what had happened. Keep in mind, by this time we had known each other and worked together for almost twenty-four years. I lived in a high-rise on the corner of 14th Street and 6th Ave. in Manhattan, which was a six-block walk to Barnes & Noble. I put on my coat and hat and set out on my journey for the truth.

When I arrived, a long line zigzagged through the children's section. I saw her at the signing table, but I made sure she didn't see me hiding behind people on the line. Carly focused on the fans in front of her, so when the last person in front of me stepped up, Carly's eyes remained on the eager fan. She still didn't see me. This would be a friggin 'ambush, and I was excited. The fan thanked her and turned to walk away. Carly looked up and our eyes met. Her expression changed from that of a cheerful, in-demand celebrity to a trapped animal. She had no choice but to talk to me, and I held no book for her to sign. When someone is my friend for twenty-four years, they don't get to ghost me without a damn good reason. I walked up and stood in front of her, then leaned in a bit closer...

"Hi Carly."

"Jimmy! I didn't expect to see you here."

I responded as politely as I could, "I know. That was the idea. You've avoided talking to me for a couple of years. You neither answer nor return my calls. The last time I saw you, we were fine. Please tell me what I did to deserve being ghosted."

She just looked at me. Her face grew a little chilly, and she said, "After all we've been through, why would you tell Teese I was a cheapskate?"

Me: "Wait... what?? What the hell are you talking about? You're one of the most generous people I've ever known. I would have no reason to say that to Teese or anyone else. That's complete crap. Teese told you that??? OMG."

Well, not exactly and probably not intentionally. Let's call it an inadvertent, careless character assassination. Teese had been staying in that little bungalow I mentioned during our visit for the party. He had written a letter to his fiancée about the day's events. She was away for a week, and in those days, if lovers were out of town, they'd exchange letters. Remember, text and email had not yet been invented. Terribly romantic. Anyway, in this letter, Teese did a little gossiping of his own. He said that on the plane, he was surprised I had called Carly a cheapskate. Remember I said he was distracted when I was relating Carly's feelings about Billy Joel not leaving her any food? Teese misheard me and thought I was dissing Carly, not gossiping about what Carly had said to me about Billy. Jesus. Teese placed the letter on the little desk in the bungalow, meaning to ask Carly for a stamp and envelope to mail it. He forgot about it and left it behind. Many weeks later, the housekeeper discovered the letter while cleaning the bungalow. She passed it on to Carly.

I reasoned with her and did my best to present the truth, that I had simply passed her comment about Billy on to Teese, but I'm not sure to this day if she believed me. She did believe in my value to her career though, and called me to play on her next album, *Letters Never Sent*. She called me for two songs, a good start. On the second one, "I'd Rather It Was You", I surprised the team (and myself) by being able to play hammered dulcimer, and when I did the Dobro slide guitar solo, they gave me a standing ovation. With that, I was sure we had repaired our relationship, but I was wrong. Silence for months. I got her new number from a friend and finally mustered up the courage to call her. She was curt and told me this was her private number and asked who gave it to me. I told her and changed the subject to live performances. She hadn't performed for a long time, and I asked if touring was a possibility. She dodged the question, saying she was in the middle of something, and we'd talk later - she'd call me. The call never came. Instead, I received a letter a week later. I had thought to post a copy here, but in the interests of her privacy, I'll paraphrase. She had decided to do six live dates, culminating with the now famous concert at Grand Central Station in Manhattan. When we talked, she realized that the way I mentioned touring, I was really saying, "Why don't we tour?" Peter Calo, a fine guitarist and friend, happened to be in the right place at the right time, had worked with her in the past and got the gig. We would not be touring. Remember what I said about words that are better left in your mind, better left unspoken? I had been a bloody gossip, Teese misheard me, Carly got the wrong idea, and who knows? Just that faint petty annoyance may well have cost me my job with her. She did not invite me to do any of the last couple of years' TV appearances, nor be a part of her opera, *Romulus Hunt*. The last time I saw her was on the *Letters Never Sent* sessions. She finished the letter with love and "Some day, we'll sit down, just you and me and talk about all of it."

I'll end the stories and formidable episodes of my life with Carly Simon on this note: In 2013, my friend Jimmy Bralower, who had contributed drum programming to many of Carly's recordings, had the occasion to work on a project with her. My name came up, she seemed very interested, and he asked if he could give me her email address. She enthusiastically said yes, and we have been in touch by email ever since. An occasion came up for us to meet in person after so many years. Michael Dorf, who promotes charity concerts at Carnegie Hall, created a star-studded tribute to Carly. The date was to be March 19th, 2020. Many artists signed on to be part of it, and she contacted me to perform on a few of the songs. We were to get together while I was in town, hang out and at least in my mind, heal the past. COVID-19 descended on the planet, and as a result, Carnegie cancelled all concerts through the end of 2020. The "Tribute To Carly Simon" had been rescheduled for March 1, 2021. That date has come and gone. We shall see what unfolded, but as I write this, on May 22, 2021, the pandemic is still here, though slightly diminished. I think the earliest this concert could happen would be the fall. To close, I'll say again, Carly was like a big sister to me, a mentor, and in the early days, an unfulfilled crush. I loved her then, I love her now, and I'll leave it at that.

Chapter Seven
The Hit Men

Hello It's Me

I'm going to make a big jump on the timeline now. In 1985 I veered away from being a studio musician and took on a new career as a TV composer. I wrote jingles, TV promos, movie scores and theme music for a bunch of news shows including all the shows currently running on CNBC daytime. I won't list everything here, as this section of my life in the corporate world could fill its own book... and may do just that, but suffice to say, at one point or another, I worked for every major TV network.

But for now, let's climb in the time machine and move forward to 2008. Avery and I had decided to end our marriage in March of that year. The lesbian revelation was a surprise to say the least, but beyond that, we had been drifting apart for a while. Though deeply saddened by my second marriage crashing on the rocks, I vowed to stay open to new possibilities. Within a relatively short time, I met a wonderful woman named Gitam at a spiritual retreat in Colorado. While I was mourning my loss, Gitam became my best friend and coached me through one of the most difficult times of my life. We stayed in touch for many months over email, and then her marriage also ended. To make a long story short, our emails fostered deep understanding and camaraderie, friendship turned to love, and eventually, after the ink dried on our respective divorce decrees, she joined me in New York, and we moved in together.

So now, it's August 2010, and here I am, staring at my computer in my home at 308 Franklin Ave., Sea Cliff, NY. It's a hot summer day with nothing much happening in my neck of the woods. I'm just reading the news and enjoying a latte when the phone rings. I answer and hear a familiar voice:

"Is this Jim Ryan?"

"Yep. How may I direct your call?"

"Jim - It's Don Ciccone."

I hadn't spoken to Don in thirty years, but he sounded exactly the same.

"Don! Wow, long time. What's up?"

We chatted for a few minutes, sharing our adventures over the last three decades, and then he popped a question: "I know I've asked you to re-form The Critters on many occasions, and you weren't interested."

"Yeah. After you went into the Air Force, we ran the band into the

210

ground. With no more hits, few profits and fewer fans, it seemed pointless to continue."

"Understood. I have another proposal."

I groan quietly to myself as he continues...

"I'm putting together a new band with an interesting slant - ex stars of previous bands unite to form a supergroup. We would only perform #1 hit songs. The show would feature bands we played with and records we played on."

"Ok, I'm listening."

"So far we have three of the Four Seasons, Frankie Valli's most famous band, Lee Shapiro, Gerry Polci, and me." (After his stint in the air force, Frankie Valli and the Four Seasons recruited Don to be their bassist. He sang the lead on "Who Loves You" and second lead on "December '63 / Oh What A Night".)

"Wait, you've got Polci, the guy who sang 'Oh What A Night', to be in this band?"

"Yes. We also have Larry Gates, an amazing singer and musician, to play bass. He has a pro-level recording studio where we can record the full band live."

"Are you inviting me to be part of this?"

"Don't want to twist your arm. Are you interested?"

"If Polci is in, I'm in. When do we start?"

"We already have. Are you free any days this week?"

"I've got some time. When and where would you like to meet?"

Don Ciccone, 2011

He gave me Larry's address, and we got together the next day. My job would be to play guitar and supply the falsetto and lead voice of Frankie Valli. That could be a challenge, but what the hell; nothing to lose by trying. What I didn't realize was that this rehearsal would be an audition.

Lee Shapiro and I had known each other off and on for thirty-two years, but Larry and Polci were new to me. With nothing pressing in my schedule that I couldn't work around, I accepted the challenge. I hopped into my car, guitar and pedalboard on the back seat, and headed over the George Washington Bridge to Fair Lawn, NJ, home of Larry Gates. As I entered Larry's studio, the first thing I noticed was everybody's greying hair and wrinkles. Those young, fit, handsome rockers had vanished. Don, Lee and Gerry all had expanded waistlines, while Larry, eight years younger than me and skinnier than all of us, still had some black hair left. The optics could be a challenge, but nonetheless, we did hugs, handshakes and the usual guy ball-busting.

Once the meet and greet was complete, we plugged in our instruments and took a shot at a song. First off, we created a short instrumental track for the Four Seasons song "Sherry". Larry hit record, and Lee counted us in. Amazing. As studio musicians, we all knew the song, but something more became apparent. We played it like we made it. It was every bit as good as the record. Maybe even better! Next, we worked on vocals. During my stint on Broadway, I had trained heavily with a vocal coach named David Soren Collyer. He gave me exercises to extend the high end of my vocal range, and this would be the test. I stepped up to the mike, put on my headphones, Larry again hit record, and I sang in my best falsetto:" Shehh - ehh - ehh - ehh - ehh - ehh - erry - bay - yay - beee…" David's technique worked like a charm, and I sang

Don Ciccone, Lee Shapiro, Me, Gerry Polci, Larry Gates, Russ Velazquez Recording vocals on "Sherry"

the high notes with ease. We stood in a circle around a mike, Lee assigned each of us harmony parts, and we recorded the group vocals. This band rocked, despite the many years away from the live concert circuit. All agreed this would be our top priority.

In the ensuing week, we threw some names around and decided on

The Hit Men, an acknowledgment to the fact that we had all been involved with hit records. The next task was to put a show together. I was now commuting daily to NJ, working hard with my new bandmates to rehearse and polish fifteen hit songs from our respective resumes. On Don's suggestion, we included The Critters" 'Younger Girl" and "Mr. Dieingly Sad". in the set. This was particularly poignant. As I mentioned in an earlier chapter, Don enlisted in the Air Force prior to the release of these two songs, and he and I had never played them on stage together. Now, for the first time, we would, and what a delight to be doing them with the vocals and instrumentals every bit as good as the original recordings. In the Critters 'days, I had gotten so used to the sound of Kenny Gorka's and my failed attempts to sound like our records, I forgot how they *could* sound. Being back in a band with Don was such a breath of fresh air. These two songs were easy, so we didn't have to spend hours perfecting them. The Four Seasons songs required a lot more work, as they were sometimes complicated instrumentally and always complicated vocally. Each one required four-part harmony. Since all of us had worked with Tommy James, we sprinkled in a few of his songs. The bottom line for repertoire was, if one of us had worked with a hit artist, songs by them were legal for the show. The Broadway play *Jersey Boys*, the story of Frankie Valli and the Four Seasons, was breaking box office records in many cities, so our big selling point was we had three of the *Jersey Boys*, the actual Four Seasons, in our band. Hell, Gerry and Don were the lead singers on The Four Seasons 'biggest hits.

In Da Club

Lee and Larry had connections at a local club called Mexicali. It seemed like a perfect place to launch our new band project, with its decent sized stage and a two-tier audience section with tables and chairs - perfect for our aging audience-to-be. We negotiated with the owner for a reasonable fee and started making plans. Larry would break out a small recording system from his studio, including his laptop, mikes and preamps, and record the show so we'd have music for future promos, CDs and our not yet created website. We set the date for November 11, 2010, and our look would be dark suits to emulate real hit men, sans sniper rifles. We did not know if anyone would show up, and we didn't care. This would be a dry run, a live rehearsal for future gigs. Nothing could have prepared us for what happened that night. Speaking of preparation, it never occurred to us to hang posters around Teaneck, NJ, where Mexicali was located. The club placed one in their window, and kept some flyers at the door, but Facebook and word of mouth were our only publicity.

We showed up around 3pm for load-in and set-up. Sound check proceeded well, but a dead channel appeared in the house mixing console, giving us a slight problem. Nothing show-threatening - just an annoying case of slack maintenance, and we had all the channels we needed for our live recording. Mexicali billed itself as a restaurant bar, so the doors opened at 6pm for dinner and an 8pm show. By 5pm, we saw a line forming outside. At first, we thought it was just the usual dinner crowd or just curiosity seekers, but then the line got longer… and longer… and longer, until it stretched around the block. Apparently, our three Four Seasons still had fans, and those fans were lining up in numbers. The show quickly sold out and fire regulations forced the club to turn many sad fans away. Though I hated to disappoint them, it's every band's dream to be that popular.

7:45pm rolled around. Time to put my contact lenses in. Well, no actually. Time to panic and start cursing. They wouldn't go in. They were being brilliant at sticking to every surface except my eyes. I rushed out

The Hit Men - Lee, Don, Gerry, Me, Larry & Russ at Mexicali

of the men's room and grabbed Gitam to see if she could help. I couldn't get away with going into the ladies' room with her, so I dragged her into the men's room. She's an RN, so when anyone came in, I just said, "Don't worry - she's a nurse. We're having an optical emergency!" She grabbed my lower eyelid and pulled it down. With the lens on the tip of her finger, she gently placed it on my eye, and in turn, the lens flipped inside out and wrapped around the tip of her finger. After about six attempts, we bagged it. By now, without any contact lens solution, the lenses were dry and dirty, so with an annoyed sigh, I put on my super thick glasses and tossed vanity to the wind. We hopped on stage to loud cheers and began our show with The Four Seasons" 'Who Loves You". And off we went, cranking through our first of two sets.

Ok, truth be told, I thought we sucked. I had not yet come up with stage appropriate equipment. I cobbled some gear from my studio, but these rack-mount devices weren't designed for the road, and my guitar sound ended up being pretty limp. Also, it's one thing to sing these high notes in a studio environment where you can stop if you get tired, rest, have a drink of water and try again. But when you're on stage with the spotlight in your face, you have no choice but to press on, no matter what. I did, but IMO, my voice sounded weak. Our harmonies sounded genuine and correct, but slightly out of tune. None of us had done this for years, and we were rusty. Don, Gerry and Larry did a good job on their lead vocals, but I felt I needed a lot more work on mine, especially the Cat Stevens and Carly songs. Also, our chatter between songs sounded dumb and self-conscious, often talking over each other and appearing disorganized and semi-pro. Chalk it up to nerves and a fledgling project, but do you think the audience cared? You'd be wrong if you said yes. Tremendous cheers and standing ovations. We knew this was just the beginning, but never expected a reception like this. Our audience forgave our faults and showered us with love. On that Thursday, November 11th, we launched a megalith that would occupy almost every day of my life for the next ten years.

Though our enthusiasm was through the ceiling, The Hit Men got off to a slow start. Despite our individual credits, with no band name recognition, we faced a pretty high wall of resistance. I played with Carly Simon, but Carly would not be on stage with us, nor would Rod Stewart, Cat Stevens, or Jim Croce. Lee, Gerry and Don performed on the biggest hits The Four Seasons ever had, but Frankie Valli did not join us, nor did the stars of *Jersey Boys*. Larry had worked with Carole King, Tommy James and Phoebe Snow, but where were they when we performed? Because the artists we honored in our shows were only names on our resume, we had a problem. We backed these stars up, but for booking purposes, we might as well have been their dog walkers.

Time and perseverance were on our side, and eventually we overcame that stigma. The shows became so good that word of mouth had us packing thousand-seat theaters regularly. In these early days, while on stage performing, I often recalled a famous photo taken from behind the Beatles in 1964 with the audience cheering in front of them. That's what I saw, but this time it was *my band*. I had stepped to the front of the stage once again, and it wasn't just fun - it was exhilarating!

215

Now for some silliness. After we sold out the Broadway Theater in Pitman NJ, where people danced in the aisles and hung over the balconies, BiCoastal landed us a booking at Harrah's Casino in Phoenix, NV. Exciting as this booking seemed at first, it turned out to be an almost comical fiasco, spawning multiple stories for my not-yet-born grandkids. Harrah's is not The Las Vegas Sands. It's a small casino. Very small. The stage began where the bar ended, making it a challenge to not kick over a blender or bottles of liquor while performing. Beer bottles were safe, as they were stored in a glass door fridge under the stage - no danger of punting a Pilsner. A small sitting area and dance floor faced us just past the bar, and beyond that lay a sea of slot machines.

In America, many casinos are owned by Native Americans. Harrah's was no exception, owned by the Ak-Chin Indians. History tells us we learned to cultivate tobacco from our Native American brothers and sisters, and though many of us have abandoned that nasty, addictive, monster of a habit, others enjoy a cancer stick hanging off the side of their mouth while pumping fortunes into slot machines. I was a smoker in my youth and loved it. I just didn't love the idea of lung cancer. Anyway, Harrah's was a smokers-welcome establishment, so most of its customers relished the opportunity to lose money by the bucket loads without being harassed by militant ex-smokers (like me). Now... if everyone is smoking, everyone will soon choke on smoke without an efficient ventilating system. No problem at Harrah's of Phoenix. They keep a six-foot exhaust fan rolling at all times. Where is this six-foot fan located, you ask? Behind us, pulling all that toxic smoke towards us in an endless cloud of lung defecation, while we try to sing. Even with gallons of water and an Olympic vocal warmup before the show, I am dying. The high Frankie Valli notes are killing me. Fortunately, we space those songs out, so I never have to sing more than two in a row, but still...! We include some slow songs in the set too. "My Eyes Adored You" "Can't Take My Eyes Off Of You" and of course, "Mr. Dieingly Sad". Imagine Don's soft voice crooning "You're just too good to be true" and right at his feet, the barmaid hits the blender and BRRRRRRREEEEGGGGGZZZZZ, as it pulverizes the ice for a round of Margaritas... every ten minutes.

Despite our compromised lungs, Harrah's was a success. We had played our first casino, and the owners and patrons were very happy. That was June. By the middle of July, we got some terrible news. Larry Gates, our bass player, had contracted multiple myeloma. He kept it quiet for almost a year, but the symptoms now encroached on his ability to perform. His back almost collapsed, and he desperately needed surgery. Replacing him, or at least finding a sub to fill in, was our next task, and it was a big one. Singer/musicians in NYC were plentiful, but it's so important to match personalities and musical taste when replacing a band member. A recording session is a one-shot deal, so talent is the most important requirement. Bands can go on performing for decades, so a negative personality can quickly become intolerable. We all had a favorite singer we worked with in the jingle business, Russ Velazquez, who was cheerful and ridiculously talented, but would he be interested? He had a good business going in New York, so would hitting the road with us be of interest to him? I put in a call to find out. Russ seemed into it, but his enthusiasm dropped a few notches when we told him he'd be playing bass. Nonetheless, he overcame his doubts and rose to the occasion, joining the band and adding a new, extraordinary lead voice to the mix. One unfortunate caveat - often while singing, he'd forget to play his bass, and the bottom would drop out of our sound. We thought, "all in good time," but then came some good news.

Larry's surgery was successful... to a degree. They glued his spine together. The bad news? They glued it together somewhat crooked, causing uneven weight distribution, so he had chronic back pain. He didn't let that stop him. This band was his dream come true, and he was determined to keep performing with us as long as he could. But... with Larry returning, what do we do with Russ? This issue reared its ugly head when we called a rehearsal, and both Larry and Russ showed up with bass guitars ready to play. Larry, with complete disregard for our WTF looks in his direction, re-commandeered the role of bass player and couldn't care less that Russ was there. No one was sure what to say or do - you know, two basses, one amp. Ultimately, Russ relented, since he considered himself a sub. I intervened, pulling Russ aside and advising him to just sing his parts, and we'd figure out how to balance things later. I wasn't about to let him go, with or without Larry. All agreed that Russ, because of his extraordinary voice, was too valuable to send home, and besides, he enjoyed the gig. The solution was simple - grow the band from five to six players. Why not? He told us he played keyboards and would set to work creating percussion, synth and horn parts to round out the band if we wanted to keep him. We did, and he did. With modern sampling technology, he created keyboard triggered parts that made us sound twice as big. It also enabled him to do solo vocals out front like a modern James Brown, and he took it to the bank. His energy and dance steps were astounding, and our fans never missed an opportunity to tell him so. Everyone was thrilled. We now had five lead singers, exceptional harmonies, and sounded as big as a house with the additional keyboard. Onward!

The rest of summer 2011 entailed small outdoor gigs in places like Chicago, Oyster Bay, and Saratoga, NY, where the world-famous Travers Festival (horse races) would be held. We thought we'd be playing at the Saratoga Performing Arts Center, a beautiful indoor/outdoor venue much like Tanglewood. Silly us for not asking. BiCoastal booked us in a bar with a central outdoor dance floor. The evening brought torrential rain, and because of the sweltering summer heat, no one cared. They danced and danced, getting soaked like they went swimming in their clothes. Fun, but not the big time we had hoped for.

Gotta mention one silly educational moment for naïve me - we did two sets as always, taking a fifteen-minute break between shows. I stood side-stage with Gerry and across the floor at the bar, a woman appeared out of nowhere. She was the spitting image of Jessica Rabbit from *Who Killed Roger Rabbit*, or maybe a cross between Marilyn Monroe and Sharon Stone. Despite her stunning appearance, something seemed odd about her. Who wears a skin-tight, low-cut sheath and spike heels to a funky outside bar where most people are wearing Old Navy? She stuck out like a tomato in a snowdrift.

Gerry says to me, "Wow, now that's a pro."

Naive me replies, "Pro what? Golfer? No way she's a pro golfer."

Gerry cracks up, "Hahahaha, no you fucking idiot, a HOOKER."

In NYC, hookers tended to look pretty shaggy, kind of like the ladies in *Pretty Woman*. This one looked like she flew up to Saratoga in a Lear Jet and just stepped out of a Lamborghini - classy, with supermodel looks.

Gerry says, "Keep an eye on her, you'll see."

"But what is she doing at this bar? Wouldn't she be more likely to hit a fancy club?"

"A fancy club in a conservative town like this wouldn't tolerate her. They'd spot her a mile off. This place is perfect. The horse races bring in thousands of people with deep pockets - everyone here is pretty well off. They're all getting drunk, because today, they either lost or won money. She knows that and knows what she's doing. Keep watching..."

Sure enough, she'd stroll up to a gentleman and start chatting. Then five minutes later she'd walk away, get a drink but not return to him... pause, sip her drink, check her phone, then approach another gentleman like a Victoria's Secret runway model in a dreamy, slow-motion vampire movie. I was too busy gawking to check my watch, but I estimated it was about a three-to-five-minute window with each prospect. Now I could see it, and Gerry nailed it on all accounts. Lady OMG was a top-of-the-line, Ride-her rental. Over forty, casually dressed men seemed to be the targets, while she ignored up and coming young lads in sweats and sneakers, no matter how good looking. After about five unsuccessful sales pitches, she seemed to engage with a medium-height, average-looking geezer, likely in his fifties. Within minutes they clinked glasses, settled the tab and left arm in arm - him like a kid in a candy store, her like a shark in a goldfish tank. Amazing, the unexpected lessons you learn about life while on the road. I was getting the education I never got at St. Cletus Elementary School during my altar boy days.

Still The One

As a rule I rarely played for weddings. For the following gig, I made an exception. On January 24, 2015, an older female fan of ours decided to throw a renewal of vows celebration with her husband of fifty years. Money was not an issue, so they rented Mar-a-Lago, Donald Trump's private residence and club in Palm Beach, FL, and hired us to perform. I looked forward to the possibility of meeting and thanking DJT for his show, *The Apprentice*, which gave rise to a big royalty bump for me on my CNBC financial shows. Composers on cable shows earn minor royalties compared to network shows. When *The Apprentice* moved to the NBC network as well as still playing on CNBC, ASCAP had to pay all CNBC composers like they were on the main NBC network. My checks tripled. Remember, this was 2015 - he had not yet run for president, nor did he show up that night.

The guys in the band who'd worked society gigs pre-Hit Men warned me about this one. I had the delusional belief that they would treat us like royalty. They paid us like royalty, so why not? Well... they treated us like dish washers, serving us our dinner in the kitchen, and it was not the meal enjoyed by the guests. It wasn't quite tuna sandwiches, but close. The Mar-a-Lago staff instructed us to remain out of sight and not mix with the guests until performance time. I ate outside in the warm Florida evening. It was actually quite pleasant and helped me get over feeling like a serf.

Now the fun. No one at the re-nuptials but the couple had heard of The Hit Men or that we would be performing. As far as they knew, two society bands would be providing the entertainment and dance music. Everything changed when we showed our introductory video on the big screens above the stage. We then came out on stage, opening with "Workin 'My Way Back To You" and a medley of Four Seasons songs. I looked out at our previously stuck-up audience and witnessed a sea of "Oh" faces. By the end of the evening, they were practically throwing bras and panties at us. So amazing how perceptions change when someone is discovered to be famous. One minute you're dish washer class; next, without changing a hair on your head, you're royalty.

As for Mar-a-Lago, the decor seemed like Louis XIV on crack. All surfaces in the ballroom, floor, ceiling and walls had been appointed in either marble or gold. For the band, it meant horrible sound - hard surfaces are reflective, causing harsh reverberation and standing waves. For me, it seemed a tasteless and flagrant display of nouveau riche gloat. But... despite my harsh opinions here, I did enjoy the experience. Once we got going, everybody was warm and friendly, and we always had fun when we performed. I'm just not a gold, marble, keep-the-help-out-of-sight kind of guy.

Anyway, it was an odd, surprising and educational outing. One last detail. I love to admire expensive, handmade sports cars. I wouldn't own one, but I appreciate the technology, design and hard work that goes into making one. So, it's a sunny Saturday afternoon, and we're coming down South Ocean Boulevard on our way to the club. Approaching us is a Bugatti Veyron, list price, $1.9 mil. Top speed 253 mph. A man in his eighties was driving, and he was going twenty-two miles per hour, holding up traffic. I appreciate that he had lived more years than Mount Rushmore and had realized a dream come true with his wonderful automobile... but DAMN, MAN - DRIVE THAT BEAST, FOR THE LOVE OF GOD! What I would have given to walk up and knock on his window, saying, "Hi mister. Can I please test-drive your Bugatti? Just a few blocks? Ten minutes, tops! I'll be real careful!"

No Secrets Revisited

Though it had been many years since my last gig with Carly Simon, a very cool event involving her came up on Nov 5, 2016. I got a surprise email from a gentleman named Guy Evans, a BBC producer, informing me of a documentary series called *Classic Albums*. At first I thought it was junk mail until I noticed Carly's name. Upon closer reading, he was preparing to shoot a BBC feature on the making of Carly's *No Secrets* album and was inquiring if I would like to be involved. Of course, I said yes. Would they be flying me to London? How would this work? Once I agreed, he said he'd be in touch with the details.

A week later he emailed me again, asking if I knew of an available studio or music making space where I would be comfortable doing interviews. Of course, my new home studio would be perfect, so I presented that idea and sent him pictures of the space. Upon reviewing them, he said the studio would be perfect. He then asked if I had some free time in the next few weeks. They would send a video and lighting crew to me, and all I had to do was answer questions and demonstrate how I came up with my guitar parts on the album. This was going to be one of the highlights of my year.

On Dec 5, 2016, a BBC video crew showed up at my house with a truckload of recording equipment. I should have realized they're a global organization and have crews available in all the major cities in the world.

In my studio playing "You're So Vain" for BBC Classic Albums

I now lived in Fairfield, IA, and this one came down from Iowa City, about ninety miles away. I led them upstairs to my studio, and we spent the morning setting up lights, cameras and audio, plus makeup. The next step was a marvel of modern technology. The plan was Guy Evans would call me on FaceTime from London, I'd answer on my iPad, and set it up behind the cameras so I could see him, he could see me and direct the shoot from London. It worked without a hitch. He would ask me questions, I'd respond with my memories of the events, and the best part - I got to play my original guitar parts on camera. These would be edited into the final video, interspersed with Carly's and all the other players 'videos and commentary. Not only was this a fun and very special project - it affirmed my choice to move to Fairfield, out of the insanity of the congested, expensive, crime-ridden New York area, and settle in an area with fresh air, wildlife, forests, organic farms and an easy-going lifestyle. It proved that for recordings of almost any kind, location had become a non-issue. You can stream *BBC Four - Classic Albums, Carly Simon: No Secrets* on Amazon Prime.

Goodbye Yellow Brick Road

Most bands go through some personnel changes over their years together, and we were no exception. Gerry Polci was our drummer, and in his previous career, the lead singer on The Four Seasons 'mega-hit, "December '63 (Oh What A Night)". On one of our jaunts to Florida, he met an heiress, the daughter of a former Florida governor, Rhea Chiles. They fell in love and within a few months, he left the band, moved to Florida, and married Rhea. There were personality issues starting to crack our happy-brothers facade, so although we missed his talent, all felt some relief from the rancor when he departed. We replaced Gerry with a powerful drummer and lead singer, Steve Murphy, who brought new life and new performance possibilities to the band with his stratospheric vocals and killer drumming. Upon the advent of this welcome changeup, our sound moved forward a couple of decades, and our audience expanded to a younger generation.

Unfortunately, like many rock bands, tragedy also added to our loss. In 2011, Don Ciccone was blessed with good fortune similar to Gerry's, meeting Stephanie Mennen, heiress to the Mennen Corporation. They fell in love and got married, and with his newfound wealth, Don also handed in his resignation. It was a personal loss for me as he was my lifelong friend, fellow Critter and college roommate, and added an essential voice and personality to the band. We all came to love Stephanie as well, so it was a double loss no longer having them around. Sadly, Don's retirement and good fortune were short-lived. On October 8, 2016, he suffered a massive heart attack, and his life came to an end. We mourned the loss of our friend and brother, but as we bid him farewell, we knew in our hearts there was more tragedy right around the corner. Larry Gates, our bass player, was still battling multiple myeloma, and the odds were not in his favor. Again, tragedy struck. On December 29 that same year, Larry passed away peacefully in his home with his wife and daughter by his side.

Though the losses took their toll on our ambitions, we decided the show must go on. Our time in the spotlight had not yet ended, and The Hit Men continued to book dates into the ensuing years. We replaced Larry with an amazing bass player/singer named Jeff Ganz. Jeff had a multi-page resume and a quirky and fun personality, and he immediately fit in like a founding member. With the loss of Don, Larry and Gerry, and the addition of Steve and Jeff, we left our Four Seasons roots behind and became the new champions of classic rock - still The Hit Men, but no longer a golden oldies band.

In early 2020, PBS, along with several theaters, asked me if I had a video of the full Hit Men show. I did not, but I liked the idea of creating one. American Public Television videoed our show at Mohegan Sun Casino in 2013 with the original Hit Men. They used it as a fundraiser, which also promoted us, and theaters posted it on their websites to generate excitement and sales for our upcoming shows. It worked very well, so why not do it again with the new band members? Everyone loved this idea, and we decided to spend some money. One of our editor friends recommended a reasonably priced video production company out of Miami. We called them, hammered out an agreement and a price, and hired a four-camera video team. They would shoot us on March 5, 2020 at the Barbara B. Mann Performance Hall in Fort Myers, FL.

On the day of the shoot, everything looked top notch, including the crew showing up early, scoping out the best locations and camera angles. We had a preproduction meeting with the company a few days earlier, where I described what we wanted and nailed down the logistics. We performed as we always did, assuming our songs, stories, video backdrops and interactions would be brilliantly captured in 4K ultra high-definition video. Though I was anxious to see the footage after the show, the crew left before I could catch them. It took several days to offload the shoot to a hard drive, as there was just short of a terabyte of data - 4K video creates very large files. They agreed to FedEx the hard drive to us as soon as the transfer was complete.

A week later, I received a one-terabyte hard drive with the footage from each of the four cameras that had captured our show. It was a complete and utter fucking disaster. I instructed the production company to always shoot wide and capture the whole band. Then I'd zoom in on the right guys at the right time in the edit. This info never made it to the camera operators. Instead, they panned around the stage, zooming in and out with no coherent plan, often missing the important moments by focusing on the wrong band member. I expected brilliant color and sharp focus. Instead, I got dull, washed-out color and lots of blurring and jitter. I asked them to be sure to capture the standing ovation at the end and take plenty of shots of the audience having fun. They gave me about twenty seconds of audience, and two standing ovations went by with all cameras on us, not the audience. And how about a dramatic moment in "I Want To Know What Love Is", where the camera zoomed in on a couple in the audience staring at their phones? In the end, there were few usable audience shots, again with the constant panning, jiggling and blurring. I wanted to scream. We had just dropped about five grand, and somehow, I had to cobble together a riveting one-hour show out of this mess. Florida State University and PBS were waiting...

It took three months to assemble something worth looking at, and it was a monster, eight-hours-per-day, seven-days-per-week job. For the first two weeks I was tearing my hair out and cursing. I had to hand-add color where there was none. The theater had minimal, boring lighting, so I had to use graphics to create artificial lighting. I even created faux lasers. Our video backgrounds were so washed out by the house lights, I had to superimpose the original videos over the on-camera backup screens to make them look acceptable. The hand-held camera had the most interesting shots but didn't use "steady cam," so it looked like he was shooting on a pogo stick. I had to correct the jerking around one frame at a time. There are twenty-five video frames in one second, so a five second jittery clip required one hundred and twenty-five corrections. The biggest faux pas - they did not connect the cameras to the PA system, so there was no usable audio - on a live concert shoot!! We had many excellent live audio recordings from other concerts, but no two performances were ever exactly the same - tempos wound not be in sync with the new footage. I combined audio from these previous performances with the current video and had to time correct each one, adjusting almost second by second, every song, four cameras. It was about as speedy and exciting as gene sequencing.

To list all the frustrating oversights and fuckups with this shoot would get me enraged all over again, but there is a happy ending. In three months, I made it all work, often grabbing shots from previous songs and even previous video shoots when I had nothing for the current one. Everyone who saw it loved it, but remember that shoot date? March 5, 2020? Yep, the year the music died. Some theaters posted the video on their websites for their patrons in hopes we'd come back at a future date, but it was not to be. All our future gigs, one by one, cancelled or moved to 2021 and some to 2022. Lee, our keyboardist, was suffering from acute neuropathy and multiple sclerosis, and his symptoms had reached a level so intense, touring was no longer an option. By July, Russ, one of our lead singers and second keyboardist, gave up and went back to his previous job scoring music for *Sesame Street*. I had neither the will nor the energy to train two new replacements. That would also leave me as the only original member, so I bowed out. And that, dear reader, was the end of the most amazing band with whom I had ever played. The COVID-19 pandemic killed our careers as a touring band along with everybody else in the touring business, the broadway actors, the support industries including stagehands, roadies, sound engineers, makeup people, ushers, ticket takers, merchandise venders, restaurants, clubs - anything that involved people gathering. Huge legacy performers were selling their homes because without touring, they had little income. Current stars had royalty income, but touring brought in the big bucks, and touring was dead. But alas, I'm telling you what you already know if you lived through this pandemic.

The Hit Men were a phenomenon that by all rights shouldn't have made it. We put on a show of songs by the artists on whose records we played or on whose tours we took part, but we weren't those artists. For most of the records we emulated, we were the accompanists - I wasn't Jim Croce, Lee wasn't Frankie Valli, Russ wasn't Carole King, Jeff wasn't Johnny Winter, and Steve wasn't Alan Parsons. You could have called us a glorified cover band, but that would not do us justice. The Hit Men had a selling point no cover band could match - we had stories of our days with the stars, from the dressing rooms, the planes, the tour busses and the crazy parties, some of which I've shared in this book. We were like a singing stack of *People* magazines (or occasionally, *National*

Enquirers), and people ate it up. Our agents made such a big deal promoting us as "Legendary, Award Winning Artists Who Performed With The Stars," people would often show up just out of curiosity. In

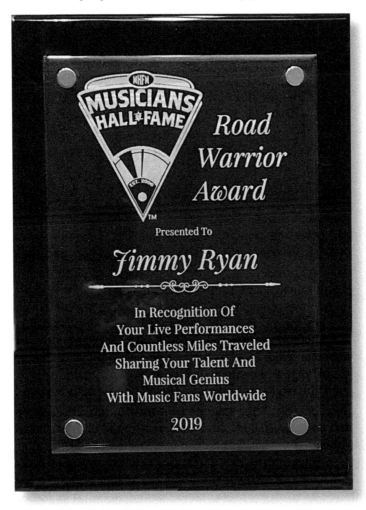

2019 we were honored with the first ever Road Warrior Award from *The Musicians Hall of Fame*. My musical brothers and I contributed to some of the biggest records of our time, and with The Hit Men, we delivered those songs to audiences all over the US and Canada, live and raw for ten years. We got together like a garage band performing the songs of *Jersey Boys*, because we had three of the Jersey Boys in the band. Then we started adding songs featuring the rest of our credits including Cat Stevens, Carly Simon, Jim Croce, Toto, Foreigner, Three Dog Night, Carole King, and even Mungo Jerry. I know it sounds boastful, but it was an amazing show by musicians who weren't imitating anyone but themselves, sometimes with the original videos flying behind us to prove that point.

And In The End

So in the end, did I learn anything through all these adventures? I started this book talking about my obsession with music and how I didn't want to just watch the stars of my day - I wanted to be them. Now that I have worked with so many gifted artists, my perspective has changed a bit. Life brought a different experience. I tried my best to stay in the spotlight, but now I'm actually grateful for how well my career chugged along out of the spotlight, but still close enough to the action to prosper and thoroughly enjoy myself. In retrospect, if I had rocketed to stardom with The Critters, rather than a Grammy or an Oscar, I could well have ended up with a Darwin Award. Like many who went before me, I wasn't ready for it, and I embodied more than my share of stupid. Instead, I watched from a very close vantage point as drugs, booze and lifestyle excesses ended the lives of many stars that I practically worshiped - artists that helped me shape my writing, playing and singing styles. I admired them, and learned from them, but someone or something always intervened when I was tempted to follow them down that dark corridor.

And the business? Sure, I was disappointed when my bands got dropped by their record companies, or the songs on which I worked so long and hard failed to move the needle. And yet... my time behind the stars, behind the film, behind the TV has been so richly rewarding in so many ways, I have few complaints or regrets. I found this wonderful world that I didn't even know existed when I was searching for that pot of gold at the end of the illusive rainbow.

To all those who inspired me and gave me reason to write this memoir and reflect on sixty-two years in both the front and the back of the stage, I give my humble thanks. When as a newbie, I thought it was fine to sit on a chair and look at my hands while playing, Elvis Presley taught me how to move, dance and actually enjoy myself on stage or at very least, act like it. He taught me that enjoyment is contagious. Same with Chuck Berry, Jerry Lee Lewis, all those dancing Motown singers... and even crazy Arthur Brown. When I was feeling my playing couldn't get much sappier, Jimi Hendrix came along and showed me that the guitar could be used for far more interesting things than chords. With his, Eric Clapton's and Jimmy Page's inspiration, I learned to improvise and play with passion. When I was unable to sing from the heart, I looked to

The Righteous Brothers, Otis Redding and my own band mate, Don Ciccone, for guidance and inspiration. Sometimes I tried to copy these artists, and sometimes that went well, but it was always better when I found my own voice through their inspiration, not imitation.

I leave you with these thoughts: If you're a music lover and have a passion to win that Grammy or score that major film, go for it and put your whole heart into it. Practice your butt off, hone your people skills, take inspiration from the greats that have gone before... but don't be discouraged if your results don't quite live up to your dreams. There are only a handful of people that reach the dizzy heights of artists like The Beatles, Bruce Springsteen, Led Zeppelin, Carly Simon or Aretha Franklin. Being a star isn't just blissful glory. More often, fame can be a super pain in the ass for you and those around you. Just watch *Bohemian Rhapsody* or *Rocket Man* to see how much more difficult, excessive and heartbreaking life can be at the top. If it's the money you want, there are far easier ways to earn it. But if you really love music or any of the arts, and you want to be part of this world, but your Facebook, Instagram or TikTok pages aren't drawing fans, consider moving to the support side. There are a hell of a lot more jobs and careers there. I had the good fortune to taste a sample of both worlds, and I am grateful to have stood in the spotlight, relishing those standing ovations and winning my share of awards, but even more grateful to have been able to live a normal life.

So go for it. Enjoy yourself. Let this magical, invisible force we call music inspire your life, fill you with joy, help you express your deepest emotions whether you create that music or enjoy the beautiful sounds that others have created for you. May your journey be happy and fruitful, and if you choose this musical path, may you find all the success and joy your heart desires.

Jimmy Ryan
28 July, 2021

Aftermath

I've mentioned a lot of bands and artists that I've worked with or been inspired by in this book. If you are among my younger readers, and some of these names are unfamiliar, I urge you to look them up on YouTube, Spotify, Apple Music, Amazon Music or any streaming service. Many of these were the big stars of my time, others were dear to me and were important to my career but didn't make it into the Billboard Top 100. Here's most of them in the order which they appeared in this book:

Elvis Presley - "Hound Dog," "Jailhouse Rock," "Don't Be Cruel," "Teddy Bear."

Buddy Holly - "Maybe Baby," "It's So Easy," "That'll Be The Day."

Chuck Berry - "Johnny B. Goode," "Sweet Little Sixteen," "Maybelline."

Fats Domino - "Blueberry Hill," "Ain't That a Shame," "I'm Walkin'."

Jerry Lee Lewis - "Whole Lotta Shakin' Goin' On," "Great Balls of Fire."

Bill Haley & The Comets: "Rock Around The Clock," Shake, Rattle & Roll."

Bobby Darin - "Splish Splash," "Mack The Knife," "Beyond The Sea."

Connie Francis - "Lipstick On Your Collar," "Who's Sorry Now," "Where The Boys Are."

The Dell Vikings - "Come And Go With Me."

Frankie Lymon & The Teenagers - "Why Do Fools Fall In Love."

Little Richard - "Long Tall Sally," "Good Golly Miss Molly," "Tutti Frutti," "Rip It Up," "Lucile," "Ready Teddy."

The Critters - "Georgianna," "Children And Flowers," "Younger Girl," "Mr. Dieingly Sad," "Don't Let The Rain Fall Down On Me."

Peter Paul and Mary - "If I Had A Hammer," "Puff The Magic Dragon," "The Great Mandala."

The Kingston Trio - "Tom Dooley," "MTA," "Scotch & Soda," "Sloop John B."

Bobby Lewis - "Tossin' & Turnin'."

Tony Orlando - "Half Way To Paradise," "Knock Three Times."

The Ronettes - "Be My Baby," "Walking In The Rain."

Jay & The Americans - "Only In America," "Cara Mia," "This Magic Moment," "Come A Little Bit Closer."

Little Anthony and the Imperials - "I Think I'm Going Out Of My Head," "Hurt So Bad," "Tears On My Pillow."

The Young Rascals - "Good Lovin'," "Groovin'," "A Beautiful Morning," "People Got To Be Free."

Paul Revere & The Raiders - "Kicks," "Good Thing."

B.J. Thomas - "Raindrops Keep Falling On My Head," "Hooked On A Feeling."

The Kinks - "You Really Got Me," "All Day and All of the Night," "Sunny Afternoon."

The Dave Clark Five - "Glad All Over," "Bits And Pieces," "Because."

Otis Redding - "I've Been Loving You Too Long," "Sittin' On The Dock of the Bay," "Try A Little Tenderness," "I Can't Turn You Loose," "Satisfaction," "So Hard To Handle."

Jimi Hendrix - "Foxy Lady," "Purple Haze," "All Along The Watchtower," "The Wind Cries Mary."

Booker T. & The M.G.s - "Green Onions."

Arthur Brown - "Fire."

Carly Simon - "That's The Way I've Always Heard It Should Be," "Anticipation," "You're So Vain," "Coming Around Again," "You Belong To Me," "Let The River Run."

Cat Stevens - "Wild World," "Oh Very Young," "Morning Has Broken," "Father And Son," "Peace Train," "Sad Lisa," "The First Cut Is The Deepest."

Derek and the Dominos - "Layla," "Bell Bottom Blues."

Traffic - "Dear Mr. Fantasy," "Paper Sun / Freedom Rider."

Spencer Davis Group - "Gimme Some Lovin'," "I'm A Man."

Sly and the Family Stone - "Dance To The Music," "I Want To Take You Higher," "Everyday People," "Stand!"

Kris Kristofferson - "Sunday Morning Coming Down," "Me And Bobbie McGee," "For The Good Times."

Jim Croce - "You Don't Mess Around With Jim," "Time In A Bottle," "Bad, Bad, Leroy Brown."

The Doors - "Light My Fire," "Riders on the Storm," "LA Woman," "When The Music's Over."

Bread - "Baby I'm a 'Want You," "Diary."

Bitch - "Good Time Coming," "I Won't Be Home Tonight."

Jimmy Webb - (as writer) "Up, Up And Away," "Galveston," "Wichita Lineman," "MacArthur Park."

Procol Harum - "Whiter Shade of Pale, "A Salty Dog," "Conquistador."

Rod Stewart - "Maggie May," "Da Ya Think I'm Sexy," "Forever Young," "Tonight's The Night."

Lesley Duncan - "Sing Children Sing," "Everything Changes," "Love Song" (As performed by Elton John on *Tumbleweed Connection*).

Chris Jagger - "Yesterday's Sun."

Kiki Dee - "Amoureuse," "I've Got The Music In Me," "Don't Go Breaking My Heart."

Karla DeVito - "Cool World," "Heaven Can Wait," "Almost Saturday Night."

Billy Joel - "Uptown Girl," "Piano Man," "Honesty," "Movin' Out," "You May Be Right," "Big Shot," "Only The Good Die Young," "Allentown."

The Four Seasons - "Sherry," "Big Girls Don't Cry," "Working My Way Back To You," "Let's Hang On," "Bye Bye Baby," "Rag Doll," "Ronnie," "Who Loves You," "December '63 (Oh What A Night)."

The Righteous Brothers - "You Lost That Loving Feeling," "Unchained Melody," "Soul and Inspiration."

Photo Credits

Page 205	The Hit Men in the studio	Jimmy Ryan Personal Photo Collection
Page 207	The Hit Men at Mexicali	Credit: Bobby Bank
Page 213	JR playing guitar	Credit: Gitam Ryan
Page 217	Musicians Hall of Fame Road Warrior Award	Credit: Jimmy Ryan

While every effort has been made to trace and contact the owners of copyright material reproduced herein and secure permissions, the publishers would like to apologise for any omissions and will be pleased to incorporate missing acknowledgements in any future edition of this book.

CPSIA information can be obtained
at www.ICGtesting.com
Printed in the USA
LVHW021029100921
697438LV00011B/569

9 781912 587612